the *flowering* garden

the *flowering* garden

choosing and growing glorious flowers for every season

andrew mikolajski
consultant: john swithinbank

southwater

This edition is published by Southwater

Southwater is an imprint of Anness Publishing Ltd
Hermes House, 88-89 Blackfriars Road, London SE1 8HA
tel. 020 7401 2077; fax 020 7633 9499
www.southwaterbooks.com; info@anness.com

This edition distributed in the UK by The Manning Partnership Ltd, 6 The Old Dairy
Melcombe Road, Bath BA2 3LR; tel. 01225 478 444; fax 01225 478 440
sales@manning-partnership.co.uk

This edition distributed in the USA and Canada by National Book Network, 4720 Boston Way
Lanham, MD 20706; tel. 301 459 3366; fax 301 459 1705; www.nbnbooks.com

This edition distributed in Australia by Pan Macmillan Australia, Level 18, St Martins Tower
31 Market St, Sydney, NSW 2000; tel. 1300 135 113; fax 1300 135 103
customer.service@macmillan.com.au

This edition distributed in New Zealand by The Five Mile Press (NZ) Ltd, PO Box 33-1071
Takapuna, Unit 11/101-111 Diana Drive, Glenfield, Auckland 10; tel. (09) 444 4144
fax (09) 444 4518; fivemilenz@clear.net.nz

A CIP catalogue record for this book is available from the British Library.

Publisher: Joanna Lorenz
Managing Editor: Judith Simons
Executive Editor: Caroline Davison
Project Editors: Claire Folkard & Mariano Kalfors
Designer: Michael Morey
Jacket Design: Balley Design Associates
Editorial Reader: Richard McGinlay
Picture Research: Gary Murphy, Joanna Skordis, Nansong Lue
Production Controller: Ben Worley

Previously published as part of a larger compendium, *An Encyclopedia of Garden Plants*

10 9 8 7 6 5 4 3 2 1

CONTENTS

INTRODUCTION

This directory is intended to be of practical value to gardeners. Plants are grouped according to type (perennials, annuals, bulbs, etc) and the descriptions are designed not only to allow for identification but to suggest how the plants can be used in the garden. Strictly speaking, bulbs are perennials, since they also persist from year to year, but they are treated separately in this book.

The number of plants available is constantly expanding, and it is obviously impossible to keep pace with every new introduction. One of the aims of this book is to bring together tried and tested plants, which have already proved their value in gardens and can be expected to perform reliably for many years to come alongside newer introductions that are likely to appear on the market. A few unusual plants are included, plants that need no special cosseting but simply deserve to be better known. It is often only the difficulties of producing stocks in large quantities that have kept them out of gardens.

This border has been designed in a "hot" colour scheme with a combination of red-flowered and purple-leaved plants, both hardy and tender.

The summer-flowering *Itea ilicifolia*, though hardy, benefits from the shelter of a warm wall.

Hardiness

All of the plants in this book have been assessed for their hardiness, and for the USA, the range of zones where they can be grown outdoors is also given (see Plant Hardiness Zones). Most of the varieties listed can be grown outdoors in most temperate areas, and are able to withstand lows of -15°C (5°F). Plants described as "borderline hardy" will need some form of protection from the coldest weather, either by growing them in a warm, sheltered spot (for instance in the lee of a sunny wall) or by covering them in winter with a dry mulch of straw or other similar material. However, severe lows in themselves are less detrimental to plants than cold, drying winds.

Hardiness in any case is relative, and the ability of many plants at least to survive cold is largely dependent on how hot the weather is the previous summer. Deciduous trees and shrubs, herbaceous bulbs that disappear below ground in winter have an in-built mechanism for surviving unfavourable weather. During hot, dry periods, plant growth stops altogether. As the soil dries out, roots delve deeper in search of moisture, while bark thickens in the heat. The result is a tough, sturdy plant with an extensive root system that is better able to withstand severe cold than one that has grown sappy through excess moisture during the growing season. These plants are able to survive colder winters than usual, simply because the preceding summer was a hot one. Winter temperatures in certain regions with a Mediterranean climate for instance can drop as low as they do in temperate areas, but plants such as olives are able to survive simply because of the long hot summers that ripen the wood. Hence the necessity of growing plants of borderline hardiness in a microclimate where they can ripen sufficiently. The same applies to many bulbs, which are adapted to long dry summers and indeed need a good summer roasting in order to flower successfully.

How to use the directory

The directory section is divided into five plant categories: perennials; annuals (including biennials); bulbs (including corms and tubers); roses; and alpines.

Each category features genus introductions in alphabetical order, accompanied by concise information on cultivation. These are followed by a selection of plant entries also organized alphabetically according to their most common and internationally accepted names.

A plant entry might be a species, hybrid or group of hybrids, a variant, or a cultivar. As well as a brief description, information is given on height and spread; best time of interest for flowers, foliage and fruits/berries/hips; and hardiness/zones.

Caption
A full botanical name is given with each photograph

Genus name
This gives the botanical name for a group of related species

Common name or names
These apply to the whole genus, if given

Genus introduction
This is a general description of the genus and may give the number of species or state that the genus is monotypic (there is only one species in the whole genus). There is also some information on preferred conditions and natural habitat, country or countries of origin, and occasional advice on how the plants can be used in the garden.

Cultivation
This section gives the level of sun or shade that the plants described in the selection either require or tolerate as well as advice on the type of soil in which they should be grown.

Hybrids
Occasionally, there is one entry for a group of hybrids.

Varieties and cultivars
The descriptions of cultivars, forms, subspecies, and varieties appears within the main plant entry. Heights and spreads are only included if they differ from those of the main plant entry.

Erigeron 'Quakeress'

ERIGERON
Fleabane
Useful daisy plants, suitable for a sunny border, these suit cottage garden-style plantings. There are a large number of hybrids; only the species described is well-represented in gardens.
Cultivation Best in fertile, moist but well-drained soil in sun. Taller varieties may benefit from light staking.

E. karvinskianus
(syn. *E. muconatus*)
Wall daisy
This spreading species has dainty white flowers from late spring to autumn. H to 30cm (1ft), S 1m (3ft). Hardy/Z 8–9.

E. hybrids
The following hybrids flower throughout summer but can also flower intermittently at other times. They are all hardy/Z 2–7. **'Dignity'** has violet-blue flowers. H and S 45cm (18in). **'Dunkelste Aller'** (syn. 'Darkest of All') has deep purple flowers with yellow eyes. H 60cm (24in), S 45cm (18in). **'Gaiety'** has mid-pink flowers. H 60cm (24in), S 45cm (18in). The deservedly popular **'Quakeress'** has white flowers flushed with pale lilac-pink. H 60cm (24in), S 45cm (18in). **'Schneewittchen'** (syn. 'Snow White') has pure white flowers, which turn pink as they age. H 60cm (24in), S 45cm (18in).

Main plant entry
This gives the current botanical name of the plant in bold and can refer to a species, hybrid or hybrids, a variant, or a cultivar.

Synonym or synonyms
If given, this provides the synonym or synonyms for the main plant entry. A synonym is an alternative name for the same plant.

Common name or names
If given, this provides the common name or names for the main plant entry.

Hardiness ratings/Zones
This gives the plant's temperature tolerance as either tender, down to 5°C (41°F); half-hardy, down to 0°C (32°F); or hardy, down to -15°C. Plants described as "Borderline hardy" will need some form of protection from the coldest weather. A slightly different system is used in the US and Canada. Zones are based on the average annual minimum temperature for each zone. The smaller number indicates the northernmost zone it can survive in and the higher number the southernmost zone the plant will tolerate. In some cases only one zone is given for a plant entry. See page 122 for details of zones and a zone map.

Height and spread
This gives the average expected height and spread, though growth rates may vary, depending on location and conditions. If the height and spread are the same, then only one measurement is given. Metric measurements always precede standard measurements.

How plants are named

All living things are classified according to the binomial system, devised by the Swedish taxonomist Carl Linnaeus (1707–78) in his *Species Plantarum* (1753). Under the rules of this system, plants have Latin names consisting of the genus name (e.g. *Viburnum*) followed by the species epithet (e.g. *davidii*). Some genera comprise only one species, while others are vast. *Euphorbia*, for instance, is made up of some 2000 plants, annuals, perennials, shrubs and trees as well as some cactus-like plants, and is widely distributed. (Such genera are sometimes rather grandly described as "cosmopolitan".)

All members of a genus are assumed to have some relationship to each other (though this may not necessarily be immediately apparent to the naked eye) and different species can often be crossed with each other. At the higher level, some genera seem to be related to each other (roses, pyracanthas and rowans, for instance, which all have cup-shaped flowers in their wild state), suggesting some common ancestry, though much remains conjectural or relies on the evidence of fossilized remains.

Naming plants

Nomenclature is not an exact science, and although there are certain internationally agreed rules, how they are put into use is often a matter of individual prejudice. Botanists and taxonomists frequently disagree over which name certain plants should bear, and in many cases there can be no "right" answer, since much depends on individual opinion. Hence the advisability of retaining synonyms, which can be as valid as the name officially sanctioned. The well-known mile-a-minute plant (here *Fallopia baldschuanica*) has

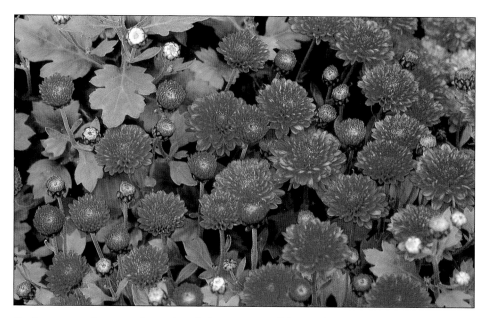

Plant names can be a complex and confusing matter, and few gardening subjects have aroused such controversy in recent years as the naming of chrysanthemums.

migrated several times between *Polygonum* and *Fallopia*, with ports of call at *Bilderdykia*. The most radical and controversial changes in recent years involved those to *Chrysanthemum*, which properly is made up exclusively of annual species from the Mediterranean. The perennials (which include the many garden forms that are such a feature of the autumn garden, the so-called florists' chrysanthemums) have been assigned to *Dendranthema*. However, so deeply entrenched is the name *Chrysanthemum* that it has been widely retained both within the nursery trade and in a number of plant dictionaries, this one included.

It occasionally happens that two plants thought to be distinct, with two separate names, are discovered to be, in fact, one and the same, and here a decision has to be taken as to which name has precedence.

Cultivars

Many plant species have the genetic potential to assume different characteristics to adapt to changes in the environment. In the wild, the

habitat will favour seedlings best suited to the prevailing conditions, while the rest will not survive. Hence any population of a particular species in the wild will look more or less the same.

In the more controlled conditions of a garden, the genetic potential becomes manifest, since gardeners are able to germinate and grow on a larger proportion of the seed. All manner of variations can arise: double flowers, albino forms, plants with variegated leaves, etc. Such forms, if they have garden potential and are sufficiently distinct from the species, are given names and known as cultivars (a contraction of "cultivated varieties") or selections of the species, and the name is put in single quotes as, for instance, *Viburnum tinus* 'Eve Price'.

Hybrids

Certain species can be crossed with each other to produce hybrids. This can occur in nature, but is more usually deliberately practised by plant breeders. Hybridization generally results in robust plants with bigger flowers. For instance, at Bodnant in Wales, *Viburnum farreri* was crossed with *V. grandiflorum* to produce *V.* × *bodnantense* (the cross indicating that the plant is a hybrid). Outstanding seedlings were given names, including 'Dawn' and 'Deben'.

Hybrids can be back-crossed with one of the parents, to consolidate a particular feature, or can be crossed with other species or hybrids. Some garden forms have such complex parentage that it becomes meaningless to try to ascribe them to one or other species or hybrid group. Indeed, if precise records were not kept, the ancestry of a plant can only be guess-work. Such plants are styled with the genus name followed by the cultivar name, e.g. *Campanula* 'Burghaltii'. Many roses and rhododendrons come into this category.

In general, garden forms can only be propagated vegetatively (cloning). Seedlings will revert back to the parent species (or one of them). Over time, the quality tends to deteriorate: repeated vegetative propagation is like photocopying a

photocopy of a photocopy. Hence only the most vigorous of the older cultivars will stand the test of time, and there is good reason for replacing them with newly created hybrids. Many gardeners regret this, but while there is every reason to wish to preserve species that may be under threat in the wild to maintain the biodiversity of the planet, the disappearance of certain garden forms from cultivation does not represent a comparable loss.

Garden forms usually do not survive in the wild, but some species have been known to "escape", as with *Rhododendron ponticum*, from the Mediterranean, which has colonized areas of the UK and Ireland, to the extent that it has become a weed.

Name changes

As previously mentioned, nomenclature is never precise and can lead to disputes amongst botanists. For instance, the genera *Berberis* and *Mahonia* were formerly united in a single genus, and members of the two will in fact hybridize, suggesting that there is

some close relationship between them. Many botanists would like to see them reunited. Recent research into cacti and bamboos has resulted in reclassification, and some species formerly considered to belong to separate genera are now thought to be related, and some species have been switched from one genus to another.

Name changes result in synonyms. A new name is not necessarily more valid than the old, and merely represents the opinion of whoever has come up with the new name. Although many gardeners despair at what seem like constant changes, there is usually a good reason for a change (even though agreement may not be universal). Sometimes it is best to be practical. *Chrysanthemum* is a case in point.

Names of cultivars that have been bred abroad and given foreign names are often given translated names (or even new names) once imported. There are arguments for and against this: on the plus side, it results in names that are easier to remember and spell; on the down side, it leads to potential confusion. Modern rules require translated names to be set in a different font and without quotes.

Hybrids with the same parentage are sometimes given group names. This usually happens when all the seedlings share similar characteristics and, while varying, make good garden plants. A case in point is *Lilium* African Queen Group, plants of which all have orange flowers, but with differing intensity of colour. Conversely, the same name is sometimes ascribed to two different plants, as is the case with the clematis 'Princess of Wales', a name that applies to two cultivars, one honouring Alexandra, wife of Edward VII, the other Princess Diana.

The breeding of orchids has been scrupulously recorded. This hybrid **Cymbidium** Summer Pearl 'Sonya' has complex parentage.

Choosing plants for your garden

Choosing plants on aesthetic grounds alone – for form or flower colour, for instance – is not really a successful method of gardening, though nearly all gardeners fall victim to some ravishing specimen spotted at a garden centre or garden show. Since not all plants will thrive in the same conditions, it makes sense to limit your choice to what will do well in your garden. One of the most important lessons for any gardener is that you cannot grow what you want wherever you please.

The plants chosen for this scheme, including *Artemisia* and *Sisyrinchium*, are perfectly adapted to hot, dry conditions.

The aspect

Light is essential to all plants as it provides the energy that is needed to manufacture food during daylight hours, so providing the right levels of light is crucial if the plants are to thrive. For this reason, one of the first considerations is the aspect of your garden. You will need to study your garden to work out which areas are sunny, shady or in partial shade at different times of the day. In their natural environment, some plants will grow in dense shade on the forest floor while others are exposed to intense bright sunlight for long periods of time. This wide diversity of natural habitat explains why so many of the different ornamental plants we grow require different conditions. The ability to adapt to unfamiliar conditions is a major reason for the popularity of many common plants.

The soil

It is worth finding out whether your soil is acid or alkaline, since not all plants will do equally well in both (though the majority are indifferent). The most reliable method is with a chemical soil testing kit, or you can make an educated guess by looking to see what is growing successfully in the surrounding countryside, or in other people's gardens if you live in a built-up area. Geological maps also indicate the presence of limestone or silt, for instance.

Equally important, perhaps more so, is the soil profile. The ideal – a loam that binds easily into crumbs, allowing for both moisture-retention and free drainage of excess water – suits nearly all plants. Stiff clays, cold and heavy to work, are usually nutrient high, suiting bog plants and others adapted to reliably wet conditions. Dry, sandy soils, easy to work and quick to warm up in spring, are nutrient poor but are the ideal medium for many of the Mediterranean plants and herbs. All soils can be improved by digging in

Dainty *Iris sibirica* is one of the many irises that appreciate a damp site. It looks exquisite grown near to water.

organic matter, in the form of garden compost or well-rotted farmyard manure, greatly increasing the range of plants you can grow.

If a plant is doing well in your garden, either plant more of the same, or some of its near relatives or others that enjoy the same conditions. The reverse is also true. If you have trouble establishing a particular plant, you are also unlikely to succeed with others of its ilk.

Designing with plants

A garden is more than just a collection of plants, and relies for much of its impact on the way these are grouped together. If you have a flair for design, devising effective groupings may be no problem. If you do not, there are any number of strategies you can adopt that will lead to pleasing combinations.

When choosing plants for beds and borders, formal gardens for instance tend to dictate themselves. A formal rose garden will clearly feature roses, with only the "filler" plants left debatable. An island bed

is meant to be viewed from all sides, so the tallest plants will usually go in the centre and smaller ones around the edges. Try planting a small tree such as *Malus floribunda* to create plenty of height.

Most gardens will feature single-sided borders, and the secret of a successful design is planning for a long period of interest. A border will not remain attractive for more than a month if all the plants flower briefly, at the same time. The plants you choose should also not only look pleasing when flowering, but also when out of bloom. A series of plants that bloom at different times can lead to an uncoordinated appearance of plants in flower dotted

amid swathes of foliage at varying stages of growth. If you have space you can easily devote separate borders for spring, summer and autumn/winter interest. Otherwise, try a mixed border incorporating many different kinds of plants arranged in bold groups, rather than as isolated specimens. If you want to cut down on the regular replanting work, you can also use dwarf shrubs as backbone plants, then include flowering ground-cover plants, such as hardy geraniums and spring bulbs, to provide flowers over a long period.

The following pages should help you find useful suggestions as to which plants to place where.

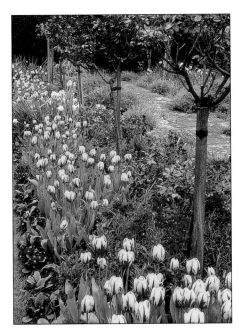

Here, tulips and primulas provide the interest before the standard roses come into bloom.

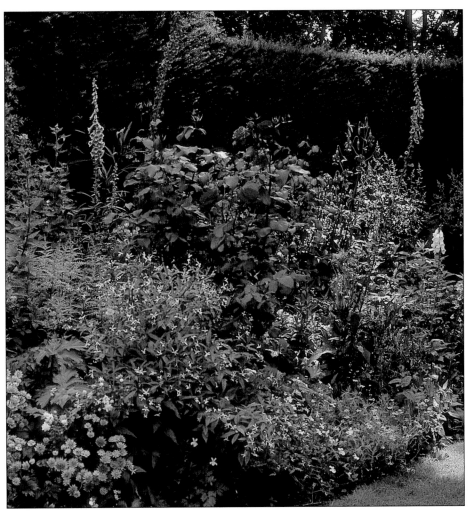

A classic mixed border, combining roses, lilies, and a range of easily pleased perennials against a backdrop of clipped yew.

Perennials

For many, a garden just would not be a garden without the contribution of perennials, often long-lived plants that provide interest year on year, usually with very little maintenance required. A herbaceous border can provide interest for many weeks in summer, but perennials also encompass many early-flowering plants (usually low-growing) that are delightful with spring bulbs, as well as plants that carry the flowering season into autumn and continue to provide colour in the garden as the days grow shorter and cooler.

Most perennials are easy to care for and provide colour for many weeks during the summer months.

Growing perennials

Perennials should be considered permanent residents of the garden and so soil improvement should be carried out before planting. If you are planting a new bed, dig the area thoroughly and remove all weeds and other debris, including the roots of perennial weeds. Improve the soil by incorporating plenty of well-rotted organic matter, such as farmyard manure or garden compost. Also add a base dressing of a slow-release fertilizer, such as bonemeal.

Planting

Nearly all perennials are now sold as container-grown specimens, which means that they can be planted out at any time of the year as long as the ground is not frozen or waterlogged. However, they will establish a lot more quickly if they are planted either in spring or autumn. Summer planting can be hard work, because new additions will need regular watering during dry spells.

Before removing the plants from their pots place them on the bed and adjust the arrangement until you are satisfied with the result. Larger specimens can be used individually, but smaller perennials and ground cover plants are best grouped in odd numbers of threes or fives if you want to achieve a natural-looking scheme. Also bear in mind that herbaceous perennials die back in winter, so you might want to include a proportion of evergreen plants or evergreen trees and shrubs to provide structure and interest throughout the coldest months.

Water the perennials thoroughly while they are still in their containers and leave to drain. When you have decided on the positions of the plants, dig planting holes. Starting with the central perennials, plant them at the same depth as they are

HOW TO PLANT PERENNIALS

1 Always prepare the soil first. Dig it deeply, remove weeds, and incorporate a fertilizer and well-rotted garden compost if the soil is impoverished. Most perennials are sold in pots, so space them out according to your plan. Change positions if the associations don't look right.

2 Water thoroughly about half an hour before knocking the plant from its pot, then dig a planting hole with a trowel. If the roots are wound tightly around the rootball, carefully tease out a few of them first. Work methodically from the back of the border or from one end.

3 Carefully firm the soil around the roots to remove any large pockets of air.

4 Always water thoroughly after planting and keep plants well watered in dry weather for the first few months.

in their pots. Firm the soil around them, not too heavily, and water well. Finally, apply a mulch, 5–8cm (2–3in) deep, of loose organic material, taking care not to pile it up against the plant stems.

Raising perennials from seed

Many perennials are also easy to grow from seed. This is much cheaper than buying container-grown

plants and many perennials grown this way will flower in their first year, while nearly all will be in bloom by their second summer. It is particularly well worth raising plants from seed if you want a lot of one variety such as ground cover plants, or are planting a new garden from scratch.

Seed can be sown in several ways: outside in a well-prepared seedbed; in a cold frame between early spring

Good perennials to raise from seed

Achillea	Helenium
Aquilegia	Lobelia
Coreopsis	Lupinus
Gaillardia	Polemonium
Geum	Viola

and midsummer; or in pots of fresh compost (soil mix) as you would sow bedding plants and vegetables. When the seedlings are large enough to handle, prick them out into 8cm (3in) pots. As soon as the young plants are well established they can be planted out into their final flowering positions.

Lupins make a good border plant, and their attractive flowers also have a distinctive, peppery scent. If you want a massed planting of lupins it may be worth raising them from seed.

HOW TO SOW SEED IN OPEN GROUND

1 Prepare the soil in the bed thoroughly, carefully removing all weeds and the roots of perennial weeds and breaking the soil down into a fine tilth with a rake.

2 Draw out a shallow drill with a corner of a hoe. It should be about 1cm (½in) deep. Keep the drill straight by using a garden line as a guide.

3 If the soil is dry, water the drill with a watering can and wait until the water has soaked in before sowing.

4 It is essential to mark the ends of the row, to help you identify the seedling flowers when weeding and hoeing later on.

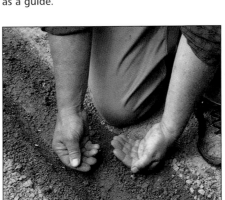

5 Sow the seed thinly along the drill. Larger seed can be "station sown" at intervals.

6 Gently rake the soil back into the drill, covering over the seed. In dry weather water regularly and do not allow the soil to dry out.

Acanthus mollis

Achillea filipendulina 'Gold Plate'

Aconitum 'Stainless Steel'

ACANTHUS
Bear's breeches

These stately, hardy perennials, mostly from Mediterranean countries, are of unquestioned value in the garden, in sun or shade, although they have rather sinister-looking hooded flowers. They are colonizing plants, which can be difficult to eradicate once they are established, so choose where you plant them with care. The flowers can be dried for winter arrangements.
Cultivation Grow in any well-drained fertile soil in sun or light shade. Flowering is best in sun.

A. mollis
Tall spikes of hooded mauve and white flowers appear in early summer above the large, handsome, glossy green leaves. H 1.2m (4ft), S 1m (3ft). Hardy/Z 7–9.

A. spinosus
A species that resembles *A. mollis* in all respects but for its deeply cut leaves. H 1.2m (4ft), S 60cm (2ft). Hardy/Z 6–10.

ACHILLEA
Yarrow

More than 80 species are included in this genus. Yarrows are tough plants, with flat heads of flowers in mid- to late summer on stout stems. The majority of them have feathery, aromatic foliage. They are indispensable for providing colour – if not vibrant – in the late summer border, working well with grasses, but some tend to be short-lived. The flowers can be dried and hold their colour well.
Cultivation Grow in free-draining, preferably moist, soil in full sun.

A. filipendulina
(syn. *A. eupatorium*)
This species has flat heads of sulphur-yellow flowers in late summer. H 1.5m (5ft), S 1m (3ft). Hardy/Z 3–9. The selection **'Gold Plate'**, which bears slightly domed flowerheads, is more robust. H 1.2m (4ft), S 60cm (2ft).

A. 'Moonshine'
This hybrid is grown as much for its ferny, grey-green leaves as its pale yellow flowerheads. H and S 60cm (2ft). Hardy/Z 4–8.

A. ptarmica 'The Pearl'
A dainty plant, with heads of button-like, white flowers in summer. Plants sold under this name probably belong to The Pearl Group – in other words they have been seed-raised and thus may differ in some respects. H and S 60cm (2ft). Hardy/ Z 4–9.

ACONITUM
Monkshood, wolf's bane

These tall plants with hooded flowers are a useful shade of rich blue. All species in the genus are poisonous.
Cultivation Any soil is suitable, but they do best in moisture-retentive soil in full sun, although they will also do well in shade.

A. 'Spark's Variety'
Of all the available hybrids, this is probably the best known, with spires of rich, dark violet-blue flowers from early to midsummer. H 1.5m (5ft), S 45cm (18in). Hardy/Z 5–8.

A. 'Stainless Steel'
This cultivar has subtly coloured, beautiful pewter grey flowers. H 1.5m (5ft), S 45cm (18in). Hardy/Z 6.

AGAPANTHUS
African lily

These elegant and desirable plants produce umbels of refreshing blue or white flowers in late summer. They contrast well with yellow flowers, of which there will be many at flowering time, as well as blending easily with softer tones. They also thrive in containers, in which they look very handsome. Overcrowding seems to intensify the flower power, so divide them only when absolutely necessary. They are easily raised from seed.
Cultivation Grow in fertile, reliably moist (but not boggy) soil in full sun.

A. 'Ben Hope'
This hybrid has umbels of rich blue flowers from mid- to late summer. H 1.2m (4ft), S 60cm (2ft). Hardy/Z 7–10.

A. 'Castle of Mey'
This is one of the daintier hybrids, producing rich dark blue flowers on erect stems in late summer. H 60cm (2ft), S 30cm (1ft). Hardy/Z 7.

AJUGA
Bugle

Useful as groundcover, these plants are grown mostly for their evergreen leaves, although the blue spring flowers make an attractive bonus. They spread by runners and will colonize any area where the conditions suit them.
Cultivation Grow in moisture-retentive soil in sun or light shade.

A. reptans
This is the most widely grown bugle, although it is seldom seen in its typical form in gardens. H 10cm (5in), S 1m (3ft). Hardy/Z 3–9. Selections available include **'Atropurpurea'** (syn. 'Purpurea'), which has rich burgundy-purple leaves; **'Jungle Beauty'** (syn. 'Jumbo'), with large

Agapanthus 'Castle of Mey'

Ajuga reptans 'Jungle Beauty'

Alchemilla mollis

Alstroemeria 'Apollo'

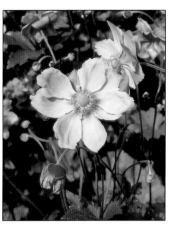

Anemone × hybrida 'Königin Charlotte'

green leaves that turn warm brown in winter; and **'Variegata'** (syn. 'Argentea'), which has leaves splashed with cream and grey.

ALCHEMILLA
Lady's mantle
The species described, which comes from Turkey and the Caucasus, is an essential garden plant. It is an excellent filler for gaps in borders and the frothy, lime-green flowers, also good for cutting, blend with almost anything else. It makes excellent groundcover but can be invasive, and its habit of self-seeding everywhere makes it a menace in some gardens. To prevent this from happening, cut off the flowers as they fade (this will also encourage further flowers). It makes a marvellous foil to old roses and looks charming where allowed to seed in the cracks between paving.
Cultivation These extremely tolerant plants will grow in almost any soil in sun or light shade.

A. mollis
The soft, almost felted, pleated, fan-like leaves emerge in early spring, followed by masses of tiny, star-like, lime green flowers throughout summer. H and S 50cm (20in). Hardy/Z 3–7.

ALSTROEMERIA
Peruvian lily, lily of the Incas
These exquisite plants, long associated with cottage gardens, are of undoubted distinction. The newer hybrids may be hardier and have a longer flowering season than some of the older ones, but

they have not supplanted them. Excellent in a warm, sunny border, in cold areas they need the shelter of a wall. Leave them undisturbed after planting; they may take some years to establish, but thereafter are extremely reliable plants.
Cultivation Peruvian lilies need reasonably fertile, well-drained soil in sun, with some shelter in cold areas. Most are best when staked, but they can be supported by neighbouring plants.

A. 'Apollo'
This outstanding hybrid has large, white flowers marked with yellow within and flecked with brown appearing from mid-summer to autumn. H and S 60cm (2ft). Borderline hardy/Z 8.

A. ligtu hybrids
This group of hybrids includes plants with varying flower colour, including pink, coral and salmon orange, but all are desirable. They

flower in early to midsummer. They are seed-raised, so buy plants in flower to ensure getting the desired colour. The plants can be invasive. H and S 60cm (2ft). Borderline hardy/Z 7–10.

A. 'Morning Star'
A hybrid with rich purplish-pink flowers fading to yellow and flecked with brown from midsummer to autumn. H and S 45cm (18in). Borderline hardy/Z 8.

ANEMONE
Windflower
This large genus includes a few perennials of undoubted merit. Their late season and tolerance of a range of conditions make them essential plants for any garden, to say nothing of the beauty of the flowers, carried on tall, elegant, wiry stems. They are ravishing in drifts under

deciduous trees, or they can be used more formally in borders planned for late interest. They are sometimes informally referred to as Japanese anemones.
Cultivation These anemones do best on moisture-retentive soil in sun or shade, although they do tolerate drier, lighter soils.

A. hupehensis
This elegant species, with white or pink, bowl-shaped flowers that seem to float at the tops of wiry stems, is rare in cultivation. H 75cm (30in), S 45cm (18in). Hardy/Z 5–8. More common is the distinguished selection **'Hadspen Abundance'**, which has rich deep pink flowers. H and S 1m (3ft).

A. × hybrida
(syn. *A. japonica* of gardens)
This large group of hybrids are the true Japanese anemones (the plant sometimes referred to as *A. japonica* does not seem to exist). Seedlings often appear in gardens, and all are worth growing, but named forms worthy of note include **'Honorine Jobert'**, which has white flowers; **'Königin Charlotte'** (syn. 'Queen Charlotte'), which has semi-double, purplish-pink flowers with frilly petals; **'Luise Uhink'**, which has chalk-white flowers; and **'Whirlwind'**, which has semi-double, green-tinged, white flowers with twisted petals. H 1.5m (5ft), S 60cm (2ft). Hardy/Z 5–8.

Alstroemeria 'Morning Star'

Anemone × hybrida 'Luise Uhink'

Anthemis tinctoria

Argyranthemum 'Mary Wootton'

Artemisia absinthium

ANTHEMIS

These cheerful plants with their daisy-like flowers are indispensable for the flower gardener because of the length of their flowering season and the freedom with which blooms are produced. Although the plants will provide endless material for cutting, they may be short-lived.
Cultivation Grow in well-drained soil in full sun. Regular division in spring helps maintain health.

A. tinctoria
The species has parsley-like leaves with masses of yellow daisies in summer. H and S 60cm (2ft). Hardy/Z 4–8. The selection **'E.C. Buxton'** is widely available. This essential plant has lemon-yellow flowers throughout summer that look good with blue flowers (especially campanulas) and border phlox. H and S 1m (3ft).

AQUILEGIA
Columbine
These short-lived perennials are notorious for seeding themselves in the garden. Unfortunately, not all seedlings develop into attractive plants, as they sometimes produce flowers of an indifferent pink or murky purple, but the best ones make elegant additions to the border, with their distinctive, spurred flowers, and usefully fill the flowering gap between spring bulbs and summer perennials. They are probably at their best when grown in informal clumps in light woodland but also blend well with irises, catmint and poppies in

cottage garden-style plantings. The genus also includes some alpines.
Cultivation Grow in any well-drained soil in sun or light shade.

A. 'Lavender and White'
This hybrid has distinctive bi-coloured flowers in early summer, in lavender and creamy white, as the name suggests. H 60cm (24in), S 45cm (18in). Hardy/Z 4.

A. vulgaris
Granny's bonnets
This is one of the most familiar garden plants, with its dumpy purple, pink, crimson or white flowers appearing in late spring to early summer. Some of the many selections available include **'Nivea'** (syn. 'Munstead's White'), which has bright white flowers; and the distinctive *A. vulgaris* **var. stellata 'Norah Barlow'**, which

Aquilegia 'Lavender and White'

has pompon-like pink, green and white double flowers. H 60cm (24in), S 45cm (18in). Hardy/Z 4–9.

ARGYRANTHEMUM
Marguerite, Paris daisy
These plants are in flower for longer than any other perennial – almost throughout the growing season. They are woody plants and, as well as their obvious value in borders, they can also be grown as standards.
Cultivation Argyranthemums will grow in sun in most well-drained, reasonably fertile soils. Pinching out the tips of the shoots in early spring can encourage bushiness and extra flowers.

A. gracile 'Chelsea Girl'
One of the best known cultivars, this has attractive, ferny grey leaves and an abundance of

Artemisia absinthium 'Lambrook Silver'

yellow-centred, white daisies from spring to autumn. H and S 60cm (2ft). Half-hardy/Z 9.

A. 'Jamaica Primrose'
An equally valuable hybrid, this bears long-stalked, cool lemon-yellow daisies throughout the growing season. H and S 1m (3ft). Half-hardy/Z 9.

A. 'Mary Wootton'
This fine hybrid has double, pompon-like, peach pink flowers. H and S 1m (3ft). Half-hardy/Z 9.

A. 'Snow Storm'
(syn. 'Jamaica Snowstorm')
This compact form has blue-green leaves and yellow-centred, white flowers. H and S 30cm (1ft). Borderline hardy/Z 9.

ARTEMISIA
Wormwood, mugwort
These are excellent foliage plants for borders, particularly hot, dry ones. The silvery foliage blends well with roses as well as with a range of herbaceous perennials. Artemisias, some of which are shrubby, also have aromatic foliage which has herbal applications.
Cultivation Grow artemisias in any well-drained, preferably gritty, soil in full sun. Prune straggly plants in spring.

A. absinthium
Absinthe, wormwood
This is the plant from which the spirit absinthe is distilled. In the garden it is valued chiefly for its silky-grey, divided leaves. The daisy-like flowers, produced in late summer, are insignificant. H and S 1m (3ft). Hardy/Z 5–8.

Asphodeline lutea

'**Lambrook Silver**' is more compact and has more finely dissected foliage. It is an excellent foil to purple-leaved plants. H and S 75cm (30in).

A. ludoviciana
(syn. *A. palmeri, A. purshiana*)
Western mugwort
This species has dissected silver grey leaves that look as if they are lightly dusted with powder. H 1.2m (4ft), S 60cm (2ft). Hardy/Z 4–8. *A. lucoviciana* var. *latiloba* is shorter growing, and, like the species, looks well grown in association with pink or crimson flowering plants. H and S 60cm (2ft).

ASPHODELINE
Jacob's rod
These stately plants, native to Mediterranean countries, are ideal for giving structure to a border.
Cultivation Grow in any well-drained soil in full sun.

A. lutea
(syn. *Asphodelus luteus*)
Spires of fragrant, bright yellow flowers appear from spring to early summer above clusters of bluish-grey leaves. After flowering, the developing bead-like, green seeds continue to provide interest. H 1.2m (4ft), S 30cm (1ft). Hardy/Z 6–8.

ASTER
This large genus includes the well-known Michaelmas daisies, essential plants for the autumn garden, many of which flower

from late summer until the first frosts. Most also last well as cut flowers. The species are as worthy of consideration as the hybrids, some of which have an annoying tendency towards mildew (although all those described are trouble-free). The genus also includes annuals.
Cultivation Asters will grow in any reasonably fertile soil, in sun or light shade. Some will do well in poor soil. The taller forms often benefit from staking.

A. ericoides
The species, which is native to North America, has given rise to several garden-worthy forms. These have wiry stems that are starred with flowers, all with yellow centres, in autumn. H 75cm (30in), S 30cm (12in). Hardy/Z 5–8. '**Blue Star**' has pale blue flowers; '**Golden Spray**' has white flowers; '**Pink Cloud**' has light mauve-pink flowers.

A. × frikartii
This group of vigorous hybrids includes some of the best of the Michaelmas daisies, all with a long flowering season. H 75cm (30in), S 38cm (15in). Hardy/Z 5–8. '**Mönch**' is an outstanding selection, which has large, lavender-blue flowers carried freely on branching stems; it is an excellent companion to shrubby lavateras. '**Wunder von Stäfa**' (syn. 'Wonder of Stafa') usually needs staking and has pinkish-blue flowers. H 1m (3ft), S 75cm (30in).

Aster × frikartii '*Mönch*'

A. laterifolius
(syn. *A. diffusus*)
The species has an unusual habit in that the erect stems produce flowering sideshoots, almost at right angles, giving a tiered effect. The flowers are white to pale lilac. H 1m (3ft), S 30cm (1ft). Hardy/Z 4–8. '**Horizontalis**', which is rather more spreading, has pale lilac flowers. The coppery tinges acquired by its dainty leaves as the weather turns colder enhance its appeal. H 60cm (2ft), S 30cm (1ft).

A. novae-angliae
New England aster
The tough, tolerant species flowers from late summer to early autumn, and is rarer in gardens than its many progeny. Hardy/Z 5–8. '**Andenken an Alma Pötschke**' (syn. 'Alma Pötschke') has rich pink flowers. H 1.2m (4ft),

S 60cm (2ft). '**Harrington's Pink**' has clear pink flowers. H 1m (3ft), S 60cm (2ft). '**Herbstschnee**' (syn. 'Autumn Snow') has white, yellow-centred flowers. H 1.2m (4ft), S 60cm (2ft).

A. novi-belgii
Michaelmas daisy
Although generally applied to the whole genus, strictly the common name belongs to this species alone, the parent of a bewildering number of garden forms. It is often found growing as a weed, brightening up railway cuttings and areas of rough land with its violet-blue flowers in early autumn, which suggests a use in a wild garden or grass. The colours of the garden forms range from white, through all shades of pink, to pale and dark lavender-blue and some purples. They vary in height from dwarf forms, which are good at the edge of a border, to more substantial plants. All are hardy/Z 4–8. One of the best of the taller varieties is '**Climax**', which has pale lavender-blue flowers in early autumn. H 1.2m (4ft), S 60cm (2ft). Among the good dwarf forms are '**Jenny**', which has purplish-red flowers, and '**Lady in Blue**', which has lavender-blue flowers. H 30cm (12in), S 45cm (18in).

A. turbinellus
A refined-looking species from the United States, this has wiry stems that carry violet-blue daisies in autumn. H 1.2m (4ft), S 2ft (60cm). Hardy/Z 4–8.

Aster ericoides '*Pink Cloud*'

Aster laterifolius

Aster turbinellus

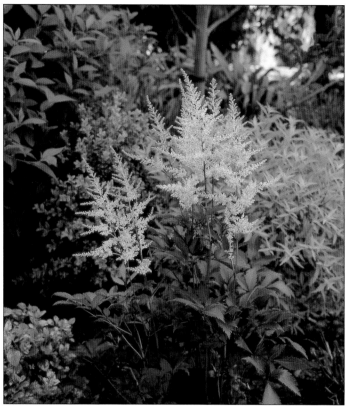

Astilbe × arendsii 'Elizabeth Bloom'

ASTILBE

These sturdy border plants, which have striking feathery plumes of flowers in mid- to late summer, have been bred to produce a range of plants of different sizes. Since the plants appreciate damp conditions, they associate well with hostas (to which they provide a strong contrast with their attractive, ferny foliage) and *Iris sibirica*. Leave the faded flowers on the plant: they will turn a rich brown, providing continued interest through the winter months. Most of the astilbes grown in gardens are hybrids.
Cultivation Grow in fertile, reliably moist soil in sun or light shade. However, they will tolerate dry soil if they are grown in shade.

A. × arendsii

This large hybrid group includes the following outstanding forms. H and S to 1m (3ft) unless otherwise indicated. All are hardy/Z 6. **'Bergkristall'** has white flowers. The late-flowering **'Elizabeth Bloom'** (syn. 'Eliblo') has pale pink flowers and bronze leaves. **'Fanal'** has long-lasting, dark crimson flowers. **'Glut'** (syn.

'Glow') is rich ruby red and flowers late. The white flowers of **'Irrlicht'** are a dramatic contrast to the dark green leaves. H and S 45cm (18in). **'Weisse Gloria'** (syn. 'White Gloria') is also white, but is bigger and early flowering. H and S 60cm (2ft).

A. 'Bronce Elegans' (syn. A. 'Bronze Elegance')

This hybrid bears plumes of pinkish-red flowers above bronze foliage. H and S 45cm (18in). Hardy/Z 6.

Astilbe × arendsii 'Fanal'

A. × crispa 'Perkeo'

This is the outstanding member of this hybrid group with deep pink flowers borne in pyramidal spires. The young leaves are tinged with bronze as they emerge. H and S to 45cm (18in). Hardy/Z 4–8.

ASTILBOIDES

Despite the name, the single species in this genus bears little resemblance to *Astilbe*. In fact, it looks more like a dwarf gunnera, for which it makes a good substitute in small gardens. It is a dramatic-looking foliage plant for a waterside location.
Cultivation This needs fertile, reliably moist soil in sun or light shade.

A. tabularis (syn. Rodgersia tabularis)

The large, light green leaves, which can be up to 1m (3ft) across, are held flat on upright stems. Small star-like white flowers appear in midsummer. H 1.5m (5ft), S 1.2m (4ft). Hardy/Z 5–7.

ASTRANTIA

Hattie's pincushion, masterwort
These perennials are not especially showy in their own right, but they combine well with other more eye-catching performers. They self-seed freely, which may become a nuisance.
Cultivation Astrantias are easy to grow in most soils in sun or light shade, and prefer fertile, well-drained ground. The species *A. major* however tolerates drier soil.

A. major
Greater masterwort
The species has straw-textured, green and pink, posy-like flowers in summer. Selections are worth growing with martagon lilies, which have similarly subdued flowers. H 60cm (24in), S 45cm (18in). Hardy/Z 5–7. The best forms include *A. major* subsp. *involucrata* **'Shaggy'**, which has clear pinkish-white flowers; *A. major* var. *rubra*, with purplish-red flowers; and **'Sunningdale Variegated'** (syn. 'Variegata'), which is a charming foliage plant with leaves generously splashed with green.

BERGENIA
Elephant's ears
These tough, hardy evergreens have stout rhizomes and leathery leaves. Most flower in early spring (some as early as late winter), producing spikes of weather-resistant, bell-shaped flowers, but they can also flower intermittently at other times of year. On some, the leaves turn beetroot (beet) purple in cold weather, retaining this colour through the winter. They look best planted en masse in an informal group near woodland and are excellent with flowering cherries. They make excellent filling for 'problem' areas of the garden, providing ideal groundcover in dry, windy sites. Most are hybrids of garden origin.
Cultivation Any soil is suitable for bergenias, which will grow in sun or shade. For the best winter leaf colour, plant in not too fertile

Astrantia major

Bergenia 'Bressingham White'

soil in an open situation. Remove damaged leaves regularly to keep plants looking their best.

B. cordifolia

This species has pink flowers among puckered leaves. H and S 30cm (12in). Hardy/Z 4–8. The selection **'Purpurea'** has rich purple flowers in spring and also later in the year. The leaves flush purple in winter.

B. hybrids

Among the best of the many forms now available are **'Baby Doll'**, which has pale pink flowers; **'Bressingham White'**, with white flowers and dark green leaves; **'Silberlicht'** (syn. 'Silverlight'), which has white flowers that fade to pink; and **'Wintermärchen'**, with deep rose-pink flowers and leaves that turn scarlet in winter. H and S to 45cm (18in). Hardy/Z 3–8.

BIDENS

Ideal hanging basket plants (and therefore often treated as annuals), these plants produce an apparently unending succession of bright yellow flowers throughout summer. *Cultivation* Grow in any well-drained soil in full sun.

B. aurea

A loosely branching, sprawling plant, this bears masses of bright yellow flowers. H 50cm (20in), S 40cm (16in). Half-hardy/ Z 8–9.

CAMPANULA
Bellflower

This is a huge genus that includes choice rock plants and biennials as well as the sturdy perennials described here. Stalwarts of the border, they combine easily with a huge range of plants, especially roses. Tough and easy to grow, they are often used to introduce their refreshing blue tones to any scheme, although other colours also occur. The common name is a perfect description of the flower shape.
Cultivation Campanulas tolerate a range of soils, provided they are well drained, and will grow in sun or light shade.

C. 'Burghaltii'

One of the subtlest campanulas, the smoky-lilac flowers are borne on erect stems in summer. Cutting back the stems after flowering can result in a second, albeit less impressive, crop of flowers. H 60cm (2ft), S 30cm (1ft). Hardy/Z 4–8.

Campanula lactiflora

C. glomerata
Clustered bellflower

This summer-flowering species is invasive in its natural form and can be troublesome, but there are several desirable cultivars. Hardy/Z 4–8. *C. glomerata* var. *alba* **'Schneekrone'** (syn. 'Crown of Snow') is a good white form. H 50cm (20in), S 60cm (2ft). **'Joan Elliott'** bears large violet flowers in early summer. H 40cm (16in), S 45cm (18in). **'Purple Pixie'** produces smaller, deep violet flowers late in the season. H 30cm (1ft), S 60cm (2ft). Possibly the best is **'Superba'**, which bears dense clusters of violet-purple flowers, ideal for adding a deeper note to plantings of red roses and peonies. H and S 60cm (2ft).

C. lactiflora
Milky bellflower

There are a number of desirable forms of this Caucasian species, all flowering in summer and early autumn. The tall, sturdy stems (taller varieties will need staking in a windy location) make them excellent for giving height to a border, and they are good as companions for shrub roses and lilies. They are also tough enough to plant in rough grass. Hardy/Z 4–8. **'Loddon Anna'** has soft lilac-pink flowers. H to 1m (3ft), S 45cm (18in). The dwarf form **'Pouffe'** makes mounds of pale blue flowers. H and S 45cm (18in). One of the grandest cultivars is **'Prichard's Variety'**, which has violet-blue flowers. H 1.5m (5ft), S 60cm (2ft).

Campanula latiloba 'Percy Piper'

C. latiloba
(syn. *C. persicifolia* subsp. *sessiiflora*)
In summer this occasionally evergreen species throws up erect stems, thickly set with rich lavender-blue flowers, from the basal rosettes of leaves. H 1m (3ft), S 45cm (18in). Hardy/Z 4–8. **'Highcliffe Variety'** and **'Percy Piper'**, both of which bear stalkless lavender-blue flowers, are similar. H 70cm (30in), S 45cm (18in).

C. punctata

This species from Russia and Japan does best in a sandy (but fertile) soil in sun. Low-growing and somewhat spreading, it flowers in mid- to late summer. The flowers are white or mauve (usually with a pink flush) and spotted inside with red. H 30cm (12in), S 45cm (18in). Hardy/Z 5–8. *C. punctata* var. *hondoensis* has greyish-pink flowers.

Campanula punctata var. hondoensis

Bergenia 'Silberlicht'

Chysanthemum 'Curtain Call'

Chrysanthemum 'Southway Swan'

Chrysanthemum 'Taffy'

CHRYSANTHEMUM

This large – formerly much larger – genus has been the subject of much controversy in recent years. Strictly speaking, the name is now applied only to annual species, but it is so deeply entrenched in gardening lore that it is retained here for a range of perennials that are now sometimes assigned to the genus *Dendranthema*. Many are for enthusiasts only, bred for exhibition and requiring a good deal of care under glass if they are to produce their stunning flowers. The plants described here, while of no lesser value, are reliable garden performers that, along with Michaelmas daisies, provide a welcome warmth of colour as the days grow cooler at the end of summer and into autumn (some continue into early winter). They are effective with late-flowering grasses.

Cultivation The plants described here do best in fertile, well-drained soil in full sun. Taller varieties need staking. Dividing plants every two years or so will help to keep them fresh.

C. hybrids

There are a vast number of named chrysanthemums available in a range of colours to suit every possible garden scheme, and flowering in late summer into autumn. The following is just a small selection. All are hardy/Z 4–9 unless otherwise stated. **'Bronze Elegance'** has light bronze, pompon flowers. H and S 60cm (2ft). **'Curtain Call'** has anemone-centred, orange flowers. H and S 60cm (2ft). **'Emperor of China'** is an old variety, with double, silvery pink flowers; the leaves are tinged with red in autumn. H 1.2m (4ft),

S 60cm (2ft). **'George Griffiths'** is an early-flowering form, with large, deep red, fully reflexed flowers; it is often grown for exhibition. H 1.5m (5ft), S 75cm (30in). Half-hardy/Z 7–9. **'Glamour'** has warm, reddish-pink pompon flowers. H and S 1m (3ft). As the name suggests, **'Goldengreenheart'** has single, gold flowers with green centres; it is late flowering. H and S 60cm (2ft). **'Mei-kyo'** is an early-flowering plant with pink pompon flowers. H and S 60cm (2ft). **'Pennine Oriel'**, an early-flowering plant, has anemone-centred, white flowers. H 1.2m (4ft), S 75cm (30in). **'Primrose Allouise'** is an early-flowering sport of 'White Allouise', with weather-resistant, incurving, soft yellow flowers. H 1.2 (4ft), S 75cm (30in). Half-hardy/Z 7–9. **'Southway Swan'**

has single flowers, with silvery pink petals surrounding yellow-green centres. H 1.2 (4ft), S 75cm (30in). **'Taffy'** has rich bronze-orange flowers. H 1.2 (4ft), S 75cm (30in).

CIMICIFUGA

Bugbane, cohash

The imposing perennials in this genus are useful for the back of a border. The upright spikes of flowers do not need staking.
Cultivation Bugbanes do best when planted in reliably moist soil in a cool position.

C. racemosa
Black snake root

This excellent plant has elegant, ferny foliage and tall bottlebrush-like spikes of white flowers throughout summer. H 2m (6ft), S 60cm (2ft). Hardy/Z 4–8.

C. simplex

This species is similar to *C. racemosa* but is more compact and flowers rather later in the year, from late summer into autumn. H 1.2m (4ft), S 60cm (2ft). Hardy/Z 3–8. Good garden forms include **C. simplex** var. *matsumurae* **'Elstead'**, which has purplish stems and creamy-white flowers; and **'White Pearl'**, which has pure white flowers and pale green leaves. H and S 60cm (2ft).

CLEMATIS

Most familiar in gardens are the many climbers belonging to this genus, but there are also a few perennials, worth growing for

Chysanthemum 'George Griffiths'

Chrysanthemum 'Primrose Allouise'

Cimicifuga simplex

Convallaria majalis

their quiet charm. All need staking.
Cultivation Grow in any fertile, preferably alkaline, soil in sun or light shade.

C. integrifolia
This weak-growing species has noticeably hairy leaves and stems. The indigo-violet flowers, borne in midsummer, have recurving petals like a turkscap lily. H and S 60cm (2ft). Hardy/Z 3–9.

C. recta
One of the best of the herbaceous clematis, this bears masses of scented, star-like, white flowers in mid- to late summer, and is an excellent foil to blue delphiniums. H 1.2m (4ft), S 1m (3ft). Hardy/Z 3–9. 'Purpurea' is more dramatic, with dark purple stems and purple-flushed leaves, but plants sold under this name can vary, some being more intensely

coloured than others. H 1.2m (4ft), S 75cm (30in).

CONVALLARIA
Lily-of-the-valley
With flowers of unsurpassed and instantly recognizable fragrance, you would think that these would be in every garden. They can be troublesome, however: difficult to establish in some cases and annoyingly rampant if they find situations they like. The flowers are excellent for cutting. The plants can also be potted up and forced under glass for early flowers. All are toxic.
Cultivation Lily-of-the-valley is best grown in fertile soil in light shade, but it also tolerates sun.

C. majalis
This species spreads by means of branching underground rhizomes. The handsome leaves emerge in spring and are followed in late spring by elegant sprays of bell-shaped, fragrant, white flowers. H 23cm (9in), S indefinite. Hardy/Z 2–9. 'Albostriata' is a choice selection, with leaves striped with silvery white. 'Fortin's Giant' is larger altogether and later flowering. H and S 30cm (1ft).

COREOPSIS
Tickseed
The genus includes perennials and annuals with daisy-like flowers in summer, all excellent in borders and ideal for cutting.
Cultivation Coreopsis does best in fertile, well-drained soil in sun. Tall varieties benefit from staking.

Coreopsis verticillata 'Moonbeam'

C. grandiflora 'Mayfield Giant'
This selection has large, single, yellow flowers in mid- to late summer. H 1m (3ft), S 60cm (2ft) Hardy/Z 4–9.

C. verticillata
The best-known species in the genus, with a number of selected forms, this is a bushy plant with star-shaped, bright yellow flowers in early summer. H 45cm (18in), S 30cm (12in). Hardy/Z 4–9. 'Golden Gain' has golden-yellow flowers from early to midsummer. Flowering later in the year, 'Grandiflora' (syn. 'Golden Shower') has rich yellow daisies and filigree foliage. H 60cm

(24in), S 45cm (18in). Also late-flowering is the versatile 'Moonbeam', which has pale yellow flowers. H 40cm (16in), S 30cm (12in).

CRAMBE
These large, rather coarse but undeniably dramatic plants are excellent for giving height and structure to borders. They are magnificent as the dominant feature of a white garden. After flowering, leave the flower stem intact and use it as a support for a late climbing annual such as sweet peas.
Cultivation Crambes will do well in any well-drained soil in full sun.

C. cordifolia
This species makes a mound of rough, cabbage-like, green leaves. In early to midsummer the flower stem carries a gypsophila-like cloud of scented, white flowers. H 2.5m (8ft), S 1.2m (4ft). Hardy/Z 6–9.

C. maritima
Sea kale
This tolerant species, found wild in coastal areas, has tough, glaucous green leaves and large panicles of white flowers in summer. The young stems are edible. H 75cm (30in), S 1m (3ft). Hardy/Z 6–9.

Clematis recta 'Purpurea'

Crambe cordifolia

Delphinium 'Clifford Sky'

Delphinium 'Fenella'

Dianthus 'Riccardo'

Dianthus 'Uncle Teddy'

DELPHINIUM

These are grand plants but are now somewhat less popular than previously, probably because they require staking from early in the season and are susceptible to slug and snail damage, which means that a certain amount of work is necessary if they are to reach their full glory. That said, few other summer perennials can equal the colour range of these stately plants: primrose-yellow, cream, white, pale and dark blue, mauve, pink and deep purple. Recent breeding programmes (mainly in the Netherlands and the United States) have also introduced orange and red into the range, making pink strains possible. A traditional, Jekyllian-style herbaceous border would be unthinkable without them, the stronger blues associating well with *Thalictrum flavum* subsp.

glaucum. The method of propagation (cuttings) has weakened the stocks of many older selections over the years, but a revival of interest in the genus has resulted in a number of vigorous plants. All parts of the plant are harmful if eaten, and the leaves can cause irritation.
Cultivation Delphiniums need fertile, well-drained, preferably limy soil in sun. Tall varieties need staking. Cutting back stems after flowering can result in further (though much less impressive) flowers later on.

D. hybrids

While some of the species make good garden plants, they have not achieved the popularity of the many hybrids, only a few of which can be described here. **Elatum Group** plants have almost flat flowers in dense, upright spikes; **Belladonna Group** plants have branched stems and loose sprays of flowers. All cultivars are hardy/Z 2–7. **'Blue Nile'** (Elatum) is a classic pale blue delphinium, with flowers, each with a white eye, densely set on the spikes. H 1.5m (5ft), S 60cm (2ft). **'Casablanca'** (Belladonna), which has pure white flowers with yellow centres, is an excellent choice for a pale planting. H 1.2m (4ft), S 60cm (2ft). **'Clifford Sky'** (Elatum) has Wedgwood-blue flowers. H 1.5m (5ft), S 60cm (2ft). **'Fenella'** (Elatum) has stems densely set with semi-double, blue flowers, each with a black centre. H 1.5m

(5ft), S 60cm (2ft). **'Finsteraarhorn'** (Elatum) has cobalt-blue flowers touched with purple, each flower having a black eye. H 1.7m (5ft 6in), S 60cm (2ft). **'Langdon's Royal Flush'** (Elatum), a good choice among pink delphiniums, has conical spires of semi-double, purplish-pink flowers. H 1.5m (5ft), S 60cm (2ft). **'Mighty Atom'** (Elatum) has solidly packed spikes of semi-double, lavender-blue flowers with brown eyes. H 2m (6ft), S 1m (3ft). The charming **'Sandpiper'** (Elatum) is a compact plant, the pure white of its flowers enhanced by their dark brown eyes. H 1.2m (4ft), S 45cm (18in).

DIANTHUS
Carnation, pink

These appealing plants are justly popular as florist's flowers, but the genus is actually a large and complex one, simplified here as border carnations, perpetual-flowering carnations, Malmaison carnations and garden pinks. Perpetual-flowering and Malmaison carnations, which are half-hardy and can be forced into flower at any time of year, are generally grown commercially under glass.

The genus also includes many alpines, the biennial *D. barbatus* (sweet William) and some annuals. Many of the species are real enthusiasts' plants, and will not do well in all gardens. Where suited, however, they are splendid additions to any border, particularly in cottage garden-style plantings. The evergreen, bluish-grey leaves provide interest over a long period, making a particularly gracious picture when combined with old-fashioned roses. They are splendid edging plants, softening the lines of any path. Dianthus are not long-lived plants, but they are easily increased by cuttings or layering late in the season.

Border carnations, which are summer-flowering, are further divided by flower type as: selfs (a single colour); fancies (one colour spotted, flecked, blotched or striped with another); and picotees (one colour edged with another). They can also be clove-scented.

Garden pinks (sometimes just referred to as 'pinks') can be further divided into: old-fashioned pinks, which flower in early summer (they can be selfs; bicolours, with the central part of

Delphinium 'Sandpiper'

Dianthus 'Spinfield Red'

Dianthus 'Louise's Choice'

Dianthus 'Letitia Wyatt'

Dianthus 'Dawlish Joy'

Dicentra formosa

the flower a different colour; or laced, with each petal edged in a contrasting colour); and modern pinks, which can have a longer season, from early summer to autumn (these can be selfs, bicolours, fancies or laced, and can also be clove-scented).
Cultivation The plants described need well-drained, neutral or alkaline soil in sun. They will tolerate some shade if it is not directly overhead.

Border carnations
All the following border carnations are hardy/Z 4–8. H to 60cm (24in), S to 40cm (16in). Among recommended varieties are the vigorous **'Bookham Fancy'**, which has yellow flowers edged and marked with carmine-purple. **'Bookham Perfume'** has scented, deep burgundy flowers. **'Lavender Clove'** has clove-scented, lavender-pink flowers. **'Orange Maid'** has apricot flowers flecked with bronze. The flowers of **'Riccardo'** combine red and white. **'Spinfield Red'** has red flowers. **'Uncle Teddy'** is red and white.

Dianthus 'Mendlesham Maid'

Garden pinks
All the following are hardy/Z 4–8. H to 45cm (18in), S to 30cm (12in). **'Bovey Belle'** has double purple flowers. **'Brympton Red'** has fragrant, crimson flowers with darker marbling. The scented flowers of **'Dad's Favourite'** are white laced with maroon, with dark centres. **'Dawlish Joy'** has variegated pink flowers. **'Devon Dove'** is pure white. **'Doris'**, a bicolour, has pale pink flowers with maroon centres. **'Excelsior'** has large-petalled, pink flowers; the flowers of **'Freckles'** are salmon-pink, delicately blotched with red. **'Gran's Favourite'** has clove-scented, white flowers laced with maroon; **'Joy'** has salmon-pink flowers. **'Letitia Wyatt'** has pale pink flowers. The semi-double **'London Brocade'** has pale pink flowers laced with dark red. **'Louise's Choice'** has crimson laced pink flowers; the miniature **'Mendlesham Maid'** has white flowers with frilly petal edges. The bicolour **'Monica Wyatt'** has phlox-pink flowers with ruby centres; **'Mrs Sinkins'** is fragrant, with double, white, fringed flowers; **'Musgrave's Pink'**, also fragrant, has double, white flowers with green centres. **'White Ladies'** has clove-scented, double, white flowers, purer in colour than 'Mrs Sinkins'.

DIASCIA
These interesting perennials (the genus name is pronounced with a hard 'c') bear nemesia-like flowers in a range of subtle colours, centring around coppery pink, throughout summer. They are not reliably hardy in cold areas, but, as with penstemons, cuttings are easily overwintered. They tend to

sprawl and look good at the base of a warm wall or in containers.
Cultivation Grow in any fertile (but not too dry) soil in full sun. Cutting the flowered stems back in summer results in further flowers in autumn.

D. barberae 'Blackthorn Apricot'
Spires of warm apricot-pink flowers are borne from summer to autumn above the mats of dark green foliage. H 25cm (10in), S 50cm (20in). Borderline hardy/Z 8.

D. rigescens
Of the several species, this is the best for general garden use. It is a shrubby South African native, with dense spikes of coppery-pink flowers in early and late summer. H and S 45cm (18in). Borderline hardy/Z 7–9.

D. hybrids
There are many excellent garden forms, including **'Lilac Belle'**, which has purplish-pink flowers; **'Rupert Lambert'**, which has pink flowers; and **'Twinkle'**, which has purplish-pink flowers. H 45cm (18in), S 40cm (16in). Borderline hardy/Z 8.

DICENTRA
Bleeding heart
This genus contains elegant perennials with arching, glassy stems clothed with ferny foliage. The heart-shaped flowers are unique. Dicentras are excellent in shady rock gardens or light woodland, but they also tolerate more open conditions, combining

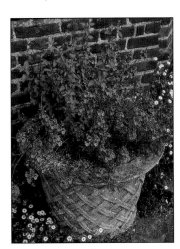

Diascia 'Rupert Lambert'

well with simple cottage garden plants, such as aquilegias, and flowering at around the same time in late spring to early summer.
Cultivation Grow in humus-rich, fertile soil in sun or light shade; they appreciate cool conditions.

D. eximia
This species is similar in appearance to *D. formosa*, and there is some confusion between the two within the nursery trade, but this is daintier with typically furry foliage and tubular, pink, purple or white flowers. H 30cm (1ft), S 45cm (18in). Hardy/ Z 4–8.

D. formosa
A species with deeply divided foliage and drooping sprays of tubular, pinkish-mauve flowers. H 45cm (18in), S 60cm (24in). Hardy/Z 3–8. *D. formosa* var. *alba* is the desirable white form.

D. spectabilis
Dutchman's breeches
The best-known species and deservedly popular, this produces fern-like foliage and masses of heart-shaped, rose-pink flowers that dangle appealingly from the arching stems. H 75cm (30in), S 60cm (24in). Hardy/Z 3–8. The selection **'Alba'** is if anything even more desirable, with white flowers and a slightly more compact habit. Both are good for cutting. H 60cm (24in), S 45cm (18in).

D. 'Stuart Boothman'
(syn. *D.* 'Boothman's Variety')
This hybrid has flesh-pink flowers on arching stems amid the bluish-grey leaves. H 30cm (12in), S 40cm (16in). Hardy/Z 4–8.

Dierama pulcherrimum

Digitalis lutea

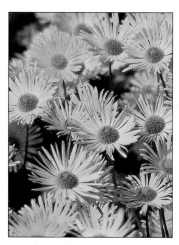

Doronicum 'Miss Mason'

ECHINACEA
Coneflower

Sturdy border plants, echinaceas are essential for providing interest from midsummer into autumn. The prominent central boss of stamens and the backwards sweeping outer petals distinguish them from all other daisy flowers. *Cultivation* Grow in any fertile, ideally humus-rich, well-drained soil in sun.

E. purpurea

This is the most widely grown species. The flowers have rich purple-crimson outer petals surrounding the prominent orange-brown centre. H 1.2m (4ft), S 45cm (18in). Hardy/Z 3–9. **'Robert Bloom'** has intense cerise-mauve flowers. **'White Swan'** is not clear white as the name suggests, but is touched with fresh pale green. H 75cm (30in), S 45cm (18in).

ECHINOPS
Globe thistle

Tolerant and undemanding, echinops are excellent in an ecological garden, since they attract bees and butterflies. *Cultivation* They will grow in any, even poor, soil in an open, sunny situation.

E. ritro

The jagged leaves are grey underneath; the ball-like flowerheads show their colour (steely blue) before the flowers open in late summer, giving a long period of interest. H 60cm (2ft), S 45cm (18in). Hardy/Z 3.

DIERAMA
Angel's fishing rods, wandflower

The common name is apt: these are plants of almost unearthly beauty, with tall, arching stems of elegant bell-shaped flowers that look well near water.
Cultivation Grow in reliably moist soil in full sun. Winter protection may be necessary in cold areas.

D. pulcherrimum
Venus' fishing rod, wandflower

From among the grassy, evergreen leaves, wiry stems emerge in mid-summer, dangling bell-shaped pink to lilac flowers. H 1.5m (5ft), S 30cm (1ft). Borderline hardy/Z 8–10. **'Blackbird'** has deep violet-mauve flowers.

DIGITALIS
Foxglove

Typical woodlanders, foxgloves also do well in more open conditions. The species described are all subtly attractive and will seed themselves where suited. They suit any cottage garden-style planting. All have spikes of characteristic, thimble-like flowers in early summer and occasionally produce lesser spikes later on, even into autumn. Poisonous.
Cultivation Foxgloves will grow in any fertile soil, but they do best in humus-rich soil, in partial shade. They will tolerate full sun.

D. lutea
(syn. D. eriostachya)

This species has small, pale yellow flowers and smooth green leaves. H 60cm (2ft), S 30cm (1ft). Hardy/Z 5–9.

D. × mertonensis

The hybrid has downward-pointing, tubular flowers the colour of crushed strawberries, a curious coppery, buff pink. The leaves are greyish-green. H 60cm (2ft), S 30cm (1ft). Hardy/Z 5–9.

D. purpurea
Common foxglove

This is the foxglove familiar in woodlands, but it makes a good garden plant, with mounds of soft, grey-green leaves, flushed purple towards the base. It is a variable species, both in flower colour, coming in shades of pink, red and purple, and height. H 1.5m (5ft), S 45cm (18in). Hardy/Z 4–8. *D. purpurea* f. *albiflora* is the delightful white-flowered form, luminous in shade. The leaves are unmarked green. The form **'Suttons Apricot'** is also desirable, with apricot-coloured flowers.

DORONICUM
Leopard's bane

These cheerful perennials have bright yellow, daisy-like flowers in spring. The species described is easily pleased and can be invasive. It is poisonous.
Cultivation Grow in any reasonable soil in sun or light shade.

D. 'Miss Mason'

This old hybrid holds its bright-yellow daisies well above the heart-shaped leaves in spring. H 45cm (18in), S 60cm (2ft). Hardy/Z 6.

D. pardalianches
Great leopard's bane

A rather coarse plant, this is suitable for colonizing light woodland and is tough enough to fill areas under deciduous trees and shrubs. The yellow, daisy-like flowers are produced in mid- to late spring. H 1m (3ft), S 60cm (2ft). Hardy/Z 4–8.

Digitalis purpurea f. albiflora

Echinacea purpurea 'White Swan'

Echinops ritro 'Veitch's Blue'

Erigeron 'Quakeress'

'Veitch's Blue' is taller, to 90cm (3ft), with darker flowerheads.

EPILOBIUM
Willowherb
These mainly tall plants are good for providing height in a border, and they flower over a long period.
Cultivation Grow in any well-drained soil that is not too rich; excessive fertility encourages leafy growth at the expense of flowers.

E. angustifolium
Rosebay willowherb
The species, attractive as it is, tends to be an invasive weed in gardens so is best confined to a wild area. H 1.5m (5ft), S 1m (3ft). Hardy/Z 3–7. **'Album'**, with spires of pure white flowers in late summer, is less rampant.

EREMURUS
Foxtail lily
Stately perennials, foxtail lilies produce tall spikes of star-shaped flowers that rise above other plants in late spring to early summer. Grow them among lower plants for maximum impact. They die back after flowering, so plant near something that will cover the gap they leave, such as *Gypsophila paniculata* or late-sown annuals. The plants may need staking in windy weather.
Cultivation Grow in any well-drained soil in sun. They tolerate dry soil.

E. × isabellinus Shelford hybrids
Under this name is a range of garden-worthy plants with tall spikes of yellow, orange, pink or white flowers. H 2m (6ft), S 1m (3ft). Hardy/Z 5.

E. stenophyllus
This lovely species has slender spikes of yellow flowers, which fade to orange-brown, giving a bicolour effect. H 1.5m (5ft), S 60cm (2ft). Hardy/Z 5.

ERIGERON
Fleabane
Useful daisy plants, suitable for a sunny border, these suit cottage garden-style plantings. There are a large number of hybrids; only the species described is well-represented in gardens.
Cultivation Best in fertile, moist but well-drained soil in sun. Taller varieties may benefit from light staking.

E. karvinskianus
(syn. E. muconatus)
Wall daisy
This spreading species has dainty white flowers from late spring to autumn. H to 30cm (1ft), S 1m (3ft). Hardy/Z 8–9.

E. hybrids
The following hybrids flower throughout summer but can also flower intermittently at other times. They are all hardy/Z 2–7. **'Dignity'** has violet-blue flowers.

H and S 45cm (18in). **'Dunkelste Aller'** (syn. 'Darkest of All') has deep purple flowers with yellow eyes. H 60cm (2ft), S 45cm (18in). **'Gaiety'** has mid-pink flowers. H 60cm (2ft), S 45cm (18in). The deservedly popular **'Quakeress'** has white flowers flushed with pale lilac-pink. H 60cm (2ft), S 45cm (18in). **'Schneewittchen'** (syn. 'Snow White') has pure white flowers, which turn pink as they age. H 60cm (2ft), S 45cm (18in).

ERYNGIUM
Eryngo, sea holly
Spiky, stiffly branched, architectural plants, eryngiums are perhaps best given space to make their own statement, ideally in a gravel garden, but they will also integrate into mixed borders, providing an excellent contrast to softer plants. Some are biennials.
Cultivation Grow in any well-drained soil in full sun. They thrive in poor, gritty soils.

E. bourgatii
This striking plant has deeply cut, bluish-grey leaves, veined white, and spiky steel-blue cones of flowers in early to midsummer. H 60cm (2ft), S 50cm (20in). Hardy/Z 5–8.

E. × tripartitum
This hybrid has wiry stems that branch freely, carrying many metallic-blue flowerheads throughout summer. It looks particularly striking with *Crambe maritima*. H 1m (3ft), S 50cm (20in). Hardy/Z 5–8.

Epilobium angustifolium 'Album'

Eremurus stenophyllus

Eryngium × *tripartitum*

Erysimum 'Bowles' Mauve'

ERYSIMUM
Wallflower

Wallflowers and tulips are a classic cottage garden combination, although bedding plants sold for this purpose are usually treated as biennials. The plants described here are all true evergreen perennials, and although they are often short-lived, they are easily increased by cuttings. All are of hybrid origin.

Cultivation Grow wallflowers in any well-drained, not too rich soil in sun, in a sheltered position. Dead-heading encourages further flowering.

E. 'Bowles' Mauve'

This truly remarkable perennial belongs in every garden. Officially it produces its four-petalled, fragrant, rich mauve flowers from late winter to early summer, but it is seldom without flowers at any time of year. H 75cm (30in), S 60cm (2ft). Hardy/Z 5–9.

E. cheiri
(**syn.** *Cheiranthus cheiri*)

This species is the parent of the many seed strains that are sold for raising bedding plants. The reliably perennial '**Harpur Crewe**' has double, rich yellow flowers from late spring to midsummer. H 30cm (12in), S 60cm (2ft). Hardy/Z 6–7.

E. 'Constant Cheer'

From mid-spring to early summer this hybrid has orange-yellow flowers that fade to purple. H 60cm (2ft), S 40cm (16in). Hardy/Z 7–10.

E. 'Parish's'

The flowers of this hybrid, produced from early spring to midsummer, open brick-red and mature to purplish-crimson. H and S 30cm (12in). Hardy/Z 7–10.

EUPATORIUM
Hemp agrimony

Somewhat coarse, but easily grown, these perennials are suitable for a wild garden or an informal border. They are valuable for their height and late season. Some are weeds.

Cultivation Any reasonable soil in sun is suitable.

E. album
(**syn.** *E. rugosum var. album*)

This species, with hairy stems and

Euphorbia cornigera

leaves, has domed heads of white flowers in late summer. H 1m (3ft), S 45cm (18in). Hardy/Z 4–9. The variant '**Braunlaub**' is similar but has brownish flowers and brown-tinged young foliage. H 1m (3ft), S 45cm (18in).

E. purpureum
Joe Pye weed, gravel root, queen of the meadow

This imposing species has characteristically rough leaves and clusters of dull pinkish-purple flowers in late summer. H 2m (6ft), S 1m (3ft). Hardy/Z 3–8. *E. purpureum* subsp. *maculatum* '**Atropurpureum**' is a superior form, with purple-flushed leaves and stems and light purple flowers. H 2m (6ft), S 1m (3ft).

EUPHORBIA

A hugely significant genus, many members of which provide interest over a long period. The true flowers are insignificant, but are surrounded by showy bracts (referred to as 'flowers' below) that continue to attract attention after the true flowers have faded. The genus encompasses a vast range of perennial plants that are at home in any garden as well as shrubs, trees, exotic succulents and annuals, in addition to the popular Christmas houseplant, *E. pulcherrima*, sold as poinsettia. Euphorbias combine happily in the border with a range of other plants. The species described here are all easy to grow, but care needs to be taken when handling them: when cut or broken, the stems exude a milky sap that can cause skin irritations.

Cultivation The euphorbias described below will grow in any well-drained fertile soil in sun. Any preferences of individual species are included in the relevant entry. To keep plants looking neat, cut back the flower stems of evergreen forms to ground level when the blooms have faded.

E. amygdaloides var. robbiae
(**syn.** *E. robbiae*)
Mrs Robb's bonnet

A good plant for a shady position under trees or for poor soil, this plant has rosettes of dark green leaves and dull green flowers in spring. H and S 60cm (2ft). Hardy/Z 5–9.

E. characias

This is a variable evergreen, rather shrubby species, happy in sun or shade, but probably better in sun. It is splendid against a warm wall, when it will send out tall, billowing shoots from ground level, clothed in narrow, grey-green leaves and topped, from early spring into summer, by lime-green flowers. H and S 1.2m (4ft). Hardy/Z 7–9. Worthwhile variants include *E. characias* subsp. *wulfenii*, which has more brilliant yellow-green flowers; and subsp. *wulfenii* '**Lambrook Gold**', which has rich golden-green flowers. H and S 1.2m (4ft).

E. cornigera
(**syn.** *E. longifolia, E. wallichii*)

An excellent border plant, this

Eupatorium album 'Braunlaub'

Euphorbia myrsinites

Euphorbia schillingii

Galega × hartlandii 'Alba'

species has dark green leaves striped centrally with paler green and, throughout summer, typical euphorbia lime-green flowers. H 50cm (20in), S 30cm (12in). Hardy/Z 7–9.

E. dulcis
This species can be invasive but makes good groundcover in shade. It has dark green leaves, sometimes tinged with bronze, and greenish-yellow flowers in early summer. H and S 30cm (12in). Hardy/Z 6. The form **'Chameleon'** is a more interesting and coveted plant than the species. It has rich purple leaves and purple-tinted flowers.

E. griffithii
This notable early summer-flowering species is invasive but desirable as groundcover in sun or light shade, especially in one

of its named varieties. It is excellent with yellow-flowered azaleas. The species has dark green, red-ribbed leaves and colourful red, yellow and orange flowerheads. H 1m (3ft), S 60cm (2ft). Hardy/Z 5–9. Among the best cultivars are **'Dixter'**, which has orange flowers and red-tinged leaves; and **'Fireglow'**, which has tomato-red flowers. H 75cm (30in), S 1m (3ft).

E. myrsinites
Myrtle euphorbia
This succulent-looking species is good in gravel gardens in full sun or in troughs, where its trailing stems are especially effective. The thick, almost triangular leaves are blue-green. The long-lasting, greenish-yellow flowers that fade to pink appear in early summer. H 15cm (6in), S 30cm (12in). Hardy/Z 6–8.

E. polychroma
(syn. E. epithymoides)
A must for the spring garden, this herbaceous perennial makes a mound of foliage that in late spring becomes a mass of brilliant yellow-green as the flowers open. It is excellent with late-flowering daffodils or *Tulipa praestans*. H and S 30cm (12in). Hardy/Z 4–9.

E. schillingii
A robust plant, this has dark green leaves and long-lasting, yellow-green flowers from midsummer to mid-autumn. It does best in light shade in reliably moist soil. H 1m (3ft), S 60cm (2ft). Hardy/Z 5–8.

FRAGARIA
Strawberry
Strawberries are usually grown exclusively in kitchen gardens for their edible fruit. The plant

described here has ornamental value, however, and makes an excellent edging plant as well as providing good groundcover.
Cultivation Grow in any moist but well-drained soil, preferably alkaline, in sun or light shade.

F. 'Pink Panda'
(syn. 'Frel')
Like the edible strawberries, this plant spreads by runners and can be invasive. It has dark green leaves and, from late spring to mid-autumn, bright pink flowers but seldom fruits. H 15cm (6in), S indefinite. Hardy/Z 4.

GALEGA
Goat's rue
This genus of large summer-flowering perennials deserve to be better known. They resemble a giant vetch with masses of pea-like flowers and are excellent for filling gaps in large borders, associating well with a wide range of other plants.
Cultivation Grow in any soil, poor or fertile, in sun or shade. Tall forms may need staking.

G. × hartlandii
This hybrid group consists of a number of worthwhile forms, usually with flowers in shades of lilac, lavender, pink or pinkish-mauve. H to 1.5m (5ft), S 1m (3ft). Hardy/Z 3–8. **'Alba'** has white flowers; **'His Majesty'** has pinkish-mauve and white flowers; and **'Lady Wilson'** is a similar bicolour, but the flowers are a more bluish-mauve.

Euphorbia polychroma

Galega × hartlandii 'Lady Wilson'

Galium odoratum

Geranium 'Ann Folkard'

Geranium macrorrhizum

GALIUM
Bedstraw

These are useful plants for filling gaps in borders, and the star-like flowers are a good foil for other, more flamboyant plants. The species described is the best known and is often included in herb gardens for its historical associations.

Cultivation Grow in any well-drained soil in sun or light shade. *G. odoratum* is one of the few plants that positively thrives in dry shade.

G. odoratum
(syn. *Asperula odorata*)
Sweet woodruff

This species cultivated as ground cover produces masses of fragrant, star-like white flowers in late spring. H 30cm (12in), S indefinite. Hardy/Z 5–8.

GERANIUM
Cranesbill

It would be difficult to over-estimate the value of these plants, which have rightly gained in popularity over recent years. Easy to grow, spreading easily and combining happily with a range of other plants, they are excellent in fairly informal, cottage-garden schemes, associating particularly well with most roses. They make excellent groundcover without being invasive. Smaller types are good in rock gardens.

Cultivation Grow hardy geraniums in any reasonable (but not boggy) soil in sun or light shade. *G. phaeum* prefers shade.

G. 'Ann Folkard'

A fine plant, this bears a succession of magenta flowers, with blackish centres and veining, throughout summer. Early in the season the flowers are pleasingly offset by yellowish leaves, but these usually turn green by midsummer. This is a good plant for growing through small shrubs in shade. H 30cm (12in), S 60cm (2ft). Hardy/Z 5–8.

G. clarkei

The spreading species, which is from India, has saucer-shaped flowers in shades of purplish-blue or white with purplish veining from early to late summer. H 50cm (20in), S indefinite. Hardy/ Z 4–8. The species is usually represented in gardens by its selected forms, outstanding among which is **'Kashmir White'** (syn. *G. pratense* 'Rectum Album'),

whose white summer flowers are delicately veined with lilac-pink. H and S 45cm (18in).

G. 'Johnson's Blue'

A plant for every garden, this hybrid has clear blue flowers in late spring over the mounds of copious green leaves. Cutting the plant back to ground level after flowering results in a fresh crop of leaves and (in a good year) a second flush of flowers. H 30cm (1ft), S 60cm (2ft). Hardy/Z 4–8.

G. macrorrhizum
(syn. *G. macrorrhizum* var. *roseum*)

The species, which spreads by means of thick rhizomes, has gummy, aromatic leaves, which assume red tinges in autumn. The liverish magenta flowers are small in relation to the size of the plant and appear in late spring. H 25cm

(10in), S 50cm (20in). Hardy/Z 3–8. The flowers of the species yield in beauty to those of **'Album'**, which are not clear white, but a delicate, pale shell pink. H 30cm (1ft), S 60cm (2ft).

G. × magnificum

This robust but sterile hybrid has handsome, slightly hairy leaves, which often redden attractively in autumn. Sticky flower stalks carry rich purple flowers, heavily pencilled with a darker shade, in late spring to early summer. H and S 60cm (2ft). Hardy/Z 4–8.

G. phaeum
Mourning widow, dusky cranesbill

The common names are appropriate: the dusky purple flowers that hang from elegant, wiry stems in mid-spring have a slightly plangent air. H 60cm (2ft), S 45cm (18in). Hardy/Z 4–9. The form **'Album'** is also desirable; it has pure white flowers and golden-yellow anthers. Where grown in proximity with the species, the two will hybridize to produce plants with pleasing soft mauve flowers. **'Lily Lovell'** is a selected form with large, mauve flowers with paler centres.

GEUM
Avens

Simple, cottage-garden-style plants, geums provide strong colour and borders over many weeks in early summer; they are good at the front of borders.

Cultivation Grow geums in any reasonable soil in sun or light shade. They benefit from division every two to three years.

G. 'Lady Stratheden'
(syn. *G.* 'Goldball')

This is one of the best known of the hybrids, with semi-double yellow flowers from late spring to midsummer. H 45cm (18in), S 30cm (12in). Hardy/Z 5–8.

G. 'Mrs J. Bradshaw'
(syn. *G.* 'Feuerball', *G.* 'Mrs Bradshaw')

The semi-double, coppery red flowers of this hybrid can be produced at any time during the summer. H 45cm (18in), S 30cm (12in). Hardy/Z 5–9.

Geranium 'Johnson's Blue'

Geranium phaeum

Geum 'Mrs J. Bradshaw'

HELENIUM
Sneezeweed, Helen's flower

These valuable daisy-like flowers are easily grown and merit a place in any border planned for late summer and autumn interest. Together with dahlias and chrysanthemums, they bring a warm glow to the garden at the end of the season, and they look good with a range of grasses and purple-leaved plants or with the strong foliage of bergenias. Most garden forms are hybrids that have been developed in Germany.
Cultivation Grow in any reasonable soil in sun. Tall forms may need staking. Regular division also prevents congestion.

H. hybrids
The following hybrids all flower from late summer to mid-autumn. All are hardy/Z 3–8. H and S 1m

(3ft). **'Gartensonne'** has light yellow flowers with dark centres; **'Indianersommer'** has rich golden-yellow flowers; **'Moerheim Beauty'**, one of the best known, has rich brownish-red flowers that age lighter brown; **'The Bishop'** has yellow flowers with dark eyes.

HELICHRYSUM

The plants in this genus are distinguished by their daisy-like, straw-textured flowers, some of which hold their colour well when dried. Some are primarily foliage plants, useful in summer bedding schemes, or in large pots or hanging baskets.
Cultivation Grow in any well-drained soil in full sun. This will not tolerate wet conditions.

H. petiolare
(syn. *H. petiolatum*)
This sprawling, evergreen subshrub is essential for hanging baskets or for trailing over the edges of a large container of seasonal plants. The typical plant has silvery, woolly leaves. H and S 1m (3ft). Half-hardy/Z 10. Selections include **'Limelight'** (syn. 'Aureum'), which has lime-green leaves; and **'Variegatum'**, which has grey-green leaves variegated with cream.

H. 'Schweffellicht'
(syn. *H.* 'Sulphur Light')
This hybrid provides interest over a long period. The white-woolly leaves are themselves a feature before the sulphur, tawny-orange daisy-like flowers appear in mid-

Helichrysum 'Schweffellicht'

to late summer. H and S 35cm (14in). Hardy/Z 5–9.

HELLEBORUS
Hellebore

An important genus from the gardener's point of view, with many desirable plants, all with nodding flowers (some a little sinister-looking, it is true) and handsome, more or less evergreen leaves. They are indispensable in the winter garden. Hellebores thrive in the shade of deciduous trees and shrubs and will even tolerate heavy shade next to a wall. All are poisonous.
Cultivation Easy to grow in any fertile, well-drained (although most prefer heavy and alkaline) soil in sun or shade.

H. argutifolius
(syn. *H. corsicus, H. lividus* subsp. *corsicus*)
Corsican hellebore
This handsome species tolerates drier conditions than most other hellebores. The firm, jade-green leaves are attractive throughout the year. The clusters of apple-green, bell-shaped flowers appear in mid-spring and last until early summer. It is a splendid foil for *Iris reticulata*. H and S 1m (3ft). Hardy/Z 6–8.

H. foetidus
Bear's foot, stinking hellebore
A dramatic species that makes a clump of blackish-green leaves. Strong stems carrying many bell-shaped, apple-green flowers (usually edged with maroon)

appear in late winter to early spring. It looks good with snowdrops. H 75cm (30in), S 60cm (2ft). Hardy/Z 4–9. Plants of the **Wester Flisk Group** have red-tinged stems and leaf and flower stalks. H 60cm (2ft), S 45cm (18in).

H. niger
Christmas rose
This is one of the most desirable of the hellebores, but unfortunately it is also one of the trickiest to grow. It has dark green, leathery leaves and large glistening white flowers in mid- to late winter. It is slow to establish and needs fertile sticky soil that does not dry out. H 30cm (12in), S 45cm (18in). Hardy/Z 4–7. **'Potter's Wheel'** is a desirable selection with larger flowers.

H. orientalis
Lenten rose
One of the easiest hellebores to grow, this is also one of the most variable species. The flowers, which appear from late winter into spring, can be white, yellowish-cream, dusky-pink, clear glowing red or plum-purple, and can also be spotted inside with a different colour to varying degrees. All are flushed green inside and out. The leaves are also handsome: firm and with serrated edges, and of varying shades of green, paler leaves being associated with paler flower colours. Blackened leaves should be removed. H 45cm (18in), S 60cm (2ft). Hardy/Z 5–9.

Helleborus foetidus

Helenium 'Indianersommer'

Helichrysum petiolare

Hemerocallis 'Golden Chimes'

Hemerocallis 'Jake Russell'

Hemerocallis 'Joan Senior'

Hemerocallis 'Ruffled Apricot'

HEMEROCALLIS
Daylily

These almost indestructible plants, with their usually trumpet-like flowers, are of increasing value in gardens. Breeding programmes (particularly in the United States) have greatly increased the number of hybrids and the length of flowering season. The colour range is also greater, but centres around yellow and orange. They make excellent border plants, rapidly forming vigorous clumps. Although the individual flowers last only a day (hence the common name), they are freely produced over a long period, and the grassy foliage is always appealing, a refreshing sight when emerging in spring and a good foil for early bulbs. Small daylilies are excellent for edging a border; the larger kinds consort happily with hostas and peonies, as well as with roses of all kinds. The species are tough enough for a wild garden or for growing in grass.

Cultivation Daylilies seem to thrive in any soil but preferably one that is not too dry. Grow in sun or light shade. Lift and divide the plants every two or three years to prevent congestion.

H. citrina
Broader leaves than average distinguish this species, whose fragrant, lemon-yellow flowers open in the evening in midsummer. H 1m (3ft), S 60cm (2ft). Hardy/Z 3–9.

H. fulva
This species is usually grown in one of its double forms. Hardy/Z 3–9. 'Flore Pleno' has sometimes muddled, rich orange flowers in summer. H and S to 1m (3ft).

'Kwans Variegata' has similar flowers but is less robust, with leaves narrowly margined with white. H and S 75cm (30in).

H. lilioasphodelus (syn. H. flava)
Late spring to early summer is the season of this semi-evergreen, evening-flowering species with scented, lemon-yellow flowers. H 75cm (30in), S 45cm (18in). Hardy/Z 3–9.

H. hybrids
There are many named hybrids, with colours and heights to fit into every garden scheme. The following, all of which are evergreen and hardy/Z 3–9 unless otherwise indicated, are just a selection. 'Cartwheels' has freely borne, orange, nocturnal flowers in midsummer. H and S 75cm (30in). The compact 'Corky' has clear yellow flowers in midsummer. H 70cm (28in), S 40cm (16in). 'Eenie Weenie', one of the first dwarfs raised, has rounded yellow flowers in early to midsummer. H 25cm (10in), S 40cm (16in). The intriguing, semi-evergreen 'Gingerbread Man' has butterscotch-orange flowers in early summer. H 70cm (28in), S 1m (3ft). Borderline hardy/Z 8–9. 'Golden Chimes' has deep yellow flowers in early summer. H 1m (3ft), S 45cm (18in). 'Green Flutter' has light yellow flowers with green throats over a long period. H 50cm (20in), S 1m (3ft). 'Jake Russell' has golden-yellow flowers with a velvety sheen in mid- to late summer. H 1m (3ft), S 45cm (18in). The semi-evergreen 'Joan Senior', the closest to a white cultivar, has pinkish-white flowers with yellow-green throats in mid- to late summer. H 60cm (2ft), S 75cm (30in). The vigorous 'Little Grapette' has deep purple flowers in midsummer. H 30cm (12in), S 45cm (18in). 'Lusty Leland' produces an abundance of scarlet and yellow flowers over a long period in summer. H 70cm (28in), S 1m (3ft). The outstanding and prolific 'Marion Vaughn' has fragrant, lemon-yellow flowers in mid- to late summer. H 85cm (34in), S 75cm (30in). 'Maura Loa' has brilliant orange flowers in summer. H 55cm (22in), S 1m (3ft). 'Prairie Blue Eyes' is semi-evergreen with lavender-purple flowers in midsummer. H 70cm (28in), S 75cm (30in). 'Ruffled Apricot' has characteristically crimped-edged, apricot flowers in early to midsummer. H 70cm (28in), S 1m (3ft). 'Scarlet Orbit' has bright red flowers with yellow-green throats in midsummer. H 50cm (20in), S 1m (3ft). 'Stafford', one of the best of its colour range, has rich scarlet flowers in midsummer. H 70cm (28in), S 1m (3ft). The vigorous 'Stella de Oro' is a dwarf selection, with rounded, bright yellow flowers in early summer, sometimes repeating in autumn. H 30cm (12in), S 45cm (18in).

HEUCHERA
Alum bell, coral bells

Invaluable plants for ground-cover, heucheras have handsome leaves, often tinted or marbled

Hemerocallis 'Little Grapette'

Hemerocallis 'Stafford'

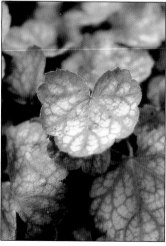
Heuchera 'Pewter Moon'

with silver-grey. There are a large number of hybrids, all making excellent companions for border carnations and pinks (*Dianthus*). **Cultivation** Grow in any reasonable soil in sun or light shade. Plants benefit from regular division.

H. micrantha var. diversifolia 'Palace Purple'

The species is most often represented in cultivation by this form, although plants sold under this name can vary. It is a striking plant with large, purple, maple-like leaves and sprays of tiny white flowers in midsummer. H 60cm (2ft), S 45cm (18in). Hardy/Z 4–8.

H. 'Pewter Moon'

This hybrid is grown primarily for the appeal of its heavily silver-marbled leaves rather than for its sprays of pink summer flowers. H 45cm (18in), S 30cm (12in). Hardy/Z 4.

H. 'Strawberry Swirl'

The hybrid has ruffled green leaves, overlaid with silver, and pale pink flowers in early summer. H 45cm (18in), S 30cm (12in). Hardy/Z 4.

× HEUCHERELLA

These dainty evergreen woodland plants, hybrids of *Heuchera* and *Tiarella*, have an old-fashioned look to them. They are clump-forming and make excellent groundcover. **Cultivation** Grow in partial shade in any soil that does not dry out completely in summer.

Hosta nigrescens

Hosta sieboldiana var. elegans

× H. tiarelloides

This beautiful evergreen ground-cover plant makes dense clusters of short leaves. The sprays of appealing, salmon-pink flowers appear in late spring. H and S 45cm (18in). Hardy/Z 4–8.

HOSTA
Funkia, plantain lily

This is an enormous genus, made larger by a huge number of hybrids, mostly of American origin. They are the ultimate foliage plants, combining handsomely with roses and a whole range of herbaceous perennials. They make good groundcover and look good with filigree ferns in shade gardens. They are also stylish in containers, although, being herbaceous, they do not provide year-round interest. The flowers, which are carried on tall 'scapes' in mid- to late summer, are of secondary interest, and some gardeners go as far as cutting them off.

Although of undoubted distinction, hostas are not universally popular, as many gardeners object to the slug and snail control that is necessary to guarantee perfect leaves. Apart from poisons, a good frog, toad and bird population or a hedgehog will control but not eradicate the pests. The parasitic nematode is effective on slugs only. An eco-friendly method that defies the cultivation hints given below is to restrict your choice to thick-leaved types and grow them in poor, gritty soil. This results in smaller but tougher leaves that are less palatable to pests. **Cultivation** Most hostas do best in fertile, humus-rich, moist soil in partial to full shade. Some will tolerate sun, but for the best leaves, the more sun, the moister the soil should be.

H. nigrescens

This large species has broadly oval, puckered leaves that are glaucous blue when mature (the emerging shoots in spring are almost black, hence the name). The near white flowers open from pale purple buds. H and S 70cm (28in). Hardy/Z 4–9.

H. sieboldiana

An impressive species with almost quilted, waxy, bluish-green leaves and almost white flowers. H 1m (3ft), S 1.2m (4ft). Hardy/Z 3–9. While of evident distinction, the species usually gives ground in gardens to *H. sieboldiana* var. *elegans* (syn. *H.* 'Elegans', *H. glauca*, *H.* 'Robusta'). This has even more thickly puckered and glaucous leaves.

H. sieboldii

One of the few naturally occurring variegated species, this should not be confused with *H. sieboldiana*, which is quite different. This has oval or lance-shaped leaves with white margins and pale mauve flowers streaked with violet. H and S 60cm (2ft). Hardy/Z 4–9.

H. ventricosa

This species has shiny green leaves with pointed tips and striking, bell-shaped, deep violet flowers. H 50cm (20in), S 1m (3ft). Hardy/Z 4–9.

H. venusta

This vigorous dwarf species is suitable for a rock garden. It has oval to lance-shaped green leaves and violet flowers, borne on scapes up to 35cm (14in) tall. H 5cm (2in), S 25cm (10in). Hardy/Z 4–9.

H. hybrids

For convenience, the following hybrids are divided into three groups: large, measuring 64cm (25in) or more from leaf tip to opposite leaf tip; medium, 40–60cm (16–24in) from leaf tip to opposite leaf tip; and small, 38cm (15in) or less from leaf tip to opposite leaf tip. All hybrids are hardy/Z 3–9 unless otherwise stated.

Hosta ventricosa

Hosta sieboldii

Hosta venusta

Hosta 'Antioch'

Large hybrids

'**Antioch**', an elegant plant, has oval leaves irregularly margined with cream or creamy white and lavender-coloured flowers. It is best in full shade. '**August Moon**' has soft yellow leaves that develop a faint greyish-blue bloom and pale greyish-lavender to white flowers. It does best in sun. '**Blue Angel**' has thick, glaucous-blue leaves (although less puckered than many of its type) and pale mauve to white flowers. '**Francee**' has leaves that are narrowly edged with white and funnel-shaped, lavender-purple flowers. '**Frances Williams**' (syn. 'Eldorado', 'Golden Circles', *H. sieboldiana* 'Frances Williams', *H. sieboldiana* 'Yellow Edge') is a famous hosta and one of the most beautiful, with deep glaucous blue leaves, margined with creamy-beige, and lavender-coloured flowers. '**Gold Standard**' has striking leaves that are generously splashed with greenish yellow, the colour becoming brighter before fading to buff beige. The flowers are greyish purple. '**Green Acres**' has

Hosta 'Gold Standard'

oval green, deeply ribbed leaves on tall petioles and near-white flowers. It is a striking plant when mature. '**Krossa Regal**', a sumptuous, urn-shaped hosta, has waxy-bloomed, bluish-green leaves and lavender-coloured flowers. '**Pearl Lake**', which has small, grey-green leaves carried on tall petioles and masses of pale lavender-coloured flowers, makes excellent groundcover. '**Piedmont Gold**' is aptly named. It has thick-textured, yellowish-green leaves with a distinct whitish bloom. The flowers are pale lavender-white. '**Sagae**' (syn. *H. fluctuans* 'Sagae', *H. fluctuans* 'Variegated') is a truly dramatic hosta with thick, blackish-green leaves margined with cream or creamy-yellow. The funnel-shaped flowers are pale lavender overlaid with purple. Sun-tolerant '**Sum and Substance**' has puckered leaves that are pointed at the tip, greenish to bright yellow in colour, depending on the amount of sun, and pale mauve flowers. '**Sun Power**' has oval to heart-shaped, yellow-green leaves and lavender flowers. '**Tall Boy**', almost uniquely among hostas, is grown for its pale purple, funnel-shaped flowers, which are carried on unusually tall scapes. The leaves are glossy mid-green. '**Wide Brim**' has puckered, bluish-green leaves that are broadly and irregularly margined with creamy white and near-white flowers. '**Zounds**' has heavily puckered, golden-yellow leaves, which develop a metallic sheen as they mature, and pale lavender-white flowers.

Medium hybrids

'**Blue Wedgwood**', an elegant plant, produces heavily puckered, intense glaucous blue leaves and pale lavender to white flowers. '**Devon Green**', a beautiful plant, has shiny dark green leaves and greyish-lavender to white flowers. '**Golden Prayers**' is a vigorous hosta, with puckered, vivid golden-yellow leaves that are held erect and almost white flowers. '**Hadspen Blue**' has substantial, glaucous-blue leaves and lavender-coloured flowers. '**Hadspen Heron**' has substantial, oval to lance-shaped, glaucous blue-green

leaves and near-white flowers. '**Halcyon**', a good choice for a container, has intensely blue leaves and near-white flowers. '**June**', an unusual hosta, has bluish-green leaves that have a strong yellow central splash, which darkens to greenish yellow. The flowers are pale lavender-grey. The sun-tolerant '**Midas Touch**' has, deeply puckered, heart-shaped, bright yellowish-green leaves and near white flowers. '**Shade Fanfare**' has yellowish-green leaves broadly margined with creamy white (both colours brighter in sun) and lavender flowers.

Small hybrids

'**Blue Cadet**' has thick, rounded, puckered leaves, which are intense glaucous blue, and purple flowers. '**Blue Moon**', which is suitable for a rock garden, has thick, puckered, dark blue leaves and pale lavender to white flowers. '**Brim Cup**' has small leaves, broadly edged with creamy white, that pucker as they age and pale lavender to white flowers. '**Ginko Craig**' has lance-shaped green leaves, crisply edged with white, and deep mauve flowers.

INULA

These robust plants have cheerful, golden-yellow daisy flowers in summer. They are undemanding cottage garden plants.
Cultivation Grow in any reasonable soil in sun. Tall species may need staking.

I. hookeri

Probably the best-known species, this coarse plant rapidly makes clumps that produce masses of acid yellow daisies in summer. H

Hosta 'Devon Green'

Hosta 'Shade Fanfare'

75cm (30in), S 60cm (2ft). Hardy/Z 4–8.

I. magnifica

As magnificent as its name implies, this is an ideal plant for a grand border, with masses of rich yellow daisies on stout stems in late summer. It combines superbly with orange-red roses and purple-leaved plants. H 2m (6ft), S 1m (3ft). Hardy/Z 5–8.

IRIS

This large genus also includes bulbs. The plants described here are rhizomatous perennials – that is, they have a fleshy rootstock (actually a modified stem) at ground level – but they represent a vast number of plants that are generally divided further as described. Irises are grown for their beautiful flowers. The combination of richness and purity of colour (in all shades except red) and elegance of form is unmatched by any other garden plant. Larger border irises are magnificent, flowering at the same time as peonies. Later on, their

Hosta 'Blue Cadet'

Inula magnifica

Iris 'Blue-Eyed Brunette'

Iris unguicularis

sword-like leaves are a good foil to other perennials and annuals. A few are best with their feet in water, in nature helping to bind the banks of streams and ponds. The winter-flowering *I. unguicularis* is unique and should be included in every garden.

Cultivation Bearded irises need well-drained soil, preferably neutral or alkaline, and a position in sun. The upper surface of the rhizome should be above ground level for a good summer baking, which promotes good flowering the next year. Beardless irises have varying requirements, as detailed in the individual entries below; the rhizomes are usually best planted below the soil surface. Crested irises (some of which are tender and excluded here) need fertile soil in a lightly shaded situation. All irises are of indefinite spread.

Bearded irises

These deciduous plants have sword-like leaves arranged like a fan; the flowers have distinctive hairs (the beard) on the falls (the three petals that hang down). The group encompasses an enormous number of hybrids, all richly coloured, of which the following are a small selection.

I. 'Blue-Eyed Brunette'
An iris with distinctive rich red-brown flowers with gold beards in late spring to early summer. H 1m (3ft). Hardy/Z 4–9.

I. 'Bold Print'
This iris has impressive flowers, basically white but heavily marked with rich purple. H 55cm (22in). Hardy/Z 4–9.

I. 'Chantilly'
An iris with pale lavender flowers in late spring to early summer. H 1m (3ft). Hardy/Z 4–9.

I. pallida
This iris, sometimes evergreen, is one of the best species for general use in the border. The warm lavender-blue flowers, good as a cut flower, open in late spring and early summer. H 1m (3ft) or more. Hardy/Z 6–9.

I. 'Peach Frost'
An iris with peach-pink standards and rich golden-orange falls in late spring to early summer. H to 1.2m (4ft). Hardy/Z 4–9.

Beardless irises

These irises, some of which are evergreen, have no hairs on the falls and generally have slimmer rhizomes than those of the bearded irises.

I. 'Arnold Sunrise'
This early spring-flowering iris has white flowers marked with orange. It needs neutral or slightly acid soil in sun or light shade. H 25cm (10in). Hardy/Z 5–9.

I. ensata
(syn. *I. kaempferi*)
Japanese water iris
This species is the parent of a large number of irises, all suitable for growing in moist, neutral to acid soil at the water's edge in full sun. Flowering is in midsummer. H to 1m (3ft). Hardy/Z 5–9. 'Ayasegawa' has white flowers edged with blue; and 'Variegata' has white markings on the leaves and deep purple flowers.

I. sibirica
This iris is a parent of a huge range of hybrids, referred to as Siberian irises, all good plants for sunny borders, but seeming to prefer damp soil. The species is an elegant plant, with narrow, grassy leaves and exquisite butterfly-like, rich violet-blue flowers, pencilled with white and gold, in early summer. H 1m (3ft). Hardy/Z 4–9. The following can be usefully grouped under this species, but are actually hybrids with other species and are therefore sometimes listed separately: 'Butter and Sugar' has white and yellow flowers. H 70cm (28in). 'Ruffled Velvet' has rich reddish-purple flowers with ruffled edges. H 55cm (22in). 'White Swirl' is a good white variety. H 1m (3ft).

I. unguicularis
(syn. *I stylosa*)
Algerian iris
One of the harbingers of spring, this iris is unique in the genus.

Among the copious grassy foliage, elegant lilac-mauve flowers with yellow markings unfurl from scrolled buds as early as midwinter, the main flowering being in late winter to early spring. This plant needs a hot spot in very well-drained soil: at the foot of a warm wall is ideal. For reliable flowering, the upper surface of the rhizome should be exposed to the sun and plants should be left undisturbed once established. H 23–30cm (9–12in).

Crested irises

These resemble bearded irises except that the beard is replaced by a raised ridge.

I. japonica
This iris has glossy green leaves and pale lavender to white flowers in mid- to late spring that are exquisitely marked with orange and purple. H to 1m (3ft). Borderline hardy/Z 8–9. In cold gardens the reputedly hardier 'Ledger's Variety', similar in all other respects, is to be preferred. H to 1m (3ft).

Iris 'Chantilly'

Iris pallida

Iris sibirica

Knautia macedonica

Kniphofia 'Alcazar'

Kniphofia 'Toffee Nosed'

KNAUTIA

The genus contains around 40 species of plants with scabious-like flowers, but only a few are widely grown. The flowers are attractive to bees, and the plants make excellent edging for the front of a border.
Cultivation Grow in any well-drained soil in sun.

K. macedonica

The best-known species, this has crimson, pincushion-like flowers on curving stems from mid- to late summer. It makes good infill in rose gardens. H and S 60cm (2ft). Hardy/Z 5–9.

KNIPHOFIA
Red hot poker, torch lily

Considered vulgar by some, there is no denying the impact that red hot pokers can have in a garden with their luminous torch-like flowers. Unfortunately, their coarse clumps of grassy foliage do not integrate well with other plants, and they tend to look best grown in isolation, for example at the foot of a warm wall. Some modern hybrids are more gently coloured and smaller, and can be grown at the front of a border. Not all kniphofias are reliably hardy, which again limits their appeal to some gardeners, but their long flowering season makes them desirable. Nearly all the plants in cultivation are hybrids of garden origin.
Cultivation Kniphofias need soil that does not dry out in summer and a position in full sun. Excessive winter wet is undesirable.

K. hybrids

There are a large number of hybrids available, ranging in size, colour and flowering time. The following are all hardy/Z 6–9. 'Alcazar', an archetypal poker, is a substantial plant with bright red flowers in midsummer. H 1.5m (5ft), S 50cm (20in). 'Candlelight' is an elegant plant, bearing slender spikes of clear yellow flowers in midsummer among long, narrow leaves. H to 50cm (20in), S 30cm (12in). 'Forncett Harvest', an autumn-flowering hybrid, has spikes of small, greenish-yellow flowers. H 1m (3ft), S 45cm (18in). One of the daintiest of recent introductions, 'Little Maid' has soft lemon-yellow flowers in summer. H 60cm (2ft), S 45cm (18in). 'Prince Igor' is a dramatic and vigorous plant, with large spikes of brick-red flowers that develop yellow touches at the base. It flowers from late summer to autumn. H 1.8m (6ft), S 1m (3ft). 'Samuel's Sensation' is a striking plant, often branched like a candelabra. It produces cream flowers tipped with coral-orange throughout the summer. H 1.2m (4ft), S 60cm (2ft). 'Toffee Nosed' is an appealing and aptly named hybrid, with cream flowers tipped with brown produced from midsummer to early autumn. H 1m (3ft), S 45cm (18in).

LAMIUM
Deadnettle

Invaluable as groundcover, these plants are considered weeds by some gardeners, but some varieties are pretty and useful for filling space under trees and shrubs.
Cultivation Grow in any well-drained soil in sun or shade.

L. maculatum

The species has mid-green leaves striped centrally with silver and whorls of reddish-purple, pink or white flowers in summer. H 20cm (8in), S 1m (3ft) or more. Hardy/Z 4–8. It is attractive enough but yields in appeal to the selections 'Beacon Silver', which has silver leaves edged in green; 'Pink Pewter', with grey-green leaves and pink flowers; and 'White Nancy', which has silver foliage and white flowers.

LEUCANTHEMUM

These daisy flowers have been included in *Chrysanthemum*. Whatever controversy may rage over their correct names, they are superb garden plants, reliably producing a show of robust daisy flowers in summer. Undemanding, they are excellent when cut, if not the most fragrant of flowers.
Cultivation Most soils are suitable, although some alkalinity seems desirable. Grow in full sun.

L. × superbum
(syn. *Chrysanthemum maximum*)
Shasta daisy

Once considered a species, this group of sturdy perennials are now known to be hybrids. All produce white flowers with yellow centres, but there are variations among the many cultivars. All are hardy/Z 5–9. 'Aglaia' has semi-double flowers. H and S 60cm (2ft). 'Everest' (syn. 'Mount Everest') has large, single flowers.

Kniphofia 'Candlelight'

Lamium maculatum 'White Nancy'

Leucanthemum × superbum 'Everest'

H to 1m (3ft), S 60cm (2ft). 'Phyllis Smith' has charming flowers, with narrow outer petals giving a dainty, feathery appearance. H to 1m (3ft), S 60cm (2ft). 'Wirral Supreme' has double flowers. H to 75cm (30in), S 60cm (2ft).

LIATRIS
Gay feather, blazing star
The feathery flowers of these perennials are unique and eye-catching, if not to all tastes. They are particularly effective as cut flowers.
Cultivation Grow in any soil that does not dry out and in a position in full sun.

L. spicata
This is the most widely grown species, with long, upright spikes of luminous mauve flowers throughout summer. H 1m (3ft), S 30cm (1ft). Hardy/Z 4–9. 'Alba' is an excellent white form.

LUPINUS
Lupin
With their tall spires of pea flowers in a range of bright colours (some being bicoloured), lupins are essential for giving height to borders in early to midsummer. Cutting them down after flowering (before they have time to set seed) can result in a second crop of (smaller) flowers in late summer, but this cannot be guaranteed so it is best to plant them behind other plants that will provide late interest. Lupins are not long-lived plants and need to be replaced regularly. They work best in groups of a single colour.
Cultivation Lupins need to grow in well-drained, lime-free soil and require a position in full sun.

L. hybrids
There are a vast number of hybrids, all of which are hardy/Z 4–8, including the following. H 1m (3ft), S 75cm (30in). The flowers of 'Blushing Bride' are white, flushed with pink; 'Catherine of York' has pinkish-orange and yellow flowers; 'Chandelier' has pale yellow flowers; 'Deborah Woodfield' is an unusual creamy pink. 'Esmerelder' has lilac flowers; 'Pope John Paul' is a good white selection; 'The Chatelaine' has pink and white flowers; 'The Governor' has blue and white flowers; 'The Page' is red.

LYCHNIS
Catchfly
These plants, with their attractive foliage, are easily grown. They look best planted en masse and blend particularly well with old roses and all cottage-garden plants.
Cultivation Grow in any well-drained soil in sun or light shade.

L. chalcedonica
Maltese cross, Jerusalem cross
This cottage-garden plant has vivid scarlet flowers in midsummer. H to 1.2m (4ft), S 40cm (16in). Hardy/Z 4–8.

L. coronaria
Dusty miller, rose campion
This species has felted grey leaves, a charming foil to the magenta flowers, which appear in midsummer. H 60cm (2ft), S 45cm (18in). Hardy/Z 4–8. The white-flowered form 'Alba' is even more desirable.

LYSIMACHIA
Loosestrife
Some of these plants are almost weed-like in their toughness and vigour, but all are useful as ground-cover, particularly in rough parts of the garden.

Lysimachia nummularia 'Aurea'

Cultivation Grow in sun in moist, well-drained, rich soil.

L. nummularia 'Aurea'
Golden creeping Jenny
The species is generally represented in cultivation by this selection, a spreading, mat-forming perennial with yellow leaves. The cup-shaped, yellow flowers, which appear throughout summer, are a bonus. In addition to its use as ground-cover, it is effective in hanging baskets or trailing over the edge of a large container. H 5cm (2in), S indefinite. Hardy/Z 4–8.

L. punctata
Dotted loosestrife
This invasive plant is almost a weed, particularly in the boggy soil in which it thrives. The bright yellow, cup-shaped flowers are carried in whorls on the upright stems in summer. H 1m (3ft), S 60cm (2ft). Hardy/Z 5–8.

Liatris spicata

Lupinus 'The Governor'

Lychnis coronaria 'Alba'

Lysimachia punctata

Lythrum salicaria 'Feuerkerze'

Macleaya cordata

Melianthus major

Melissa officinalis 'All Gold'

LYTHRUM
Loosestrife
These plants, which are suitable for a bog garden, have two seasons of interest. Not only do they attract attention when in flower in midsummer, but the whole plant often turns a vivid yellow in autumn before dying back. They self-seed prolifically unless dead-headed.
Cultivation Grow in reliably moist soil in sun. Staking may be necessary on windy sites.

L. salicaria
Purple loosestrife
This familiar plant produces tall spikes of reddish-purple flowers in summer. H 1.2m (4ft), S 45cm (18in). Hardy/Z 4–9. It has several named forms, the best of which is **'Feuerkerze'** (syn. 'Firecandle'), whose flowers are a more intense purple. H 1m (3ft), S 45cm (18in). The similar sized **'Robert'** is bright pink.

MACLEAYA
Plume poppy
These are plants for a large border. Despite their size, their overall splendour suggests that they should be grown near the front of a border, where their handsome leaves can be appreciated to the full. They work well with phlox, which flowers at around the same time, as well as helping to cool down 'hot' schemes.
Cultivation Any fertile, well-drained soil in sun or light shade is suitable. Although tall, they never need staking.

M. cordata
(syn. *Bocconia cordata*)
This is the best-known species, with plumes of cream-coloured flowers in summer. H 2m (6ft), S 60cm (2ft). Hardy/Z 4–9.

M. microcarpa
The species is broadly similar to *M. cordata*, with plumes of creamy-white flowers, but is less desirable on account of its invasive habit. The selection **'Kelway's Coral Plume'** is worthwhile, with rich pink flowers in summer. H 2m (6ft), S 1m (3ft). Hardy/Z 4–9.

MECONOPSIS
The genus includes annuals and biennials as well as the perennial described here, which is a useful addition to a wild garden.
Cultivation Grow the species described in reliably moist soil in partial shade.

M. cambrica
Welsh poppy
This European species forms clumps of dissected, bright green foliage. From spring until autumn solitary poppy flowers in yellow or orange are borne on slender stems. H 45cm (18in), S 30cm (12in). Hardy/Z 6–8.

MELIANTHUS
One of the grandest of all foliage plants, the species described becomes shrubby in warm areas where it can overwinter successfully. In cold gardens it behaves as a herbaceous perennial and is cut down by hard frosts,

usually regenerating from below ground level the following spring. It is excellent for adding height to an 'exotic' planting of cannas, dahlias and half-hardy annuals.
Cultivation Grow in any fertile, well-drained soil in full sun. In cold areas, protect the base of the plant with a dry mulch in winter.

M. major
Honey bush
Large, soft, grey divided leaves, with serrated edges, are the principal ornamental feature. In a good year plumes of brownish-red flowers can appear in summer. H 2.4m (8ft), S 2m (6ft). Half-hardy/Z 9–10.

MELISSA
Lemon balm, bee balm
An essential plant for the herb garden, lemon balm is also decorative enough for use as a foliage plant in mixed plantings. The leaves have a distinct citrus scent when crushed and can be used in herb teas.
Cultivation Grow in any well-drained soil in sun or light shade. Alkaline soil is particularly suitable.

M. officinalis 'Aurea'
(syn. *M. officinalis* 'Variegata')
The straight species bears pale yellow flowers in summer, but is of limited ornamental value. More interesting are **'All gold'**, with golden yellow leaves and lilac-tinged white flowers; and **'Aurea'** (syn *M. officinalis* 'Variegata'), with green leaves splashed with gold. H 60cm (2ft), S 45cm (18in). Hardy/Z 4–9.

MENTHA
Mint
Most mints are grown for their culinary rather than for their ornamental use, and they are indispensable in the herb garden, although they can be invasive. The flowers are of scant interest.
Cultivation Unlike most other herbs, mints prefer moist soil, but they will grow in almost any garden soil, in sun or shade. Some

Mentha suaveolens 'Variegata'

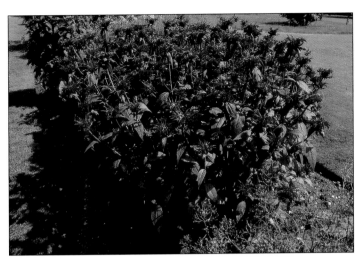

Monarda didyma

means of restraining the roots is advisable (for instance by growing them in pots sunk in the ground).

M. × gracilis
(syn. M. × gentilis)
Ginger mint, red mint
Apart from its culinary use, this hybrid, with upright, red-tinged stems and lilac-pink flowers, is of little ornamental value. Hardy/Z 4–9. More interesting is the selection **'Variegata'** (syn. 'Aurea'), which has bright green leaves speckled and striped with yellow. The best leaf colour is produced in sun. H and S 60cm (2ft).

M. suaveolens
Apple mint
This invasive mint, sometimes wrongly known as M. rotundifolia, has apple-scented leaves and pink to white flowers. H 1m (3ft), S indefinite. Hardy/Z 5–9.

'Variegata' (apple mint, pineapple mint) is a more attractive form. The leaves are marked with creamy-white, and it has a sharper fragrance (of apples) than the species. It sometimes produces plain cream leaves.

MONARDA
Bergamot
These excellent border plants bear showy heads of hooded flowers from mid- to late summer in a range of clear colours. The leaves are similar to those of mint. The stems are square in cross-section. They are ideal for a mixed or herbaceous border. Most of the plants in cultivation are hybrids.
Cultivation Monardas, particularly those with purplish flowers, prefer reliably moist soils in sun, but they will grow in most soils if improved with organic matter.

Monarda 'Snow Queen'

M. didyma
Oswego tea, sweet bergamot
This species, which is often included in herb gardens, has dense heads of pinkish-red flowers in mid- to late summer. H 1m (3ft), S 45cm (18in). Hardy/Z 4–9. **'Alba'** has white flowers.

M. hybrids
The garden hybrids, all flowering from midsummer to early autumn, and all hardy/Z 4–9, include the following. **'Beauty of Cobham'** has pale pink flowers held in purple calyces and leaves that are flushed purple. H 1m (3ft), S 45cm (18in). **'Cambridge Scarlet'**, the most widely grown cultivar, has rich red flowers held in plum red calyces. H 1m (3ft), S 45cm (18in). **'Croftway Pink'** has rose-pink flowers. H 1m (3ft), S 45cm (18in). **'Mahogany'** has purplish-red flowers. H 1m (3ft), S 45cm (18in). The tall **'Mohawk'** has light mauve flowers with paler bracts. H 1.2m (4ft), S 45cm (18in). **'Prärienacht'** (syn. 'Prairie Night') has dark lilac flowers. H 1m (3ft), S 45cm (18in). **'Snow Queen'** has pale pinkish-white flowers. H 1m (3ft), S 45cm (18in). The vigorous **'Squaw'** has scarlet flowers. H 1m (3ft), S 45cm (18in).

MORINA
Whorlflower
Elegant rather than showy, these plants need a fairly prominent position in borders among low-growing plants for their distinction to be apparent. Only the species

Morina longifolia

described is generally grown.
Cultivation Grow in fertile, well-drained but moist soil in sun. Although hardy, cold, wet conditions in winter can kill it.

M. longifolia
The species forms a rosette of thistle-like leaves, from which the flower spikes emerge in summer. These carry whorls of tubular flowers set in thorny collars that open white, turn to clear rose pink, then darken to crimson after they have been fertilized. H 1m (3ft), S 30cm (1ft). Hardy/Z 5–8.

MUSA
Banana
These exotic-looking plants are grown for their lush, tropical leaves – in cold climates, fruit is hardly likely to appear, let alone ripen. They can be used as bedding plants with cannas, dahlias and tender perennials and also look dramatic in containers. The species described is more or less hardy and can survive cold winters if given adequate protection.
Cultivation Grow in any fertile soil in full sun. Protect plants over winter with a mulch of straw or other dry material.

M. basjoo
(syn. M. japonica)
Japanese banana
This species has huge, simple, bright green leaves that tend to split horizontally and fold over. H and S 1.5m (5ft) (more in favourable conditions). Borderline hardy/Z 9–10.

Musa basjoo

Myrrhis odorata

Oenothera fruticosa subsp. glauca

MYRRHIS
Sweet cicely

A genus of one species, this is a fragrant cow-parsley-like plant that seeds itself willingly throughout the garden. It is especially effective near water or in a wild garden, and the flowers will light up any dark corner. It makes a delicate contrast to more dramatic plants such as rheums.
Cultivation Grow in any reasonable soil in sun or light shade. It prefers cool, damp situations.

M. odorata

The ferny leaves are aniseed- (anise seed-) scented and can be used in salads when young. The fluffy heads of flowers appear in early summer. H and S 1m (3ft). Hardy/Z 4–8.

NEPETA
Catmint

The catmints are essential in any garden, especially cottage gardens. They make excellent edging plants, effectively softening the hard edges of paths with their billowing habit, and are an excellent foil to herbaceous perennials and old roses. Plants become woody with age.
Cultivation Grow in any well-drained soil in full sun.

N. × faassenii
(syn. *N. mussinii*)

This hybrid is the commonly grown catmint, making mounds of aromatic, soft sage green leaves. The lavender-coloured flowers will appear in succession throughout the summer if regularly cut back as they fade. H and S 45cm (18in). Hardy/Z 4–9.

N. racemosa

A spreading catmint with soft grey-green leaves and lavender-coloured summer flowers. H 30cm (1ft), S 60cm (2ft). Hardy/Z 4–9. There are several cultivars, including **'Snowflake'**, which has white flowers; and **'Walker's Low'**, which has an arching habit and is somewhat taller. H 30–45cm (12–18in), S 60cm (2ft).

N. 'Six Hills Giant'

Generally considered the most distinguished of the catmints, this hybrid is bigger than the species in all its parts. It has the typical soft grey-green leaves and masses of lavender-coloured flowers on upright stems in summer. It can be used as a low – albeit floppy – hedge. H and S to 1m (3ft). Hardy/Z 4–9.

OENOTHERA
Evening primrose

Plants of unique charm, evening primroses have large, cool lemon-yellow flowers that open in the evening – hence the common name. They are excellent for adding dots of colour among lower-growing plants, and, because they are attractive to butterflies, are ideal for a wild garden.
Cultivation Grow in any well-drained soil in sun. Tall plants may need staking.

O. fruticosa
(syn. *O. linearis*)
Sundrops

This species is sometimes grown as a biennial and is distinct in that the flowers are open during the day. H 60cm (2ft), S 40cm (16in). Hardy/Z 4–8. On **'Fyrverkeri'** (syn. 'Fireworks') the stems and leaves are flushed with brown, and the yellow flowers open from red buds. H 45cm (18in), S 30cm (12in). *O. fruticosa* subsp. *glauca* (syn. *O. tetragona, O. tetragona* var. *fraseri*) has greyish-green leaves and pale yellow flowers. H 60cm (2ft), S 40cm (16in).

O. macrocarpa
(syn. *O missouriensis*)
Ozark sundrops

This prostrate species produces a

Nepeta racemosa 'Walker's Low'

Ophiopogon planiscapus 'Nigrescens'

Origanum vulgare 'Aureum'

Osteospermum 'Lady Leitrim'

long succession of bright yellow flowers that open from red calyces throughout summer and into autumn. It is an ideal plant for the front of a sunny border. H 23cm (9in), S 60cm (2ft). Hardy/Z 4–8.

OPHIOPOGON
Lilyturf

A genus normally represented in gardens by the form described here, which is more a conversation piece as a 'black' plant than a thing of beauty. For the most impact, grow it in gravel. It is especially effective in a Japanese-style planting.
Cultivation Grow in fertile, preferably lime-free or slightly acid soil in sun or light shade.

O. planiscapus

The straight species, an evergreen, grass-like plant with deep green leaves and small, bell-shaped pale pinkish-purple flowers, is of small distinction. Hardy/Z 6–9. Of greater interest are its cultivars, especially **'Nigrescens'** (syn. *O.* 'Arabiscus'; 'Black Dragon'; 'Ebony Knight'), with black-purple leaves and small, purplish, bell-shaped flowers. The plant spreads slowly by stolons. H and S 20cm (8in).

ORIGANUM
Oregano, marjoram

Apart from their value as culinary herbs, marjorams are of great value in the ornamental garden. In many cases the small flowers

are carried in coloured bracts that persist for several weeks, making these plants of long-lasting appeal.
Cultivation Grow in any well-drained soil in sun.

O. laevigatum

This species has dark green leaves that are less aromatic than those of some other marjorams. Its principal interest lies in its late-summer, purplish-pink flowers. It looks good with grey-leaved plants. H and S 45cm (18in). Hardy/Z 5–8.

O. vulgare
Oregano, wild marjoram

This is the species most widely grown in herb gardens, but its tiny mauve flowers in late summer are also appealing in a modest way.

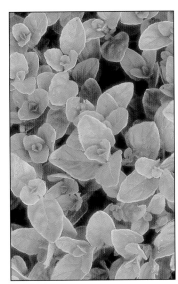

Origanum vulgare

H and S 60cm (2ft). Hardy/Z 6–9. **'Aureum'** is more compact, and grown mainly for its golden-yellow leaves, which become progressively greener during the season. It flowers only sparsely. H and S 30cm (12in).

OSTEOSPERMUM

These attractive, evergreen daisies, scarcely without a flower throughout the growing season, are of borderline hardiness and are thus often treated as summer bedding, in borders, containers and hanging baskets. However, they are reliably perennial given some shelter or can easily be overwintered as cuttings. Most of the plants sold commercially are hybrids.
Cultivation Grow in well-drained soil in full sun. To ensure winter survival in cold areas, grow them in the shelter of a warm wall. Protecting them with a dry mulch during the cold months will further increase their chances of overwintering safely.

O. hybrids

In recent years many new cultivars have been developed, extending the colour range and style of the petals. All have daisy-like flowers. **'Buttermilk'** is upright, with primrose yellow flowers. H and S 60cm (2ft). Borderline hardy/Z 9–10. **'Lady Leitrim'** has white flowers that age to pink. H and S 35cm (14in). Half-hardy/Z 9. **'Whirligig'** (syn. 'Tauranga') has flowers with distinctive, spoon-

shaped, white petals, which are mauve on the reverse, and with white centres. H and S 60cm (2ft). Half-hardy/Z 9–10. **'White Pim'** (syn. *O. ecklonis* var. *prostratum*) is low-growing. The flowers have white petals and purplish-blue centres. H 10cm (4in), S 30cm (12in). Half-hardy/Z 9.

PAEONIA
Peony

Gorgeous flowers and lustrous foliage characterize this genus. The hybrids – of which there are many – are sumptuous, but the species are equally beautiful in a different way, with simple, bowl-shaped flowers. The fact that the hybrids need staking is unlikely to deter many gardeners, for peonies are essential garden plants, either as soloists, perhaps offset by hostas or other plants with bold, simple leaves, or, where there is room, in grand groups. The species work well in light woodland. Plant spring bulbs around them, which will flower as the red peony buds appear from ground level. Peonies are usually slow to establish, but reward patience and are generally long-lived and trouble-free. The genus also includes a number of highly desirable shrubs.
Cultivation Peonies need fertile, humus-rich, well-drained soil, ideally in sun. Peonies will grow in light shade, but the flowering will be delayed and possibly impaired. They do not like being transplanted.

Paeonia lactiflora 'Alice Harding'

P. cambessedesii
Majorcan peony

This beautiful species has single, poppy-like, deep rose-pink flowers in spring, a glowing complement to the striking foliage, which is deep green suffused with crimson-purple. Unfortunately, it is not reliably hardy in cold gardens. H and S 45cm (18in). Borderline hardy/Z 7–8.

P. lactiflora
(syn. *P. albiflora*, *P. japonica* of gardens)

The species, from Russia, China and Tibet, has handsome, dark green leaves and fragrant, single, white to pale pink flowers. It has given rise to many fine cultivars. Hardy/Z 3–7. 'Adolphe Rousseau' has rich red, double flowers. H and S 60cm (2ft). 'Alice Harding' has creamy-white, double flowers. H and S to 1m (3ft). 'Bowl of Beauty', an aptly named plant, has glowing satin-pink petals, which open to reveal a central boss of cream-coloured petaloids in mid- to late spring. H and S 1m (3ft). 'Duchesse de

Nemours' (syn. 'Mrs Gwyn Lewis') has globe-shaped, double flowers in early to mid-spring. The outer petals are white, the inner creamy-yellow. H and S 60cm (2ft). 'Félix Crousse' produces a profusion of silky, clear cerise pink flowers over a long period in mid-spring. H and S 75cm (30in). The pleasingly scented 'Laura Dessert' is a ravishing plant, if rather slow to establish. It has cream or pale lemon-yellow flowers that open from pink-tinged buds to reveal a central mass of creamy-yellow inner petals. H and S 1m (3ft). 'Président Poincaré' is a tall, vigorous variety, with dark, red-veined leaves and semi-double, garnet-red flowers in mid-spring. H and S 1m (3ft). A deservedly popular cultivar with a good track record, 'Sarah Bernhardt' has large, double, soft silvery pink flowers in late spring. Strong flower stems make this a good peony for cutting. H and S 1m (3ft). 'White Wings', a cultivar flowering in late spring, has deliciously fragrant single flowers with glistening white petals surrounding golden-yellow stamens. H and S 75cm (30in).

P. mlokosewitschii
Caucasian peony

This is one of the most desirable of all the species, even if its moment of glory is all too brief. The pewter green foliage is attractive throughout the season, a splendid foil to its cool lemon-yellow flowers, which are open for no more than a week in spring.

Papaver orientale 'Effendi'

A massed planting creates a breathtaking sight. H and S 60cm (2ft). Hardy/Z 5–8.

P. officinalis

The true species has single pink or red flowers and is seldom seen in cultivation. Unnamed hybrids with fully double, white, red or pink flowers are often sold under this name, all fragrant and flowering in mid- to late spring. H and S 60cm (2ft). Hardy/Z 4–8.

PAPAVER
Poppy

Simple, beautiful plants for late spring, the flowers have silk-textured petals of unique appeal. In borders, poppies are superb curtain-raisers to the rose season. Most will have died back by midsummer, but it is possible to cover their traces with a planting of *Gypsophila paniculata* or late-flowering annuals. Many have attractive seedheads, which are

Papaver orientale 'Khedive'

good for drying for indoor decoration. Some poppies are annuals and self-seed generously. **Cultivation** Poppies do best in poor, dry soil in sun.

P. orientale

Most of the perennial poppies grown in gardens are descended from this species, although some are manifestly hybrids involving other species. They are usually grouped under *P. orientale* for practical reasons; they all produce their large, bowl-shaped flowers in late spring. All are hardy/Z 3–7. 'Beauty of Livermore' has scarlet flowers, each petal blotched with black at the base. H and S 1m (3ft). 'Black and White' has white petals blotched with black at the base. H and S 1m (3ft). 'Cedric Morris' (syn. 'Cedric's Pink') has subtly coloured greyish-pink flowers. H and S 1m (3ft). 'Effendi' has orange-red flowers. H and S 1m (3ft). 'Karine' has pale pink, flat flowers with maroon centres. H and S 80cm (32in). 'Khedive' has pale pink flowers. H and S 1m (3ft). 'Picotee' has frilly-edged flowers that are white flushed with salmon pink. H and S 1m (3ft).

PELARGONIUM

With a seemingly endless succession of cheerful flowers, in shades of white, pink and crimson, pelargoniums are the archetypal summer plant. These (usually) evergreen perennials are infinitely versatile: whether they are grown in hanging baskets, containers, windowboxes or as bedding, they belong in every

Paeonia lactiflora 'Bowl of Beauty'

Paeonia lactiflora 'Adolphe Rousseau'

Pelargonium inquinans

Pelargonium triste

Pelargonium 'Schöne Helena'

Pelargonium 'Ashley Stephenson'

summer planting, either on their own or with other bedding plants such as lobelias, alyssums and *Helichrysum petiolare*.

The genus is huge. The large number of species (native mainly to South Africa) and the sheer quantities of named varieties can seem bewildering. Breeders have devised various categories for subdividing them, as described. *Cultivation* All the plants described here are tender and are best grown in containers. Most potting composts (soil mixes) are suitable, though it is wise to add grit or perlite to the mixture to improve the drainage. Feed with a high-potassium feed when in growth to prolong flowering. Most are best in full sun, but will also tolerate light shade. Plants can be overwintered in bright, frost-free conditions. Keep the compost barely moist.

P. betulinum

This decorative plant is probably a parent to both the regal and unique pelargoniums. It has large, pink or purplish-pink (occasionally white) flowers that are heavily veined with purple-red. H and S 30–60cm (1–2ft). Tender/Z 10.

P. inquinans

This branching species has red-hairy stems, soft, almost circular leaves and scarlet, pink or white flowers. H to 1m (3ft), S 50cm (20in). Tender/Z 10.

P. triste

This appealing species has hairy, carrot-like leaves on short stems. The flowers are brownish-purple or (sometimes) yellow or brown and are remarkable in releasing a strong freesia-like scent at night. H 15cm (6in), S 45cm (18in). Tender/Z 10.

Zonal pelargoniums

The leaves are banded (or 'zoned') with a darker colour, and for most gardeners these are the typical pelargonium. This very large group is sometimes further sub-divided. All are tender/Z 10. 'Appleblossom Rosebud' has tightly clustered, double, pale pink flowers that are flushed deeper pink. H and S 35cm (14in). 'Happy Thought' has rounded leaves, with pale cream or yellow-green centres, a pale brown zone, and a broad, bright green margin. The small flowers are crimson. H and S 40–45cm (16–18in). 'Irene' has generous clusters of crimson, semi-double flowers. H and S 45cm (18in). 'Joan Fontaine', a good bedding plant, is branching and bushy, with dark green leaves and pale salmon pink flowers with small white eyes. H and S 25–30cm (10–12in). 'Lass o' Gowrie' has tri-coloured leaves, green margined with silver-green overlaid with a dark, reddish band, and bright scarlet flowers. H and S 25–30cm (10–12in). 'Mr Everaarts' is a neat, bushy plant that is ideal for windowboxes, with double, rose pink flowers. H and S to 20cm (8in). 'Mr Henry Cox' has strongly tri-coloured foliage, with a brilliant golden margin surrounding a green centre, overlaid by a deep red-black zone, and single, salmon-pink flowers. H and S 30cm (12in). 'Plum Rambler' has unusual, double, plum-red flowers. H and S 40cm (16in). 'Red Black Vesuvius' (syn. 'Black Vesuvius') has blackish-green leaves with an even darker zone and an abundance of rich scarlet flowers. H and S 13cm (5in). 'Scarlet Rambler' has clusters of eye-catching, double, brilliant scarlet flowers. H and S 40cm (16in). 'Schöne Helena' is erect and stocky, with semi-double, large, clear salmon flowers carried in large heads. H and S 40cm (16in). 'Silver Kewense' has leaves variegated silver and green and crimson flowers. H and S 13cm (5in). 'Wallis Friesdorf' has dark, blackish-green leaves and narrow-petalled, semi-double, deep rose pink to scarlet flowers. H and S to 20cm (8in).

Regal pelargoniums

These have large, richly coloured flowers. All are tender/Z 10. 'Ashley Stephenson' is compact, with creamy-pink flowers blotched and pencilled with mahogany red. H and S to 35cm (14in). 'Black Magic' produces rich blackish-red, velvety flowers. H and S to 35cm (14in). 'Fleur d'Amour' has pale leaves and soft pink and white frilly-edged flowers. H and S to 35cm (14in). 'Sunrise' has large, salmon-orange flowers that have white throats and are strikingly blazed with magenta. H and S to 40cm (16in).

Pelargonium betulinum

Pelargonium 'Irene'

Pelargonium 'Black Magic'

Pelargonium 'Moon Maiden'

Angel pelargoniums

These pelargoniums are derived from regals and are similar to them but smaller. All are tender/Z 10. **'Catford Belle'** is compact, producing an abundance of small, mauve-purple flowers that are frilled and marked with purple. H and S 30cm (12in). **'Jer'Rey'** has masses of deep red-purple flowers edged with crimson over an extended period. H and S to 35cm (14in). **'Moon Maiden'** has almost circular, pale pink flowers, which are marked with rich deep pink, and neat, dark green leaves. H and S 45–50cm (18–20in).

Decorative pelargoniums

Similar to regal pelargoniums, these have smaller leaves and flowers. All are tender/Z 10. **'Black Knight'** has masses of small, purple-black flowers that are edged with lavender. H and S 40cm (16in). **'Madame Layal'** has bicoloured flowers: deep plum-purple upper petals edged white and white lower petals marked dark purple. H and S 45cm (18in). **'Sancho Panza'**, which does well in light shade, has deep purple flowers with paler, lavender-coloured borders that are attractive to bees. H and S to 45cm (18in).

Scented-leaf pelargoniums

As the name suggests, these have aromatic leaves, and it is for these that they are grown: the flowers are small and simple, like those of the species. They are popular as houseplants. All are tender/Z 10. Members of the **Fragrans Group** make lax, open plants with pine-scented, grey-green leaves and small white flowers on trailing stems. H and S to 20–25cm (8–10in). **'Lady Scarborough'** makes a loose mound of lemon-scented foliage, above which appear small, pale pink flowers with dark purple veining. H and S to 50cm (20in). **'Little Gem'** has soft leaves that release a warm rose-lemon scent and an abundance of small mauve flowers. H and S 45cm (18in).

Unique pelargoniums

These make large, shrubby plants with soft, aromatic leaves; the flowers usually bear some mauve coloration. All are tender/Z 10. **'Pink Aurore'** has warm pink flowers, the upper petals strongly marked with a burgundy blaze. H and S to 50cm (20in). **'Rollisson's Unique'**, a lax variety, has magenta-purple flowers marked darker purple, and rose-scented leaves. H and S 40–45cm (16–18in).

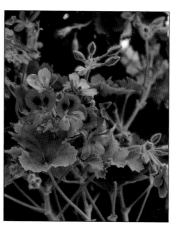

Pelargonium 'Pink Aurore'

Stellar pelargoniums

Both the flowers and leaves are roughly star shaped. All are tender/ Z 10. **'Bird Dancer'**, a neat plant, has spidery, narrow-petalled, pale pink flowers. H and S to 20cm (8in). **'Fandango'** (syn. 'Stellar Fandango') has flowers in a clear shade of salmon-pink. H and S to 18cm (7in). **'Meadowside Midnight'** has blackish-green leaves edged with paler green and orange-red flowers. H and S 18cm (7in). **'Rads Star'** has clear rose pink flowers with white eyes. H and S to 20cm (8in). **'Strawberry Fayre'** produces single to double, coral-red flowers with white eyes reliably throughout the summer. H and S to 25cm (10in).

Ivy-leaved pelargoniums

Thick, shield-like leaves are borne on trailing stems; these are ideal for hanging baskets. All are tender/Z 10. **'Eclipse'** produces large, open heads of salmon-pink flowers. S 60cm (2ft). **'Giro Fly'**

Pelargonium 'Strawberry Fayre'

has rosebud-like, double, bright purple-red flowers that are crowded together in balls. S 60cm (2ft). **'Golden Lilac Gem'** is very ornamental, with golden-green leaves and double lilac flowers. S 60cm (2ft). **'Harvard'** has semi-double, deep wine red flowers on long-jointed stems. S 60cm (2ft). **'Rigi'** is strong-growing, with semi-double, cerise pink flowers, which are feathered with burgundy red. S 60cm (2ft). **'Rio Grande'** has double, blackish-maroon flowers and shiny green leaves. S 60cm (2ft).

PENSTEMON

Penstemons are becoming increasingly popular, both for their spikes of foxglove-like flowers that appear throughout the summer and for their ease of cultivation. They make excellent border plants, but need a sheltered spot in cold areas. As a rule, the larger the flowers and leaves, the more tender the plant. Taking cuttings in late summer to autumn will ensure continuing stocks, although plants cut back by frost often regenerate from ground level. Smaller types are good in rock gardens.
Cultivation Grow in fertile, well-drained soil in full sun.

P. hybrids

The following hybrids are suitable for borders. **'Andenken an Friedrich Hahn'** (syn. 'Garnet') is useful in borders for providing the elusive clear claret red over a long period. H 75cm (30in), S 60cm (2ft). Borderline hardy/Z 7-9. **'Apple Blossom'** has soft

Pelargonium 'Black Knight'

Pelargonium 'Little Gem'

Penstemon 'Sour Grapes'

Penstemon 'Pennington Gem'

Penstemon 'Russian River'

Persicaria bistorta 'Superba'

pink flowers from midsummer until autumn. H and S 45cm (18in). Borderline hardy/Z 5–8. **'Evelyn'** is a neat-growing penstemon with slim, warm rose pink flowers striped inside with paler pink. H 45cm (18in), S 30cm (12in). Hardy/Z 6–9. **'Pennington Gem'** is a popular hybrid with large, soft pink flowers from midsummer to mid-autumn. H 75cm (30in), S 45cm (18in). Borderline hardy/Z 5–8. At its dramatic best when grown en masse, **'Russian River'** has small, dark purple flowers over a long period. H 45cm (18in), S 30cm (12in). Borderline hardy/Z 6–9. A well-known penstemon, **'Sour Grapes'** has large flowers of a rich violet-purple hue, with the characteristic white insides, striped with purple. H 60cm (2ft), S 45cm (18in). Borderline hardy/Z 6–9. An appealing plant, **'Stapleford Gem'** produces flowers that combine two colours: lilac-blue and cream. H 60cm (2ft), S 45cm (18in). Hardy/ Z 6–9. **'White Bedder'** (syn. 'Snow Storm') is a beautiful plant, which is essential in a white garden. It has pure white flowers that acquire pink tints as they age. H 60cm (2ft), S 45cm (18in). Borderline hardy/Z 6–9.

PERSICARIA
Knotweed
A genus of rampant plants that includes annuals as well as perennials, which are good for mass planting in damp soil. Most have a long flowering season. *Cultivation* Grow in reliably moist soil in full sun or light shade.

P. affinis
(**syn.** *Polygonum affine*)
The species is seldom grown in its typical form, being represented in cultivation usually by the excellent **'Darjeeling Red'**, which has drumstick-like heads of pinkish-red flowers in summer and autumn. H 25cm (10in), S 50cm (20in). **'Dimity'** is shorter with light pink flowers. H 10cm (4in), S 48cm (18in). **'Superba'**, a vigorous plant, has pale pink flowers. H 25cm (10in), S 50cm (20in). Hardy/Z 3–9. All turn rich reddish-brown in autumn, and are effective for a long time in winter.

P. amplexicaulis
(**syn.** *Bistorta amplexicaulis, Polygonum amplexicaule*)
Bistort
This semi-evergreen species has erect, lavender-like spires of pink flowers from summer to autumn. It is particularly effective with Michaelmas daisies. H and S 1.2m (4ft). Hardy/Z 5. The robust **'Firetail'** is bright red.

P. bistorta
(**syn.** *Polygonum bistorta*)
Bistort
The semi-evergreen species is almost always encountered in the form **'Superba'**, in some ways similar to *P. affinis* 'Superba' but not to be confused with it. It forms strong clumps that produce bottlebrush-like spikes of cool pink flowers on stiff stems in late spring to early summer. The damper the soil, the longer the flowering period. H and S 60cm (2ft). Hardy/Z 4.

P. virginiana
(**syn.** *Polygonum virginianum, Tovara virginiana*)
The species is seldom grown, but the following selection is a beautiful foliage plant. **'Painter's Palette'** has green-and-cream marbled leaves generously blotched with brown and touched with pink. H and S 60cm (2ft). Hardy/Z 5.

PHLOX
This is a large genus of popular evergreen and herbaceous perennials, which give an air of grandeur to borders from midsummer onwards with their pyramid-shaped heads of flowers. They are useful for providing soft colours at a time when orange and yellow are predominant in the garden, as well as being richly scented. There is a huge number of cultivars, mostly developed from *P. maculata* and *P. paniculata*, plants belonging to the former species being generally slighter and more elegant. The genus includes alpines.

Cultivation The phlox described here need humus-rich soil and a position in sun.

P. maculata
Meadow phlox
The species is characterized by hairy, often red-spotted stems. The cultivars, hardy/Z 4–8, all have flowers in the white–pink–lilac range and include **'Alpha'** with soft pink flowers; the excellent **'Omega'**, which has white flowers with violet eyes; and **'Schneelawine'** (syn. 'Avalanche') with white flowers. H 1m (3ft), S 45cm (18in).

P. paniculata
Perennial phlox
The species has smaller flowers than the many cultivars developed from it. The fragrant flowers are white or lilac. It is excellent in a wild garden. H 1.2m (4ft), S 60cm (2ft). Hardy/Z 4–8. More garden forms have been derived from this species than from *P. maculata*, all making slightly more imposing plants. **'Blue Ice'** has white flowers opening from pink buds. H 75cm (30in), S 60cm (2ft). The free-flowering **'Eve Cullum'** has rich pink flowers with deeper pink eyes. H 1.2m (4ft), S 60cm (2ft). **'Fujiyama'** has white flowers. H 75cm (30in), S 60cm (2ft). **'Little Laura'** is a compact selection with purple flowers. H 65cm (26in), S 45cm (18in). **'Mother of Pearl'** has white, pink-tinted flowers. H 1.2m (4ft), S 60cm (2ft). **'Prince of Orange'** has orange-red flowers. H 80cm (32in), S 45cm (18in).

Persicaria virginiana 'Painter's Palette'

Phlox paniculata 'Mother of Pearl'

Phormium cookianum 'Cream Delight'

PHORMIUM
Flax lily, New Zealand flax

These architectural foliage plants form imposing clumps of stiff, upright leaves, giving style and substance to borders and making an effective contrast to rounded shrubs and any plant with soft or filigree leaves. They are equally effective in containers. Be careful when handling them: the leaf tips are sharply pointed and can cause injuries. There are many selected forms with dramatically coloured leaves. The robust flowering spikes, which appear in summer, are also eye-catching.
Cultivation Grow phormiums in any, preferably reliably moist, soil in full sun or light shade. A winter mulch of straw or other dry material may be necessary in cold districts. Remove damaged leaves regularly.

P. 'Bronze Baby'
This dramatic hybrid (sometimes listed as a form of *P. tenax*) has bronze-purple, arching leaves and is useful where there is not enough room for larger forms. H and S 60cm (2ft). Borderline hardy/Z 8–10.

P. cookianum
Mountain flax
This distinguished species has plain, light green leaves and is effective where a dramatic stroke is needed. H 2m (6ft), S 1.2m (4ft). Borderline hardy/Z 8–10. *P. cookianum* '**Cream Delight**' is less vigorous. The leaves have a broad cream band along the centre. H and S 1.2m (4ft).

P. 'Sundowner'
This handsome plant has erect bronze-green leaves with deep pink edges. H and S to 2m (6ft). Borderline hardy/Z 8–10.

P. tenax
New Zealand flax
The species has smooth, grey-green, sword-shaped leaves. H 4m (13ft), S 2m (6ft). Borderline hardy/Z 8–10. Plants in the **Purpureum Group** have leaves overlaid with various shades of bronze-purple. H 2.4m (8ft), S 2m (6ft).

PHYSOSTEGIA
Obedient plant
This small genus of perennials exhibits a unique characteristic: the stems can be moved to any position, hence the common name. The species described makes a good border plant but can be invasive.
Cultivation Grow in reliably moist, humus-rich soil in sun or light shade.

Polygonatum × hybridum

P. virginiana
(syn. P. speciosa)
The species has spikes of white, red or pink flowers in late summer. H 1m (3ft), S 60cm (2ft). Hardy/Z 3–9. *P. virginiana* subsp. *speciosa* '**Variegata**' is a neater-growing form, with white-edged leaves and deep pink flowers. '**Summer Snow**' (syn. 'Snow Queen') is a good white variety. H and S 60cm (2ft).

POLYGONATUM
Solomon's seal
These quietly elegant plants are related to lily-of-the-valley and enjoy similar conditions. Their arching stems and beautiful leaves make them ideal companions for hostas and ferns, especially in woodland gardens. Sawfly caterpillars often decimate the leaves after flowering, but without affecting the plant's longevity.
Cultivation They are best in humus-rich, heavy, moisture retentive soil in shade but will tolerate most other conditions, apart from hot and dry situations.

P. × hybridum
(syn. P. multiflorum of gardens)
This, the best-known member of the genus, is a hybrid of *P. multiflorum* and *P. odoratum*. The arching stems appear in spring and bear small, lightly fragrant, bell-shaped flowers, which are white tipped with green, in late spring. H 1m (3ft), S 30cm (1ft). Hardy/Z 4–8. '**Striatum**' (syn. 'Variegatum') is a less vigorous form with cream-edged leaves. H 60cm (2ft), S 30cm (1ft).

PRIMULA
Primrose
This large and complex genus contains about 400 species of perennials, some suitable for mixed plantings, others for bedding, while a few are happiest in a rock garden. Charming though they are, they are not for all gardens, many having highly specific cultivation needs, and some particularly choice species (excluded here) are definitely best grown under glass. The plants described below do well in cool, damp atmospheres and may even seed themselves to the point of becoming a nuisance where suited. All have characteristic rosettes of spoon-shaped leaves from which the flowering stems arise. Another characteristic (but not of all) is 'farina', a flour-like bloom on the stems and leaves, which can provoke an allergic reaction.

Phormium tenax Purpureum Group

Physostegia virginiana

Physostegia virginiana 'Summer Snow'

Primula beesiana

Shorter growing primulas are delightful with dwarf spring bulbs and are good in windowboxes; primroses and polyanthus are archetypal cottage-garden plants; moisture-lovers are effective near water (preferably running water); and they are among the few plants that combine happily with rhododendrons as well as being good companions for the smaller hostas. So-called candelabra types are distinctive and graceful plants, with flowers carried in whorls up the stems.

Cultivation The plants described here are best in moisture-retentive, preferably neutral soil in sun or light shade (the more sun, the damper the soil should be). Candelabra types need moist soil.

P. beesiana
This candelabra primula, which is deciduous or semi-evergreen, produces whorls of magenta flowers from late spring to early summer. H 45cm (18in), S 30cm (12in). Hardy/Z 5–8.

P. bulleyana
The semi-evergreen species, a candelabra primula, is valued for its sharp orange flowers, which are produced throughout summer. H and S 60cm (2ft). Hardy/Z 6–8.

P. denticulata
Drumstick primula
This distinctive species has golfball-like heads of purple flowers on stout stems in spring. H and S 30cm (1ft). Hardy/ Z 4–7. **P. denticulata var. alba** is a desirable form with white flowers. 'Rubra' is one of many selections with reddish-purple flowers.

P. florindae
Giant cowslip
One of the largest species, this candelabra primula will produce satisfying mounds of foliage in damp soil, above which the erect stems carry mealy, deliciously fragrant, soft yellow flowers in early summer. It looks best planted en masse. H 1.2m (4ft), S 1m (3ft). Hardy/Z 5–8.

P. 'Inverewe'
A well-known candelabra hybrid, this has bright red flowers in summer. H 75cm (30in), S 60cm (2ft). Hardy/Z 6–8.

P. Polyanthus Group
This large hybrid group is understood here to include primroses (with flowers carried singly) and polyanthus (with clusters of flowers on upright

Primula Polyanthus Group

stems). The so-called 'hose-in-hose' polyanthus apparently have one flower emerging from the inside of another and are much sought after. Seed mixtures are available, and seed-raised plants in a range of jewel-like colours (some appealingly combining two or more) are often sold unnamed for use in bedding schemes. Depending on how they have been raised, they can flower from late winter to mid-spring in their first year. Most lose vigour the season after planting, but the following are reliably perennial and will flower in spring once established. They will grow in most garden soils that have been improved with organic matter. All are hardy/Z 6–8. Flowers of the evergreen plants in the **Gold-laced Group** (polyanthus) have an old-fashioned look, with purple-brown flowers margined with golden-yellow. H 25cm (10in), S 30cm (12in). **'Guinevere'** (syn. 'Garryarde Guinevere'; polyanthus) is distinctive, with pink flowers on red stalks and evergreen leaves suffused with bronze. H 13cm (5in), S 25cm (10in). The evergreen or semi-evergreen **'Lady Greer'** (polyanthus) has small, pale yellow flowers. H 15cm (6in), S 30cm (12in). The evergreen **'Schneekissen'** (syn. 'Snow Cushion'; primrose) has white flowers. H 10cm (4in), S 20cm (8in). Plants in the **Wanda Group** (primrose) are evergreen or semi-evergreen and have warm bluish-purple flowers. H to 15cm (6in), S 30cm (12in).

P. pulverulenta
A vigorous species, this candelabra primula has very mealy stems carrying rich pinkish-red flowers with darker eyes over a long period in summer. H 1m (3ft), S 60cm (2ft). Hardy/Z 6–8. Plants grouped as **Bartley Hybrids** vary in colour from pink to pinkish-purple and have contrasting eyes. H 1m (3ft), S 60cm (2ft).

P. veris
Cowslip
A familiar sight in damp meadows, this dainty species can be established in grass, as long as the ground is damp. The small, fragrant, yellow flowers hang from the stems in late spring. H and S 25cm (10in). Hardy/Z 6–8.

Primula denticulata

Primula pulverulenta

Primula veris

Pulmonaria saccharata

Rheum palmatum

PULMONARIA
Lungwort

Pretty plants for the spring garden, pulmonarias provide a long season of interest as the rough-textured, grey-spotted leaves expand in size. Some are more or less evergreen. Plant them with dwarf bulbs in areas around deciduous trees or shrubs. They make a good alternative to hostas for those gardeners reluctant to use slug pellets, and they are worth trying in conditions inhospitable to most other plants.
Cultivation Grow these easily pleased plants in any reasonably fertile, well-drained soil in light (or even full) shade.

P. angustifolia
Blue cowslip

This species differs from most other pulmonarias in having small, unspotted, deciduous leaves. The flowers, which open in spring, are rich blue, an effective contrast to yellow forsythias. H 23cm (9in), S 45cm (18in). Hardy/Z 4–8. Selections include **'Munstead Blue'**, which has violet flowers that age to blue. H 23cm (9in), S 45cm (18in).

P. officinalis
Jerusalem cowslip, spotted dog

This evergreen species has pink flowers, which age to violet-blue. The mid-green leaves are spotted with white. H 30cm (12in), S 45cm (18in). Hardy/Z 4–8.

P. rubra

This evergreen species, which makes excellent groundcover, has coral-red flowers that hold their colour, opening in late winter in a good year. The leaves are plain green. H 40cm (16in), S 60cm (2ft). Hardy/Z 4–8.

P. saccharata
Jerusalem sage

This species has the most heavily marked leaves – sometimes the whole leaf is silver. The spring flowers are pink, aging to blue. H 30cm (1ft), S 60cm (2ft). Hardy/Z 3–7. Plants of the **Argentea Group** have narrow leaves that are almost all silver. The flowers are red, aging to violet.

P. 'Sissinghurst White'

This outstanding hybrid, developed from *P. officinalis*, has white flowers and leaves spotted with silver. H 25cm (10in), S 45cm (18in). Essential in a white garden. Hardy/Z 4–8.

RHEUM

These are fine plants for the water's edge or for a large border. The genus includes the edible rhubarb, a handsome foliage plant in its own right. The plants described below are strictly ornamental and are especially effective as 'accent' plants in a large border but will lend an exotic touch to any garden.
Cultivation Rheums need fertile, reliably moist soil in sun or light shade.

R. 'Ace of Hearts'
(syn. *R.* 'Ace of Spades')

This hybrid is especially effective if placed where the crimson undersides of its large, heart-shaped, dark green leaves will be lit up by the sun. The plumes of tiny, pinkish-white flowers that rise up in summer are an added – if not the principal – attraction. H 1.2m (4ft), S 1m (3ft). Hardy/Z 6.

R. alexandrae

Unlike other members of the genus, this species is grown less for its glossy dark green leaves (smaller than on other species) than for its flowers, which are hooded by conspicuous cream bracts and carried on tall stems in early summer – a ghostly apparition in the twilight. It does not do well in all gardens, seeming to prefer cool, moist climates. H 1.2m (4ft), S 60cm (2ft). Hardy/Z 6–8.

R. palmatum
Chinese rhubarb

Probably the grandest rheum, this plant will command any planting. Above its mound of large, deeply cut, red-veined leaves, spires of starry, greenish flowers arise in early summer. H and S 2m (6ft). Hardy/Z 5–9. The leaves of **'Atrosanguineum'** (syn. 'Atropurpureum') are vivid red on emergence in spring, retaining that colour until the deep pinkish-red flowers appear.

ROMNEYA
Californian tree poppy, matilija poppy

The tree poppy is both beautiful and maddening in equal measure.

Pulmonaria 'Sissinghurst White'

Rudbeckia fulgida

Their deeply divided, grey foliage and huge, glistening white flowers make these plants highly desirable, but they are difficult to establish and, once at home, become aggressively rampant rapidly. Grow them in large borders and keep them well away from paths and house walls: they have been known to penetrate bricks and mortar.
Cultivation These plants do best in sun in deep, fertile, slightly heavy soil, although most types of soil are tolerated as long as it is not boggy.

R. coulteri
This striking species has large, fragrant, poppy-like flowers with crumpled white petals surrounding a central boss of deep yellow stamens. H 2.1m (7ft), S 1m (3ft). Borderline hardy/Z 6–9.

RUDBECKIA
Coneflower
Essential plants for borders in late summer, rudbeckias are sturdy and easy to grow. The petals of the daisy-like flowers droop away from the contrasting centres in a most appealing way. They combine well with grasses.
Cultivation Grow in any reasonable soil in sun. Tall varieties may need staking.

R. fulgida
Black-eyed Susan
This species makes for an excellent garden plant. The vivid yellow flowerheads with striking black centres appear from summer to autumn. H 75cm (30in), S 30cm (12in). Hardy/Z 3–9. **R. fulgida** var. **sullivantii 'Goldsturm'** has large, richer yellow flowerheads. H 60cm (2ft), S 30cm (12in).

R. 'Goldquelle'
This hybrid has double flowers with yellow petals surrounding greenish centres. It associates well with *Artemisia lactiflora*. H 1m (3ft), S 60cm (2ft). Hardy/Z 4–9.

SALVIA
Sage
In addition to important shrubby plants for the herb garden, this genus includes a number of fascinating perennials (as well as some annuals). These are becoming better known and exert a subtle attraction.
Cultivation Grow in any well-drained soil in full sun. *S. uliginosa* needs damp soil.

S. candelabrum
This woody based, almost shrubby species is rare in cultivation but of undoubted garden merit. It has wrinkled, somewhat hairy leaves and blue to violet flowers, flecked with white, in summer. H and S 1m (3ft). Borderline hardy/Z 7.

S. uliginosa
Bog sage
This full, graceful species, which sometimes needs staking, has sprays of clear blue flowers from late summer to mid-autumn. It makes a fine companion to cannas. H 1.5m (5ft), S 45cm (18in). Borderline hardy/Z 6–10.

SCHIZOSTYLIS
Kaffir lily
These plants will brighten up the autumn (and winter) garden with

Schizostylis coccinea 'Major'

their elegant spikes of fresh-looking flowers. Kaffir lilies spread rapidly, so regular division is advisable. Although there is only one species, there are a number of desirable selections.
Cultivation Grow in any but dry soil in sun. Plants will not thrive in soil that dries out in summer.

S. coccinea
The whole plant looks like a miniature gladiolus, with slender, grassy leaves and spikes of cup-shaped, bright red flowers. H 60cm (2ft), S 23cm (9in). Borderline hardy/Z 6–9. Among the many cultivars are **'Major'** (syn. 'Grandiflora'), which has bright clear red flowers; **'Sunrise'** (syn. 'Sunset'), which has salmon pink flowers; and **'Viscountess Byng'**, one of the last to flower, with pale pink flowers. H 60cm (2ft), S 23cm (9in).

Romneya coulteri

Salvia candelabrum

Schizostylis coccinea

Sedum aizoon

SEDUM
Stonecrop

These tough, hardy plants are not immediately appealing, but their merits slowly become obvious: fleshy, healthy leaves that tolerate drought and late flowers that attract bees and butterflies. They are good plants for 'problem' areas of the garden. The genus also includes small species for the rock garden and tender species, which are usually grown as houseplants.
Cultivation Sedums thrive in any well-drained, even poor, soil in full sun.

S. aizoon
(syn. *S. maximowiczii*)
One of the first sedums to flower, the star-shaped yellow flowers, held in flat heads, begin to open in midsummer. The leaves are green and toothed at the edges. H and S 45cm (18in). Hardy/Z 4–9. **'Euphorbioides'** (syn. 'Aurantiacum') is more dramatic, with red stems, darker leaves and richer yellow flowers. H 35cm (14in), S 30cm (12in).

S. 'Herbstfreude'
(syn. *S.* 'Autumn Joy')
This robust hybrid is probably the best known of all sedums. It has large, fleshy grey-green leaves and heads of scented flowers in autumn, deep pink at first, turning to salmon-pink and aging to a rich brick-red. H and S 60cm (2ft). Hardy/Z 3–9.

S. spectabile
Iceplant
Probably one of the parents of 'Herbstfreude', this species is roughly similar to the hybrid but is smaller and has pinkish-mauve flowers. H and S 45cm (18in). Hardy/Z 4–9. Among the many cultivars are **'Brilliant'**, which has bright pink flowers; and **'Iceberg'**, which is a good white.

S. 'Vera Jameson'
One of the most dramatic of the sedums, this hybrid has glaucous, purple leaves and heads of dusky-pink flowers in late summer. H 30cm (12in), S 45cm (18in). Hardy/Z 4–9.

SIDALCEA
False mallow, prairie mallow

Mallow-like flowers, like miniature hollyhocks, characterize this genus, which, from the gardener's point of view, consists mainly of hybrids. They are excellent additions to the mixed or herbaceous border and work well in cottage gardens.
Cultivation Grow in any reasonable soil in sun or light shade. Tall varieties may need staking. Cutting down the stems after flowering can result in further flowers.

S. hybrids
There are several fine hybrids, mostly developed from *S. malviflora* (checkerbloom) and flowering in early to midsummer. **'Elsie Heugh'**, one of the palest, has spikes of fringed, pink flowers. H 1m (3ft), S 45cm (18in).

Sedum 'Herbstfreude'

Sidalcea 'Elsie Heugh'

'Oberon' has clear pink flowers. H 1m (3ft), S 45cm (18in). **'Puck'**, which is more compact and robust, has deep pink flowers. H 40cm (16in), S 30cm (12in). Hardy/Z 5–7.

SISYRINCHIUM

These plants, which have iris-like leaves, have a happy knack of seeding themselves around – generally to good effect. They are excellent in gravel gardens, their stiffly upright habit providing effective contrast to mat-forming plants. They can also be grown in borders. The genus includes annuals as well as the perennials described here.
Cultivation Grow in sun in any well-drained soil that is not too fertile and preferably gritty and alkaline.

Sisyrinchium striatum

S. striatum
(syn. *Phaiophleps nigricans*)
The best-known species, this has compact tufts of sword-shaped, grey-green leaves and, in summer, slender spikes of straw yellow flowers, striped purple on the reverse of the petals. H 75cm (30in), S 23cm (9in). Hardy/Z 6–9. **'Aunt May'** (syn. 'Variegatum') has leaves edged creamy-yellow. H 50cm (20in), S 20cm (8in).

STACHYS
Betony, hedge nettle

A group of charming edging plants for a border or for a Mediterranean scheme – the hotter and drier it is, the more they like it.
Cultivation Grow in any well-drained soil in full sun.
S. macrantha will take some shade.

S. byzantina
(syn. *S. lanata*)
Lamb's ears, bunny's ears
Softly furry, silvery leaves, enhanced by hot sun, characterize the plants of this low-growing species. The flower spikes appear in summer and are also furry, swaddling the tiny pinkish-purple flowers. H 45cm (18in), S indefinite. Hardy/Z 4–8. There are a large number of selections, all of which make good edging plants to rose beds, including **'Cotton Boll'** (syn. 'Sheila McQueen'), which has flowers that look like balls of cotton wool; **'Primrose Heron'**, which

Stachys byzantina 'Silver Carpet'

Tradescantia Andersonia Group 'Innocence'

Thalictrum flavum subsp. *glaucum*

Tradescantia Andersoniana Group 'Isis'

has leaves with a pronounced soft yellow flush; and **'Silver Carpet'**, a valuable non-flowering form, which is useful where a low mat of foliage is required.

S. macrantha
(syn. S. grandiflora)
This slightly coarse plant has corrugated, dark green, hairy leaves and rich rose-mauve flowers in summer, which combine in a particularly pleasing fashion with old-fashioned roses. H 60cm (2ft), S 23cm (9in). Hardy/Z 4–8.

THALICTRUM
Meadow rue
Still all too rare in gardens, these are plants of considerable style. They combine delicacy with stature and bring a touch of freshness to borders with their frothy flowers at the height of summer. Use them as a contrast to plants that have bolder, showier flowers or combine them with the foaming *Gypsophila paniculata* for a romantic billowing cloud of blossom.
Cultivation Grow in any fertile, well-drained soil in sun or light shade.

T. aquilegiifolium
This species is distinguished by its aquilegia-like foliage, although it is much taller and the flowers are far from similar. Appearing in early summer, these are a fluffy mass of warm pinkish-lilac. H 1m (3ft), S 60cm (2ft). Hardy/Z

5–8. Also worth growing are *T. aquilegiifolium* var. *album*, which has white flowers, and **'Thundercloud'**, which has dramatic dark purple flowers.

T. flavum
Yellow meadow rue
The species has glaucous grey leaves and masses of fluffy yellow flowers in summer. H 1m (3ft), S 45cm (18in). Hardy/Z 5–9. The leaves of *T. flavum* subsp. *glaucum* (syn. *T. speciosissimum*) are more pronouncedly glaucous.

TIARELLA
Foam flower
Dainty woodland plants, tiarellas are useful as groundcover in shady areas of the garden. They are grown primarily for the appeal of their leaves; the pretty flowers are an attractive bonus.

Tiarella cordifolia

Cultivation Tiarellas do best in humus-rich, fertile soil in shade; they prefer cool conditions.

T. cordifolia
The heart-shaped leaves of this species take on bronze tints in cold weather. Upright spikes of creamy white flowers appear in summer. H and S to 30cm (12in). Hardy/Z 3–8.

T. wherryi
(syn. T. cordifolia var. collina)
Although it is broadly similar to *T. cordifolia*, this is more compact and has white or pink flowers. H and S 20cm (8in). Hardy/Z 3–8. **'Bronze Beauty'** has bronze-tinged leaves and pink flowers. H and S 20cm (8in). Hardy/Z 3–8.

TRADESCANTIA
The flowers are unusual in having only three petals, which gives them a distinctive appearance. Tradescantias are easy to grow and look good towards the front of mixed or herbaceous borders, providing thick cover and flowering reliably. The genus also includes some well-known house-plants, grown mainly for their variegated leaves.
Cultivation Grow in any well-drained soil in sun.

T. Andersoniana Group
This hybrid group includes a number of worthy garden plants, all of which are hardy/Z 4–9, including **'Innocence'**, which has

pure white flowers; **'Isis'**, with rich indigo-blue flowers; and **'J.C. Weguelin'**, with pale blue flowers. H and S 45cm (18in).

TRICYRTIS
Toad lily
These are gracious little flowers for the end of the season. They need a prominent position in borders, where their unique appeal can be appreciated. They are also effective in light woodland.
Cultivation Grow in any fertile soil in light shade.

T. formosana
This species sends up tall, thin, branching flower stems with glossy oval leaves in early autumn. The small, lily-like flowers are mauve, heavily spotted with darker mauve. H to 1m (3ft), S 45cm (18in). Hardy/Z 7.

Tricyrtis formosana

Trifolium repens 'Purpurascens Quadrifolium'

TRIFOLIUM
Clover

With the exception of the plant described, most clovers are generally considered to be weeds. Nevertheless, selected forms are effective at the front of a border and are essential in wildflower gardens, the flowers being especially attractive to bees.
Cultivation Grow clover in moist, neutral soil in sun.

T. repens
Dutch clover, shamrock

The species is normally encountered as a lawn weed but the form 'Purpurascens Quadrifolium' has attractive maroon-purple leaves edged with green and typical white clover flowers in summer. H 10cm (4in), S indefinite. Hardy/Z 4–7.

TRILLIUM
Trinity flower, wood lily

These dramatic woodlanders are among the most desirable of spring-flowering plants, but unfortunately they are not always easy to please. Where they are happy, a massed planting can be breathtaking (although isolated clumps are also effective), but they are best appreciated when kept away from daintier flowers.
Cultivation Grow in fertile soil, preferably enriched with leaf mould, in shade, ideally beneath overhanging deciduous trees.

T. grandiflorum
Wake robin

One of the grandest of the genus, this is also the best-known species. The flowers, which have three curving, pure white petals, open in spring above the large, simple leaves. H 38cm (15in), S 30cm (12in). Hardy/Z 4–9. 'Flore Pleno', which has double white flowers, is if anything even more sumptuous.

TROLLIUS
Globe flower

Pleasing perennials for the spring garden, globe flowers are good in borders with tulips, although they really prefer damp conditions and are ideal for a streamside planting or bog garden. They are also good companions to rhododendrons.
Cultivation Grow in reliably moist soil in sun or light shade. Also worth trying in ordinary soils provided they are not in full sun.

Trillium grandiflorum 'Flore Pleno'

T. × *cultorum*

The hybrid group contains a large number of selections, all of which are hardy/Z 3–7, flowering from mid-spring to midsummer. The unique 'Alabaster' has pleasing soft ivory-yellow flowers, but is none too vigorous. H 60cm (2ft), S 40cm (16in). The early-flowering 'Earliest of All' has yellow flowers. H 50cm (20in), S 40cm (16in). 'Orange Princess' is vigorous and has orange-yellow flowers. H to 60cm (2ft), S 45cm (18in).

VERBASCUM
Mullein

A genus of stately plants, many of which are grown as biennials, but including a number of perennials. They are excellent for giving height to summer borders.

Cultivation Grow in any well-drained soil in sun. Tall plants may need staking.

V. chaixii
Nettle-leaved mullein

This sturdy semi-evergreen species has woolly, upright stems, which are densely set with buttercup-like yellow flowers in summer. H 1m (3ft), S 45cm (18in). Hardy/Z 5–9. The selected form 'Album' has white flowers.

V. 'Helen Johnson'

A very desirable hybrid, this is difficult to propagate – hence the high price of plants in the nursery trade. The spikes of pinkish-brown flowers bring a unique colour into the garden. H 1m (3ft), S 45cm (18in). Hardy/Z 5–8.

V. 'Mont Blanc'

This hybrid has pure white flowers, so has an honoured place in white gardens, the grey-green leaves adding to its value. H 1m (3ft), S 30cm (1ft). Hardy/Z 6.

VERBENA

Not all verbenas are reliably hardy, and that has probably kept them out of many gardens, but the ones described here are all worth taking a chance on. They provide a long season of colour and for that reason deserve their place, even if they behave as annuals and succumb to winter frost (the

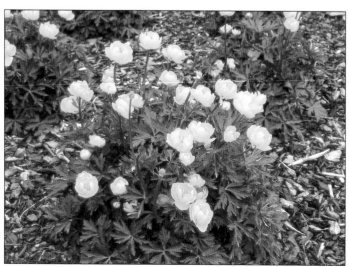

Trollius × *cultorum* 'Earliest of All'

Verbascum chaixii 'Album'

Verbena bonariensis

Viola 'Jackanapes'

V. 'Jackanapes'

A delightful hybrid with a cheeky look to its yellow and brown flowers, the yellow petals streaked with purple. It tends to be short-lived. H 12cm (5in), S 30cm (12in). Hardy/Z 5–7.

V. labradorica
Labrador violet

This species is a prolific self-seeder in conditions that suit it, and charming where allowed to naturalize beneath shrubs. Its dainty, apple purple flowers appear above the bronze-tinged leaves in spring. H to 8cm (3in), S indefinite. Hardy/Z 4–8.

genus also includes true annuals). Verbenas are delightful in borders, popular as bedding, and short varieties also work well in containers (including window-boxes) and hanging baskets.
Cultivation Grow in any well-drained soil in full sun. In cold areas a dry mulch can help them overwinter.

V. bonariensis

This is a plant that should be in every garden. The tall stems (square in cross-section) are much-branched and have a profusion of heads of small, luminous violet flowers from summer until well into autumn. It combines happily with almost every other plant in the garden, as well as adding an airy charm all of its own. Even where not hardy, it

tends to seed itself freely. For the best effect, plant in groups. H to 1.5m (5ft), S 30cm (1ft). Borderline hardy/Z 7–10.

V. 'Sissinghurst'
(syn. V. 'Saint Paul')

This is one of a number of hybrids with a low, spreading habit, and it is, therefore, ideal for the front of a border. It has heads of glowing magenta flowers throughout the growing season. H 20cm (8in), S 60cm (2ft). Borderline hardy/ Z 5–9.

VERONICA
Speedwell

These easy-to-grow plants are excellent in mixed and herbaceous borders, and the spikes of flowers are produced over a long season. Mostly in the violet-blue-lilac range, they provide an excellent contrast to orange and yellow daylilies. Small species are good in rock gardens.
Cultivation Grow in any ordinary garden soil in sun or light shade.

V. longifolia

This species has hebe-like spikes of lavender-blue flowers in late summer and autumn. H 1m (3ft), S 30cm (1ft). Hardy/ Z 4–8. **'Blauer Sommer'** is more compact and has clear blue flowers. H 50cm (20in), S 30cm (12in).

VIOLA
Violet

This huge genus containing about 500 species includes annuals

(pansies), biennials and alpines as well as a number of perennials. They are excellent for carpeting large areas, especially under trees and shrubs. There are also a huge number of hybrids, omitted here, developed for exhibiting.
Cultivation Grow in any well-drained soil in sun or light shade.

V. biflora
Twin flowered violet

This dwarf rhizomatous species is found in Europe to Northern Asia and North America. Kidney-to heart-shaped pale green leaves are borne on thin stems and lemon-yellow flowers, veined dark purple-brown on the lower petals, appear either solitary or in pairs in late spring to summer. H 5-15cm (2-6in), S 15cm (6in). Hardy/Z 4-8.

ZAUSCHNERIA
Californian fuchsia

This genus of sun-loving perennials provides brilliant material for the front of a border, the funnel-shaped flowers being a vivid scarlet in most cases.
Cultivation Good drainage is essential, as is a position in full sun. They are best with the shelter of a warm wall in cold areas, where they are not reliably hardy.

Z. californica

This, the best-known species, has attractive, lance-shaped, grey-green leaves, the perfect foil to the luminous scarlet flowers, produced from late summer to early autumn. H and S 45cm (18in). Hardy/Z 6–9. **'Dublin'** has slightly longer, bright orange-red flowers. H 25cm (10in), S 30cm (12in).

Veronica longifolia

Zauschneria californica

Annuals

Annuals are unrivalled for bringing colour into the garden throughout the warmer months. They bring any border to vivid life within a matter of weeks, and give an established air to even a new garden. Besides their use in the larger garden, they are also excellent in tubs, hanging baskets and all manner of containers. Many bring other rewards, being deliciously scented or attractive to beneficial insects, or providing cut flowers for the house.

Few plants provide the gardener with such a wide range of colour and form as the annuals.

Growing annuals

Vigorous but delicate young bedding plants need to be planted carefully at exactly the right time, otherwise they will receive a check in growth and may never recover.

Planting

Prepare the ground by digging over the soil and removing weeds and other debris. Incorporate well-rotted organic matter, such as manure or garden compost, if the soil is poor. Make sure all the plants have been hardened off well beforehand and keep tender bedding in a frost-free place until it is safe to plant outside.

The stems of young bedding plants are delicate and easily damaged, so it's advisable to handle them by their rootball or leaves rather than holding them by the stems. For this reason the best way to remove the plant from its container is by turning it upside down in the pot with the plant between two fingers and tapping the pot or pushing on its base to dislodge the rootball. Plant at the same depth as the plant was in the pot and firm the soil lightly around the rootball. Water well after planting.

HOW TO PLANT EDGING

1 Prepare the soil, removing any weeds and adding some well-rotted compost if the soil is impoverished. Break the soil down to a fairly fine consistency. Set up a garden line at an even distance from the actual edge of the border. Alternatively, for a curved border, use a standard measure, such as a length of stick, between the edge and each plant.

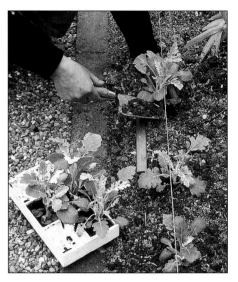

2 Plant the edging plants along the line at the correct spacing (depending on the variety), checking the distance between each one with a measuring stick. Firm in each plant and water. For an informal planting, you can use a mixture of plants in uneven rows so that the edging merges into the other plants in the border.

Late frosts

Protect new bedding from damaging late frosts by covering plants with a double layer of horticultural fleece or sheets of newspaper when late frosts are forecast. If unprotected tender plants are touched by frost, minimize the damage by covering them in the morning, before the temperature rises, to slow down the thaw. It is the rapid thaw that causes most damage to plant tissues.

Hardening off bedding plants

About two weeks before you want to set out your bedding plants, they will need to be weaned off the cosy temperatures inside the greenhouse to the harsher environment outdoors. This is known as hardening off. It simply means that you get plants slowly accustomed to conditions outside over a period of time. Normally, this is done with a cold frame. Start off by opening the top slightly on mild days and closing it at night, then increase this ventilation each day until the top is removed altogether. If you don't have a cold frame you can use shelves near vents in the roof of a greenhouse to harden plants off or construct a makeshift cold frame out of a large cardboard box cloche or layers of horticultural fleece in a sheltered part of the garden.

Puddling in

If your soil is dry or you are planting during a warm spell in summer, use a special technique called puddling in. Water the plants well in their pots as usual. Prepare the planting hole and fill it right up with water. When the water has had a chance to soak away, position the plant and replace the soil around the roots. Water thoroughly after planting and keep well watered until established.

An informal edging of *Chrysanthemum tenuiloba* 'Golden Fleck' sprawls out over a path.

Bedding planner

Bedding type	planting distance
Ageratum	20cm (8in)
Alyssum	15cm (6in)
Antirrhinum	23cm (9in)
Begonia	15cm (6in)
Dianthus	20cm (8in)
Gazania	20cm (8in)
Impatiens	20cm (8in)
Lobelia	15cm (6in)
Nemesia	20cm (8in)
Nicotiana	30cm (12in)
Pelargonium	30cm (12in)
Petunia	25cm (10in)
Salvia	20cm (8in)
Tagetes (African)	20cm (8in)
Tagetes (French)	20cm (8in)
Verbena	25cm (10in)
Viola x wittrockiana	20cm (8in)
Zinnia	25cm (10in)

HOW TO PLANT ANNUAL CELLULAR PLANTS

1 Several hours before planting out, or the evening before, water the tray of plants and leave them to stand so excess water drains away. The plants are less likely to be stressed by the move if they are growing well.

2 Remove a plant from the pack by pressing on the bottom. In strips, where the plants are not segregated, remove the lot from the pack and carefully remove one, trying not to tear off too many of its neighbour's roots.

3 Using a small trowel, dig a planting hole that is wider and slightly deeper than the plant's rootball.

4 Adjust the depth of the planting hole so that the top of the rootball is level with the surrounding soil.

5 Fill in the hole around the plant with soil and gently firm down with your hands.

6 Water the plant with a watering can fitted with a fine rose. Keep well watered thereafter until the plant is well established.

Ageratum houstonianum 'Blue Danube'

AGERATUM
Floss flower

These fluffy half-hardy annuals, mostly in shades of blue, are ideal for edging a border. They are also excellent in windowboxes.
Cultivation Grow in any soil in full sun. Sow from late winter onwards in a propagator.

A. houstonianum
Most seed and hybrid strains are listed under this species, although they may result from crosses with other species. **'Blue Danube'** forms compact hummocks of rich lavender-blue flowers; **'Blue Mink'** has powder-blue flowers; **'North Star'** has warm purplish-blue flowers; **'Pinky Improved'** is an unusual dusky pink variety; and **'Summer Snow'** is a good white form. H and S 15cm (6in) or more. Half-hardy/Z 8.

ALCEA
Hollyhock

Hollyhocks are quintessential cottage-garden plants, such that most gardeners are prepared to put up with their tendency to develop rust for the sake of their spires of mallow-like flowers. Although they can be perennial, their propensity to disease makes it advisable to treat them as biennials and discard plants that have flowered. Plant them towards the back or middle of a border. The flowers attract butterflies.
Cultivation Grow in any soil in sun. Sow in summer for flowering the following year and transplant in autumn, if necessary.

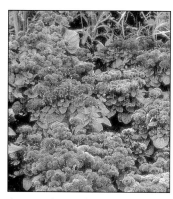

Ageratum houstonianum 'North Star'

A. rosea
(syn. *Althaea rosea*)
The papery-textured flowers, carried the length of tall, felted stems, are characteristic of this Turkish species. Named forms and strains include plants in **Chater's Double Group**, which have peony-like, double flowers in a range of colours; and the impressive **'Nigra'**, which has dramatic, rich chocolate-maroon flowers. H 2m (6ft), S 60cm (2ft). Hardy/Z 6–9.

AMARANTHUS
Love-lies-bleeding

The unusual tassel-like flowers of these half-hardy annuals are not to all tastes, although they are indispensable in a 'hot' scheme of reds, oranges and purples.
Cultivation Grow in any soil in sun or light shade. Sow in containers in early spring.

A. caudatus
The species produces pale green leaves and dangles its tassels of

Amaranthus caudatus

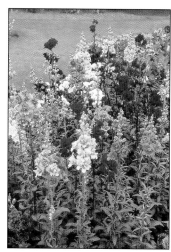

Antirrhinum majus 'Double Madam Butterfly Mixed'

tiny blood-red flowers from mid- to late summer. H and S to 1.2m (4ft). Half-hardy. **'Viridis'** has electric green flowers that fade to cream. H and S 60cm (2ft). **'Pygmy Torch'** has purple-flushed leaves and red flowers. H and S 45cm (18in).

ANGELICA

These stately biennials are well known in herb gardens, but they can also be effectively deployed in ornamental mixed borders, where they will add height and structure.
Cultivation Grow in any fertile soil in sun or light shade. Sow the seed as soon as it is ripe.

A. archangelica
(syn. *A. officinalis*)
Archangel
In its first year this species produces fresh green leaves with

Angelica archangelica

serrated edges. In the second year tall, ribbed stems carry domed heads of tiny greenish flowers. H 2m (6ft), S 1m (3ft). Hardy/Z 4–9.

ANTIRRHINUM
Snapdragon

The unique "snapping" lips of the flowers of snapdragon gives them a certain appeal to children. These half-hardy annuals provide strong blocks of colour – white, yellow, orange, pink and red (some flowers being bicoloured) – in beds and borders.
Cultivation Any soil in full sun is suitable. Sow in a propagator from midwinter.

A. majus
The many hybrids are often ascribed to this species. They are characterized by upright spikes of richly coloured flowers over a long period from summer to the first frosts. All are half-hardy. **'Black Prince'** has deep crimson flowers and bronze foliage. H 45cm (18in). **'Brazilian Carnival'** has bicoloured flowers in a combination of colours. H 60–90cm (2–3ft). **'Double Madam Butterfly Mixed'** has rather muddled, double flowers in a range of colours. The flowers are excellent for cutting. H 60–90cm (2–3ft). **'Kim Orange Bicolor'** has dazzling flowers, combining brilliant orange and yellow. H 25–30cm (10–12in). Plants from the **Royal Carpet Series** are vigorous and ideal for bedding, with flowers in a range

Antirrhinum majus 'Black Prince'

Bellis perennis 'Dresden China'

Begonia semperflorens Cocktail Series

of colours. H 25–30cm
(10–12in). Plants raised from the
Sonnet Series, which are also in
mixed colours, show good weather
resistance. H 45cm (18in).

BEGONIA
In addition to the tuberous
species and houseplants, this large
genus includes a number of
tender annuals, which are useful
for bedding or for growing in
hanging baskets.
Cultivation Grow in any soil in
sun or light shade. Sow in a
propagator from midwinter (this
is not always successful and it can
be advisable to buy in young
plants as plugs for growing on).

B. semperflorens
These versatile plants, with pink,
red, white or bicoloured flowers,
can also be used as summer houseplants. All are tender/Z 10.
The single flowers in the **Cocktail
Series** are set off by round, bronze
leaves. H 20–30cm (8–12in),
S 30cm (12in). Flowers in the
Coco Mixed Series are also offset
by rich bronze leaves. H 20–30cm
(8–12in), S 30cm (12in).
Plants in the **Options Mixed**
series can have green or bronze
leaves. H 20–30cm (8–12in),
S 30cm (12in).

BELLIS
The genus includes the attractive
lawn daisies that generally appear
unannounced in all gardens, but
the hardy biennials described here
are appealing bedding plants for
early in the season. They are also

delightful in windowboxes.
Cultivation Grow in any soil in
full sun. Sow in summer for
planting out in autumn.

B. perennis
This species, which is native to
Europe, is the parent of a number
of seed strains, all producing
rosettes of leaves and flowers in
shades of red, pink or white. All
are hardy/Z 4–8. 'Dresden
China', a dwarf form, has small,
pink, double flowers with quilled
petals. H and S to 10cm (4in).
Plants in the **Habanera Series**
have flowers with long petals,
each flower to 5cm (2in) across.
H and S to 20cm (8in). The
Pomponette Series produces
double, tightly quilled, pompon
flowers, each to 4cm (1½in)
across. H and S 15cm (6in).

BIDENS
These plants are actually perennial
in frost-free conditions but are
usually treated as annuals. Their
trailing habit and dainty, fern-like
foliage make them ideal for
hanging baskets or to soften the
edge of a large container.
Cultivation Grow in any soil in
sun or light shade. Sow in a
propagator in early spring.

B. aurea 'Sunshine'
This form is the one most
commonly seen. It has bright
yellow flowers over a long period
from early summer until the first
frosts. H 50cm (20in), S 40cm
(16in). Half-hardy/Z 8.

BRACTEANTHA
These Australian annuals have
daisy-like flowers with distinctive
papery petals. They are excellent
for filling gaps in summer
borders, holding their colour
well in hot sun.
Cultivation Grow in any well-
drained soil in sun. Sow in a
propagator in spring.

B. bracteata
(**syn. *Helichrysum bracteatum*)**
Golden everlasting, strawflower
Most of the seed strains and
cultivars are included within this
species. Tender/Z 9–10. **Bright
Bikinis Series** is a dwarf strain
with double, pompon-like flowers
in white or shades of red, pink
and yellow. H 30–45cm
(12–18in), S to 30cm (12in).
'Coco' (syn. *Helichrysum* 'Coco')
has straw white flowers with
yellow centres. H 1m (3ft), S
30cm (12in). 'Silvery Rose' has
clear pink flowers with yellow
centres. H to 75cm (30in), S
30cm (12in).

CALCEOLARIA
Slipper flower
This is a large genus containing
about 300 species, although only
a few are widely available. Selected
forms are grown as half-hardy
annuals for summer bedding.
The common name refers to the
shape of the inflated flowers.
Cultivation Grow in well-drained
soil in sun. Sow in a propagator
in spring or, for earlier flowers
the following year, in summer.

Bracteantha bracteata 'Coco'

C. Herbeohybrida Group
Most of the strains grown in
gardens belong to this complex
hybrid group, which involves a
number of species. Besides their
garden use, they can also be
grown as flowering pot plants for
conservatories. Half-hardy/Z 9.
The **Anytime Series** produces
dwarf plants in a range of colours
that are good for growing in
containers under glass. H and S
to 20cm (8in). '**Bright Bikinis'**
has dense heads of yellow, orange
or red flowers. H and S 20cm
(8in). '**Kentish Hero'** has vivid
yellow flowers marked with
orange-red to maroon. H and S
to 30cm (12in). '**Sunset Mixed'**
is a strain of bushy plants that
produce clustered flowers in
shades of red, including some
bicoloured with yellow or orange.
H and S to 30cm (12in).

Bellis perennis Pomponette Series

Calceolaria 'Kentish Hero'

Calendula officinalis 'Fiesta Gitana'

Cerinthe major

Cleome hassleriana 'Helen Campbell'

Cleome hassleriana 'Pink Queen'

CALENDULA
Pot marigold
The common name refers to the culinary use of these hardy annuals, not to their suitability for containers. They are rather coarse plants of easy cultivation (often seeding themselves indiscriminately), but valued for their cheery flowers.
Cultivation Grow in any soil in full sun. Sow in situ from autumn onwards.

C. officinalis
The straight species has single orange flowers and aromatic, light green leaves. H and S to 60cm (2ft). Hardy/Z 6. There are several named selections. Plants in the **Art Shades Mixed Series** have flowers in shades of orange, apricot or cream. H and S 60cm (2ft). **'Fiesta Gitana'** is a more compact form, which has orange or yellow (sometimes bicoloured) flowers. H and S 30cm (1ft). The flowers of **'Pacific Apricot'** have pale apricot petals, tipped in a deeper shade. H and S to 30cm (12in).

CENTAUREA
Knapweed, hardheads
The genus contains about 450 species of annuals and perennials, of which the species described is an indispensable plant for a wild-flower meadow, attracting bees and butterflies into the garden. Selected forms are good for cutting.
Cultivation Grow in any well-drained soil in sun. Sow in containers in late winter to early spring.

C. cyanus
Cornflower
The species can have blue, pink, purple or white flowers through-out summer and into autumn. H to 1m (3ft), S 30cm (1ft). Hardy/Z 7. **'Blue Diadem'** has double, rich blue flowers and is more compact. H 75cm (30in), S 30cm (12in).

CERINTHE
Honeywort
Until recently, these hardy annuals were little known, but gardeners have slowly become more aware of their subtle charms. They are grown for their coloured bracts, of interest over a long period in summer, rather than the true flowers, which are insignificant.
Cultivation Grow in any well-drained soil in sun. Sow in spring in containers or in situ.

C. major
The species, from southern Europe, has sea-green bracts tinged with yellow and purple.

H to 60cm (2ft), S 30cm (1ft). Hardy/Z 5. The flowers of the more compact **'Kiwi Blue'** are shaded more blue-purple. H 45cm (18in), S 30cm (12in). **'Purpurascens'** has rich purple-blue flowers with cream insides. H to 45cm (18in), S 30cm (12in).

CLEOME
Spider flower
These beautiful plants, with airy domed heads of scented flowers, lend elegance to any planting. They are among the tallest of the half-hardy annuals.
Cultivation Grow in any well-drained soil in sun. Sow in a propagator from late winter.

C. hassleriana
(**syn. *C. pungens*, *C. spinosa* of gardens**)
Most of the garden forms are grouped under this species. H 1.2m (4ft), S 45cm (18in). Half-hardy/Z 1–11. **'Colour Fountain'**, has flowers in shades of pink, lilac, purple and white. Single-

colour selections include **'Cherry Queen'**, with reddish flowers; **'Helen Campbell'** (syn. 'White Queen'), with pure white flowers; **'Pink Queen'**, with pinkish-white flowers; and **'Violet Queen'**, with mauve flowers.

COBAEA
Cathedral bell, cup-and-saucer vine
The common name is descriptive: the large flowers really are like cups and saucers. This tender annual (a perennial in its native Mexico) is an ideal plant for adding seasonal interest to a pergola or can be grown on a tripod to give height to a border.
Cultivation Grow in any moderately fertile soil in sun, preferably with some shelter. Sow in a propagator in spring.

C. scandens
Where grown as an annual this species, which climbs by means of tendrils, will produce large, fragrant, velvety-purple and green

Cerinthe major 'Kiwi Blue'

Cerinthe major 'Purpurascens'

Cobaea scandens

Convolvulus tricolor 'Royal Ensign'

Coreopsis grandiflora 'Early Sunrise'

Cosmos bipinnatus 'Versailles Tetra'

flowers from summer to autumn. H to 3m (10ft), more in favourable conditions. Tender/Z 9–10. The attractive **C. scandens f. alba** has white flowers aging to yellowish-cream.

CONVOLVULUS

In addition to the pernicious bindweed, this genus includes some highly desirable hardy annuals that, with their spreading habit, make excellent hanging basket plants.
Cultivation Grow in any well-drained soil in sun. Sow in situ in spring or in summer for flowers the following year.

C. tricolor
(**syn. C. minor**)
This species is actually a short-lived perennial, but is best treated as an annual. It has short-lived, blue, funnel-shaped flowers, borne in succession all summer long. H 40cm (16in), S 30cm (12in). Hardy/Z 8. Strains in single colour and mixtures are also available, of which one of the best is 'Royal Ensign'. It has rich, deep blue, trumpet-shaped flowers with yellow and white centres. H and S 35–50cm (14–20in).

COREOPSIS
Tickseed
These plants produce cheerful, usually bright yellow daisy flowers over a long period in summer.
Cultivation Grow in any well-drained soil in sun or light shade. Sow in situ from late winter, or from midsummer to autumn for early flowers the following season.

C. californica
This erect annual produces a vivid show of yellow daisies over grassy foliage. H to 45cm (18in), S to 30cm (12in). Hardy/Z 1–11.

C. grandiflora
This perennial species is parent to a number of strains that are invariably grown as annuals. All are hardy/Z 4–9. 'Early Sunrise' bears masses of semi-double, yellow flowers, which are excellent for cutting. H 45cm (18in), S 38cm (15in). 'Mayfield Giant' has large, single, bright yellow flowers. H 1m (3ft), S 45cm (18in).

COSMOS
With one of the longest flowering seasons of any annual, these half-hardies are of unquestioned value, quite apart from the distinction of the glistening flowers and feathery foliage. They are also excellent for cutting.
Cultivation Grow in any soil in sun. Sow in situ after all danger of frost has passed.

C. bipinnatus
Most of the available seed strains are ascribed to this species. All are half-hardy/Z 1–11. 'Sea Shells' has distinctive flowers, with rolled, almost tubular florets in shades of crimson, pink and white, some being bicolours. H to 1m (3ft), S 45cm (18in). The compact plants in the **Sonata Series** produce carmine, pink or white, bowl-shaped flowers. Single-colour selections include 'Sonata White', which has pure white flowers and grows to 60cm (2ft), and 'Sonata Pink', which has all-pink flowers. H 45cm (18in), S 30cm (12in). 'Versailles Tetra' has greyish-pink flowers with a darker area towards the golden-yellow centres. H 1m (3ft), S 45cm (18in).

DIANTHUS
Pink
Most dianthus are perennials or rock garden plants, but there are also a few annuals and the appealing biennial, sweet William,

a plant of old-fashioned charm that is essential for any cottage-style planting.
Cultivation Grow in any well-drained soil in sun. Sow sweet Williams in midwinter, in containers, for flowers in late summer, or in summer, in situ, for flowers the following spring. Sow annuals in containers in early spring.

D. barbatus
Sweet William
Uniquely in the genus, this biennial produces flowers in dense rounded heads. The deliciously scented flowers can be red, pink or white; some are bicoloured. Selected strains are available. H to 70cm (28in), S 30cm (12in). Hardy/Z 4. **Indian Carpet Mixed** is a dwarf strain. H and S 15cm (6in).

D. chinensis
(**syn. D. sinensis**)
Chinese pink, Indian pink
The annual pinks are usually grouped under this species. They are all excellent in containers or for edging borders. Hardy/Z 7. Plants in the **Carpet Series** have flowers in a range of colours and are good in exposed situations. H and S to 20cm (8in). 'Fire Carpet' is bright red. The **Heddewigii Group** includes 'Black and White Minstrels', an eye-catching strain, with flowers in various colours, highlighted with white. H 30–38cm (12–15in), S to 30cm (12in). Plants in the compact **Princess Series** have masses of scarlet, white, crimson or salmon-pink flowers, and usually bloom early. H and S 20cm (8in).

Cosmos bipinnatus 'Sonata Pink'

Dianthus barbatus

Echium vulgare

ECHIUM

The genus includes perennials and shrubs as well as the hardy annuals described here. They are easy to grow and the upward-facing flowers will attract bees and butterflies into the garden, making them a good choice for a wildlife border. They can also be treated as biennials. The plants contain a skin irritant.
Cultivation Grow in any soil in full sun. Sow in spring for flowers the same year, or in late summer for flowering the following spring.

E. vulgare
Viper's bugloss
This annual or biennial produces tall spikes of bell-shaped, blue, pink or white flowers over a long period. H to 1m (3ft), S 30cm (12in). Selected forms are more compact. H to 30cm (12in). 'Blue Bedder' has blue flowers; those of the **Dwarf Hybrids** can be blue, lavender, pink or white. Hardy/Z 1–11.

Echium vulgare 'Blue Bedder'

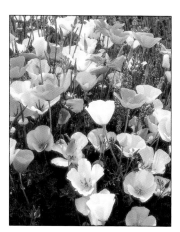

Eschscholzia californica

ESCHSCHOLZIA
California poppy
These hardy annuals are gratifyingly easy to grow, and it is possible to develop your own strains by weeding out unwanted colours as the flowers appear and letting the remainder self-seed.
Cultivation Any well-drained soil in full sun is suitable. Sow in situ from spring onwards. Late sowings will flower the following year.

E. californica
The species typically produces satiny, yellow-orange flowers (although they can also be red, yellow or white). H to 30cm (12in), S 15cm (6in). Hardy/Z 6. Plants in the **Thai Silk Series** have fluted petals (giving a double appearance) in scarlet, orange, pink-orange, yellow, cream and white, while the **Thai Lemon Silk Series** has yellow flowers only. H to 20cm (8in), S 10cm (4in).

FELICIA
Kingfisher daisy
The delightful plants described are actually tender perennials, which are ideal for use in summer hanging baskets or at the edges of large containers.
Cultivation Grow in any soil in sun. Sow in a propagator in spring; named forms are best increased by cuttings.

F. amelloides
This species has lax stems with an abundance of vivid blue, yellow-centred, daisy flowers throughout summer. H and S 30cm (12in). Tender/Z 10. 'Santa Anita' has large, deep blue flowers.

GAZANIA
Treasure flower
These half-hardy annuals would be perennials in a warm climate. Needing heat, they are ideal candidates for growing along the foot of a wall. The flowers open fully only in sunshine.
Cultivation Most soils in full sun are suitable, but a sheltered spot is desirable in cool areas. Sow in a propagator from late winter.

G. varieties
Chansonette Series, a prolific strain, produces exotic-looking flowers in shades of lemon-yellow, rich golden-yellow, apricot, orange, bronze, lavender-pink or carmine red, all zoned with a contrasting colour. H and S 23–30cm (9–12in). Plants in the **Daybreak Series** produce bronze, orange, pink, yellow or white flowers, usually with a contrasting central zone. 'Daybreak Orange', a perennial grown as an annual, has orange flowers only, which stay open longer than other varieties. H to 20cm (8in), S to 25cm (10in). Half-hardy/Z 8–10.

GLAUCIUM
Horned poppy
The species described here is a short-lived perennial best treated as a biennial. Thriving in dry spots, it is ideal for sowing in the cracks in paving or in a gravel garden. The common name refers to the curved, horn-shaped seedcases.
Cultivation Grow in well-drained, preferably dry and not too fertile soil in sun. Sow in situ in spring or autumn.

Gazania 'Daybreak Orange'

Glaucium flavum

G. flavum
Yellow horned poppy
The species forms a rosette of blue-green leaves from which arise hairy stems carrying clear yellow, poppy-like flowers in summer. H 60cm (2ft), S 30cm (1ft). Hardy/Z 7.

HELIANTHUS
Sunflower
Most sunflowers are coarse plants, although they can be very effective in splendid isolation. The seeds are a valuable food source for birds in winter, suggesting use in an ecological garden, and the temptation to cut the plants down after the flowers have faded should be resisted if possible. Shorter types are good in mixed borders. The genus includes some useful perennials, as well as the hardy annuals described here.
Cultivation Most soils are suitable (although heavy, lime clays seem to be preferred) in sun. Sow in situ in spring. Tall plants may need staking.

H. annuus
This species sends up a stout stem at the top of which is a solitary, although huge, daisy-like yellow flower with a brown or purple centre. H 2.5m (8ft), S 60cm (2ft). Hardy/Z 4–7. There are many selections. 'Moonwalker' has lemon-yellow petals surrounding chocolate brown centres. H 1.2m–1.5m (4–5ft), S 60cm (2ft). 'Music Box', a good dwarf, has a mixture of cream, yellow to dark red flowers, some being bicolours. H to 70cm (28in), S 45cm (18in).

Helianthus annuus

'Teddy Bear', very dwarf, has rounded, very double, powder-puff flowers in golden-yellow. H 45cm (18in), S 30cm (12in).

HELIOTROPIUM
Heliotrope

The species described is actually an evergreen shrub in its native Peru but is treated as a half-hardy annual in colder climates. The wrinkled leaves and fragrant, richly coloured flowers make it a distinctive bedding plant. It is also suitable for windowboxes and other containers.
Cultivation Grow in most soils in full sun. Sow in a propagator in spring. Named varieties are best raised from cuttings, although 'Marine' and its variants, such as 'Mini Marine', can be raised from seed.

H. arborescens
(syn. *H. peruvianum*)
Cherry pie

The species has rich green leaves and domed heads of violet, purple or white flowers throughout summer. H and S to 45cm (18in). Half-hardy/Z 10. Many cultivars

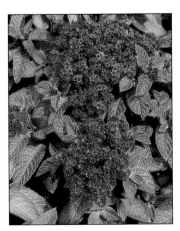

Heliotropium arborescens 'Marine'

have been developed, including the strongly growing 'Chatsworth', which has purple flowers; 'Marine', which is a dramatic and highly desirable form with very dark green leaves and deep purple flowers; and 'Mini Marine', which is roughly similar but more compact. H and S 35cm (14in).

HESPERIS
Dame's violet, sweet rocket

This cottage-garden favourite produces phlox-like flowers, which are fragrant in the evening. Perennial in favourable conditions, this is best treated as a biennial in most gardens and is indispensable in a border planned for scent.
Cultivation Grow these plants in any well-drained soil (preferably neutral to alkaline) in sun or light shade. Sow in situ in spring.

H. matronalis

The species, a good butterfly plant, produces domed heads of flowers in shades of purple (usually pale, but darker and white flowers are also possible) from late spring to midsummer. H 60cm (2ft), S 30cm (1ft). Hardy/Z 4–9. **H. matronalis var. albiflora** has white flowers only.

IMPATIENS
Busy Lizzie

These annuals are invaluable for providing colour in shady borders. Use them in borders, containers, windowboxes or – especially – hanging baskets for a long period of interest. Packed tightly, they will produce a ball of flowers.
Cultivation Grow in any soil in

Hesperis matronalis var. *albiflora*

Ipomoea tricolor 'Purpurea'

light to full shade. Sow in a propagator in late winter. Seed can be tricky to germinate and it may be more practical to buy in young plants as seedlings or plugs.

I. New Guinea Group

These striking plants have the added attraction of exotic-looking red, bronze or rich green leaves, sometimes marked with yellow and pink. The flowers can be pink, red, purple, orange or white. H 45cm (18in), S 40cm (16in). Tender/Z 10. 'Tango' is a superb selection, with deep orange flowers offset by rich bronze leaves. H 35cm (14in), S 30cm (12in).

I. walleriana

Most of the seed strains are grouped under this species. **Double Carousel Mixed** produces well-branched plants with double, rose-like flowers in orange, pink, red and white, with some bicolours. H and S 23–30cm (9–12in). Plants of the **Super Elfin Series** are free-flowering and compact, with flowers in a range of dazzling colours. H and S 15cm (6in). 'Tempo Peach Frost' has pink flowers edged scarlet. H and S to 25cm (10in). 'Victoria Rose' has pink flowers. H and S 23–30cm (9–12in). Tender/Z 10.

Impatiens walleriana 'Victoria Rose'

Ipomoea lobata

IPOMOEA
Morning glory

With their trumpet-shaped, convolvulus-like flowers, these tender plants are true glories of the garden, with a shade of blue probably unmatched by any other summer flowers. The species described here are twining climbers, which look charming when they are allowed to wander through other plants, but they can also be more formally trained on vertical wires or other supports.
Cultivation Morning glories need well-drained soil in sun, preferably in a sheltered site. Sow in a propagator from late winter.

I. lobata
(syn. *Mina lobata*)
Spanish flag

This climber is grown for its variety of beak-like flowers. Initially scarlet, they age to orange, yellow and finally white, all colours appearing simultaneously. H and S 1.2–2m (4–6ft) or more. Tender/Z 10.

I. tricolor

The straight species is well worth growing, for the joy of its clear blue, white-throated flowers. H to 4m (13ft), but probably less in cool gardens. Tender/Z 8. Selected forms include 'Flying Saucers', which has larger flowers striped blue and white; and 'Heavenly Blue', which has richer blue flowers with white throats and 'Purpurea', with rich purple, white-throated flowers.

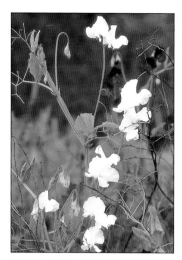

Lathyrus odoratus 'White Supreme'

LATHYRUS

For many gardeners, summer would not be summer without the delicious scent of these tendril climbers. Cutting the flowers for arrangements is actually to the benefit of the plant, since it will greatly extend the flowering season. Some gardeners like to grow them for this purpose alone and relegate them to the vegetable plot trained on cordons, which seems a pity, because their flower colours blend so happily with other plants. In borders they have great charm if allowed to climb over wigwams of peasticks or trellis obelisks.

Cultivation Grow in any soil in full sun. Sweet peas need a long growing season, so sow from late autumn in special sweet pea tubes, which will minimize disturbance to the roots on planting out.

L. odoratus
Sweet pea
Both the specific name and common name are slightly misleading. Not all strains are scented, and some are distinctly more fragrant than others (the sweet peas described are all richly scented unless otherwise indicated). H to 2m (6ft) unless otherwise stated. Hardy/Z 1–11. **'Cream Southborne'** produces large, frilled, cream flowers. The prolific **'Firecrest'** has unusual bicoloured flowers of fiery red and orange. **'King Size Navy Blue'**, one of the darkest blues, has wavy-edged flowers on long slender stems. **'Orange Dragon'**

has startling orange (only lightly scented) flowers, which hold their colour best in a position that is sheltered from hot sun. Plants of the **Snoopea Group** are compact and have no tendrils. The flowers can be white, pink, red or purple. H to 60cm (2ft). One of the best white varieties available is **'White Supreme'** with outstandingly fragrant flowers produced on long, strong stems.

LAVATERA

Among the 25 species in the genus are a number of perennials. The annuals are easy and resilient hardy plants, which are ideal for plugging summer gaps in borders.
Cultivation Any soil in full sun is suitable. Sow in containers from late winter or in situ in mid-spring.

L. trimestris
Most of the annual lavateras are listed under this species. They make bushy plants with mallow flowers. Selections include **'Mont Blanc'**, which has dark leaves and glistening white flowers; and **'Silver Cup'**, a very weather-resistant form, which has glowing silvery pink flowers with darker veins. H to 1m (3ft), S 45cm (18in). Hardy/Z 5–9.

LIMNANTHES
Poached egg plant
These hardy annuals, with their simple white and yellow flowers, will attract a wide range of beneficial insects (especially bees) into the garden. They seed themselves readily, particularly in gravel.

Limnanthes douglasii

Cultivation Most well-drained soils in full sun are suitable. Sow in situ in spring or in early autumn for early flowers the following year.

L. douglasii
This easily grown species has gleaming yellow, buttercup-like flowers, with white edges to the petals, throughout summer. H 15cm (6in), S 20cm (8in). Hardy/Z 8.

LOBELIA

Given the chance, these half-hardy annuals would be perennial, but they are usually raised annually from seed. Compact forms are the mainstay of park bedding schemes, while a hanging basket would be virtually unthinkable without the trailing kinds. Lobelias are among the precious few shade-tolerant annuals. Most are blue, although there are also selections in other

Lobelia erinus 'Cambridge Blue'

colours. The genus also includes true perennials and shrubs.
Cultivation Grow in any soil in sun or light shade. Sow in a propagator from late winter.

L. erinus
The annuals are usually usefully grouped under this species. All are hardy/Z 5–8. The compact **'Cambridge Blue'**, which is suitable for bedding, has clear sky-blue flowers. H and S 10cm (4in). Trailing varieties suitable for hanging baskets include those in the **Cascade Series**. Individual colour selections are **'Blue Cascade'**, **'Crimson Cascade'**, **'Lilac Cascade'**, **'Red Cascade'** and **'White Cascade'**. H 15cm (6in), S 30cm (12in). **'Crystal Palace'**, a compact form suitable for bedding, has dark blue flowers. H and S 10cm (4in). **'Sapphire'** has rich blue flowers with white eyes. H and S 15cm (6in).

LOBULARIA
Sweet alyssum
These tough little hardy annuals are very useful. They will seed themselves in various nooks and crannies around the garden, generally to good effect. Easy to grow, they are excellent for edging a path or border and are especially tolerant of coastal conditions. They also work well in containers and windowboxes. The flowers are scented.
Cultivation Alyssums will grow in any well-drained soil in sun. Sow in containers in late winter or in situ in spring.

Lavatera trimestris 'Mont Blanc'

Lobularia maritima 'Carpet of Snow'

L. maritima
(syn. *Alyssum maritimum*)
This species, native to the Canary Islands, has a huge range of selections. Most make compact hummocks. All are hardy/Z 1–11. **'Carpet of Snow'**, which is neat-growing and ground-hugging, has white flowers. H 10cm (4in), S 30cm (12in). **'Oriental Night'** has rich purple flowers. H 10cm (4in), S 30cm (12in). The flowers of **'Sweet White'** are white and smell of honey. H 10cm (4in), S 30cm (12in). **'Trailing Rosy Red'**, which has pinkish-purple flowers, is less compact than the others; its trailing habit makes it ideal for hanging baskets. H 10cm (4in), S 40cm (16in).

LUNARIA
Honesty, satin flower
These modest biennials (some-times persisting a bit longer) have two seasons of interest. The pretty spring flowers are followed by distinctive, papery, oval seedheads, which are excellent in dried arrangements. Honesty often appears unbidden in gardens and once established is unlikely to die out.
Cultivation Honesty tolerates most soil, in sun or light shade. Sow in situ from late spring to early summer.

L. annua
(syn. *L. biennis*)
This European species has usually purple, sometimes white, flowers in spring followed by translucent white seedheads in autumn. H 1m (3ft), S 30cm (1ft). Hardy. For white flowers only, sow seeds of *L. annua* var. *albiflora*. **'Alba Variegata'** is a desirable garden form with white variegated leaves and white flowers. 'Variegata' has similar leaves but flowers in shades of purple.

MATTHIOLA
Stock, gillyflower
Among the most fragrant of all flowers, these beautiful, hardy biennials (which can also be treated as annuals) can be sown in succession for an extended season. The flowers, which are white, pink, lavender, lilac or crimson, blend well with virtually all others. Night-scented stock, the most fragrant of all, has rather insignificant looking flowers of light mauve. Seed can usefully be scattered among showier but scentless plants.

Lunaria annua

Cultivation Any soil in sun is suitable. Sow seed from summer onwards for flowers the following year and from late winter for flowers the same year.

M. incana
Most strains are usefully gathered within this species and include Brompton stocks and Ten Week stocks. So-called Brompton stocks, which are biennials, are available in a wide colour range. H 50cm (20in), S 30cm (12in). There are many dwarf strains including the **Cinderella Series**, plants of which produce multiple spikes of double flowers. H 30cm (12in), S 10cm (4in). **'Cinderella Antique Pink'** is a selection with flowers in a unique shade of bronze-pink. **Ten Week Mixed** are annuals, with branching spikes of usually double flowers in a range of colours. H 30cm (12in), S 20cm (8in). Hardy/Z 6.

M. longipetala subsp. bicornis
(syn. *M. bicornis*)
Night-scented stock
This annual species is grown for the power of its scent alone. The lilac-mauve flowers open, modest in appearance and sparsely scattered up the stems, in the evening. H 30cm (1ft), S 23cm (9in). Hardy/Z 5.

MYOSOTIS
Forget-me-not
Although they will seed on their own freely, it is worth sowing these biennials afresh every season – the named forms always have flowers of a more intense colour than their natural progeny. Indispensable for most spring bedding schemes, forget-me-nots make a classic cottage-garden combination with pink tulips.
Cultivation Forget-me-nots will grow in most well-drained soils in sun or, preferably, light shade. Sow outdoors in early summer.

M. sylvatica
The straight species has mid-blue, yellow-eyed flowers in spring and early summer and grey-green leaves. H 30cm (12in), S 15cm, (6in). All forms are hardy/Z 5–8. **'Blue Ball'** is a more compact form with indigo flowers. H and

Matthiola longipetala subsp. *bicornis*

S 15–20cm (6–8in). The flowers of **'Compindi'**, another dwarf form, are even darker. H and S 15–20cm (6–8in). **'Rosylva'** is something of a novelty, with large flowers of clear pink. H 30cm (12in), S 15cm (6in).

NEMOPHILA
These hardy annuals have delightfully marked, cup-shaped flowers. They should be planted near the edge of a border or in a container or windowbox where this feature can be fully appreciated best.
Cultivation Most soils are suitable, although it should ideally be re-liably moist. Plant in sun or light shade. Sow in situ in spring, or in autumn for larger plants that will flower earlier the following year.

N. maculata
Five spot
The common name is descriptive. Each pale blue petal is marked at the edge with a dark blue spot. This is a charming plant for a hanging basket. H and S to 30cm (12in). Hardy/Z 1–11.

N. menziesii
Baby blue eyes
In summer, this carpeting species is smothered in sky-blue flowers with paler centres. It is excellent for adding late colour to a rock garden. H 15cm (6in), S 30cm (12in). Hardy/Z 1–11. **'Pennie Black'** has blackish-purple flowers with scalloped, silvery edges and is more ground hugging. H 10cm (4in), S 30cm (12in).

Nemophila menziesii

Nicotiana 'Lime Green'

NICOTIANA
Tobacco plant

These sticky, half-hardy annuals (actually tender perennials) bear flowers that remain closed at daytime but perk up at dusk and give off an incense-like fragrance. Modern selections are more compact and floriferous, but have not displaced older varieties.
Cultivation Grow in any soil in full sun or light shade. Sow in a propagator in spring.

N. langsdorfii
This distinctive annual is one of few species grown in its straight form. The branching stems carry drooping, pale, lime-green flowers. It combines well with a wide variety of border plants. H 1.5m (5ft), S 35cm (14in). Half-hardy/Z 7.

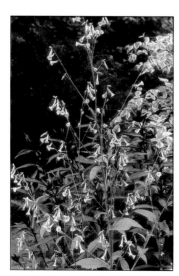

Nicotiana langsdorfii

N. 'Lime Green'
Blending with all other flowers, this popular selection produces lime sherbet flowers throughout the summer. H 60cm (2ft), S 20cm (8in). Half-hardy/Z 7.

N. × sanderae
Most of the annual strains are considered to belong to this hybrid group. All are half-hardy/Z 7. Plants of the **Domino Series** are branching and bushy, with red, white, pink or green flowers. Domino Series **'Salmon Pink'** is only lightly scented but produces unique salmon-pink flowers. H 30–45cm (12–18in), S 25cm (10in). Plants in the **Havana Series** are compact. The selection **'Apple Blossom'** has unusually coloured flowers: pale pink with darker pink reverses, giving a two-tone effect. H 30cm (12in), S 20cm (8in). Plants in the **Merlin Series** are compact and bushy, ideal for containers or the front of a border. The flowers can be purple, crimson, lime green or white (bicolours being a possibility). Seed is also often sold as single colour selections; the white-flowered ones are usually the most potently scented. H and S 23–25cm (9–10in).

N. sylvestris
This beautiful Argentinean species, which is actually a short-lived perennial, sometimes behaves as a biennial, surviving winter cold and flowering only in its second year. The fragrant, white flowers

are carried in a candelabra-like arrangement on tall plants in summer, making this an excellent 'dot' plant. H 1–1.2m (3–4ft), S 60cm (2ft). Half-hardy/Z 9–10.

NIGELLA
Love-in-a-mist

These charming and elegant annuals are dainty cottage-garden stalwarts, almost as attractive when the seedheads develop as when they are in flower; the feathery foliage is a definite bonus. They are easy to grow.
Cultivation Grow in any soil in sun. Sow in situ from spring onwards.

N. damascena
The species is the parent of the garden strains, all of which are hardy/Z 1–11. **'Dwarf Moody Blue'** is a compact form, which can be used to make a temporary low hedge at the margin of a border. The flowers are sky blue. H 15–20cm (6–8in), S 10cm (4in). The popular and widely grown **'Miss Jekyll'** has bright blue, semi-double flowers. H 45cm (18in), S 15cm (6in). The rarer and desirable **'Miss Jekyll Alba'** is white. H 45cm (18in), S 15cm (6in). Plants in the **Persian Jewel Series** have flowers in a range of colours: pink, blue, violet and white. H 38cm (15in), S 15cm (6in).

OENOTHERA
Evening primrose

These stately annuals and biennials produce a succession of

Nigella damascena 'Miss Jekyll'

Oenothera biennis

flowers over the summer months that are valuable for attracting butterflies and other beneficial insects into the garden. Some open only in the evening – hence the plant's common name. All have a cool beauty. The genus includes some perennials.
Cultivation Evening primroses will grow in any well-drained soil in sun. Sow in situ in autumn; annuals can also be sown in containers in spring.

O. biennis
This species can be treated as an annual or a biennial and will usually seed itself. From basal rosettes of leaves emerge tall stems carrying shorter leaves and the large, cup-shaped, scented yellow flowers. H 1m (3ft), S 40cm (16in). Hardy/Z 4.

Papaver rhoeas

Papaver somniferum

PAPAVER
Poppy

Annual and biennial poppies, all hardy and easy to grow, are as valuable in gardens as their perennial cousins. Some will seed themselves, often to good effect, but sometimes to the point of becoming weeds. All have characteristically silky-textured flowers and are excellent in wildflower gardens as well as in borders.

Cultivation Any soil in sun is suitable. Sow annuals in situ in early spring, or in autumn for earlier flowers the following season. Biennials can be sown in situ in summer.

P. croceum
(syn. P. nudicaule of gardens)
Arctic poppy, Icelandic poppy

The species, usually grown as a biennial, has blue-grey leaves and fragrant, yellow, white or pale orange flowers. H to 30cm (12in), S 15cm (6in). Hardy/Z 4–8. Some ravishing strains, all with glistening flowers, including some doubles, have been developed. **Meadow Pastels** is a mixture that produces large, single flowers in shades of white, pink, rose pink, yellow and orange on sturdy stems. Early sowings can flower the same year. They are excellent for cutting. H to 30cm (12in), S 15cm (6in). **Oregon Rainbows** produces smaller plants, with flower colours including apricot, pink, soft cream and lemon-yellow. H to 25cm (10in), S 10cm (4in).

P. rhoeas
Corn poppy, field poppy

This is the annual species that appears on arable land that has been recently cultivated, the soil disturbance effectively breaking the seed's dormancy. The typically red flowers are a familiar sight, blanketing entire fields in summer. H to 1m (3ft), S to 30cm (1ft). Hardy/Z 5. Selected strains include the well-known **Shirley Series**, which produces semi-double or double flowers in red, pink, lilac and white, some flowers uniting two colours. Self-sown seedlings that revert to type should be weeded out if the characteristics of the strain are to be maintained. H 60cm (2ft), S 30cm (1ft).

P. somniferum
Opium poppy

The species, which has blue-green leaves, produces pink, purplish, red or white flowers, followed by striking seedheads. H 1m (3ft), S 30cm (1ft). Hardy/Z 7. Double forms have distinctive ruffled petals. **'Hen and Chickens'** has pink flowers, but is really grown for its larger than average seedheads, which can be dried for winter decoration. H 30cm (12in), S 20cm (4in). Plants raised from the **Peony Flowered** group live up to their name and have double flowers in red, purplish-pink, pink or white. H 1m (3ft), S 30cm (1ft). **'White Cloud'** has large, double white flowers. H 1m (3ft), S 30cm (1ft).

PETUNIA

The trumpet flowers of these sticky, half-hardy annuals have an immediate appeal. Most are ideal bedding plants, but recent introductions with trailing stems are best in hanging baskets. Blue-flowered plants are often heavily scented. All petunias grown in gardens are hybrids (sometimes lumped under the catch-all name *P.* × *hybrida*). According to flower size, they are usually divided among the three groups specified below (some seed merchants have created other divisions).

Cultivation Petunias need well-drained soil in sun. Sow in a propagator from late winter.

Petunia 'Blue Daddy'

P. Grandiflora Group

Plants in this group produce the largest flowers. The **Aladdin Series** has wavy-edged flowers in an impressive colour range, including blue, red, burgundy, pink, lilac and white. H to 30cm (12in), S to 1m (3ft). The **Daddy Series** has flowers in unique shades of plum burgundy, orchid lavender, pink, blue and red, all with a velvety texture and darker veins. **'Blue Daddy'** has silver-blue flowers with darker veins and is early-flowering. H to 35cm (14in), S 1m (3ft). The well-known **Surfinia Series** produces vigorous plants of trailing habit that makes them ideal for hanging baskets. Flower colours include pink, red and blue. H 40cm (16in), S 1m (3ft). Half-hardy/Z 7.

P. Milliflora Group

Plants in this group produce quantities of small flowers. H and S to 30cm (12in). **Fantasy Series** plants are smothered with flowers in a range of colours throughout summer. They are ideal for containers and hanging baskets. H 15cm (6in), S to 30cm (12in). Half-hardy/Z 7.

P. Multiflora Group

This, the largest group, is characterized by medium-sized flowers on bushy plants. Plants in this group are the most weather resistant. **Carpet Mixed** produce low-growing, spreading plants that flower early in shades of pink, red, plum purple, rich blue and white. **'Carpet Buttercream'** is a selection that has creamy-yellow flowers only. H to 25cm (10in), S to 1m (3ft). Petunias belonging to the **Duo Series** have double flowers in a range of colours, including some strongly veined flowers and some bicolours. H to 30cm (1ft), S to 1m (3ft). The **Mirage Series** has plants with red, pink, blue and lavender flowers, all attractively veined with darker shades. H to 30cm (1ft), S to 1m (3ft). **Storm Mixed** petunias produce rain-resistant flowers in shades of salmon, white, pink and lavender. Single colour selections are available. **'Lavender Storm'** is vigorous, with pale yellow-throated lavender flowers. H 20–30cm (8–12in), S to 1m (3ft). Half-hardy/Z 7.

Petunia 'Lavender Storm'

Salvia fulgens

SALVIA
Sage

In addition to the well-known culinary herb, this large genus includes several annuals, as well as some perennials and subshrubs that can be treated as annuals or biennials in cool climates. Most have spikes of vivid flowers, while some are grown more for the appeal of the conspicuous bracts that surround them.
Cultivation Salvias prefer light, well-drained soil and a position in sun. Sow even hardy varieties in a propagator in mid-spring, or in situ once all danger of frost has passed; late sowings flower later.

S. fulgens
(syn. *S. cardinalis*)
A woody-based perennial or sub-shrub in its native Mexico, this upright plant produces spikes of vivid red flowers in summer. It is electric with *Verbena bonariensis*. H 1.2m (4ft), S 75cm (30in). Half-hardy/Z 9–10.

S. patens
This species is of borderline hardiness, but most gardeners are prepared to persevere with it for the sake of the very vivid blue flowers produced from summer to autumn. H 60cm (2ft), S 45cm (18in). It sometimes survives as a perennial. Borderline hardy/Z 7–9. Among the cultivars are **'Cambridge Blue'**, which has paler blue flowers; and **'White Trophy'**, which has white flowers.

S. sclarea var. turkestanica
The species is most often seen in this naturally occurring form. It is a hardy perennial best treated as a biennial. The plant is branching, with erect, pink stems and pink-flecked white flowers held in purple bracts. A choice plant for the border. H to 1m (3ft), S 30cm (1ft). Hardy/Z 4–7.

S. splendens
Scarlet sage
This species includes the vivid red cultivars familiar in park bedding schemes, although other colours also occur. **'Blaze of Fire'** is a compact and early-flowering form. H 30cm (12in), S 20cm (8in). Plants belonging to the **Phoenix Series** can have pink, purple, white, red or lilac flowers. H 25–30cm (10–12in), S 20cm (8in). **'Red Arrows'** has the advantage of deep green leaves to set off the scarlet flowers. H 30cm (12in), S 20cm (8in). The flowers of **'Sizzler Burgundy'**, also red, are long-lasting. H 30cm (12in), S 20cm (8in).

S. viridis
(syn. *S. horminum*)
Annual clary
This species is grown for its pink, purple or white bracts. The stems can be dried for winter decoration. H to 50cm (20in), S 23cm (9in). Hardy/Z 4–7. **'Claryssa'** is a dwarf form with somewhat more brightly coloured bracts. H to 40cm (16in), S 20cm (8in).

Salvia sclarea var. turkestanica

Tagetes erecta Jubilee Series 'Golden'

TAGETES
Marigold

These are among the easiest of half-hardy annuals to grow, and provide a reliable, long-lasting display throughout summer. There are two large groups, African marigolds and French marigolds, African marigolds tending to be taller and less spreading than the French. Hybrids between the two groups also exist, as well as a range deriving from *T. tenuifolia*. Single-flowered French marigolds make good companions for plants that are attacked by aphids: they attract hoverflies, which will help control the pests.
Cultivation Any fertile soil in sun is suitable. Sow in a propagator in spring.

T. erecta
African marigold
These plants have fully double, daisy-like flowers, in shades of cream, yellow and orange. Half-hardy/Z 9. **Crackerjack Mixed** plants have bold, double flowers in orange, golden-yellow and lemon-yellow. H 60cm (2ft), S 30cm (1ft). The **Gold 'n' Vanilla Series** includes creamy white flowers. H 50–75cm (20–30in), S 30cm (1ft). **Jubilee Series 'Golden'** is a single

Tagetes erecta Gold 'n' Vanilla Series

colour selection with golden-yellow flowers. H 50cm (20in), S 30cm (1ft).

T. patula
French marigold
The flowers of these marigolds can include more than one colour. Plants of the **Boy O' Boy Series** are neat and compact, making them very suitable for window-boxes. The double flowers, with crested centres, can be yellow, orange or rich brownish-red. H and S 15cm (6in). **'Gypsy Sunshine'** bears a heavy crop of double butter-yellow flowers. H and S 15–20cm (6–8in). **'Naughty Marietta'** has single deep yellow flowers marked with maroon. H 30–40cm (12–16in), S 25cm (10in). Half-hardy/Z 9.

T. tenuifolia
These marigolds are bushy and produce domes of flowers. Half-hardy/Z 9. Plants of the **Gem Series** have single flowers in shades of yellow or orange, marked with darker colours. **'Golden Gem'** is a selection with golden-yellow flowers. H and S 15–23cm (6–9in). **Starfire Mixed** has red and yellow flowers, some dramatically bicoloured. H and S 15–23cm (6–9in).

Tagetes tenuifolia 'Golden Gem'

Tropaeolum majus Alaska Series

TROPAEOLUM
Nasturtium

These half-hardy annuals, which are perennials in warm climates, are gratifyingly easy to grow. Some strains make large plants with trailing stems, which are useful for providing quick cover, although the large leaves tend to mask the flowers. The more compact forms are good for bedding or, more informally, for slipping into the cracks in paving. The young leaves and the flowers are edible. The genus also includes some hardy perennials.
Cultivation Grow in any, but not too fertile, soil in sun. Sow in situ from mid-spring onwards.

T. majus
This is the species to which the annual strains are most usually ascribed. All are half-hardy/Z 8–9. The **Alaska Series** produces plants with leaves that are attractively marbled with cream and pink; the flowers can be brilliant orange, red or yellow. H 20–30cm (8–12in), S 45cm (18in). **'Empress of India'** is a compact form, with rich purplish-green leaves and bright scarlet flowers. H to 30cm (12in), S 45cm (18in). Plants raised from seed of the **Gleam Series** are trailing, with semi-double flowers in yellow, red or orange. H to 40cm (16in), S to 60cm (2ft). Plants in the **Whirlybird Series** make low mounds, with upward-facing yellow or red flowers. H to 25cm (10in), S to 40cm (16in).

VIOLA
Pansy

An endearing genus that includes perennials and rock garden plants as well as the charming hardy annuals and biennials described here. Attractive as the self-coloured strains are, most gardeners find the bicolours more appealing: the mask-like markings make the flowers look like faces. So-called winter pansies will flower intermittently from late autumn onwards, reaching their peak in spring. With successive sowings it is possible to produce flowering plants throughout the year. All pansies make ideal bedding and container plants; a winter windowbox is virtually

Tropaeolum majus 'Whirlybird Gold'

Viola 'Padparadja'

unthinkable without them.
Cultivation Any soil in sun or light shade is suitable. Seed germinates best at low temperatures (maximum 10°C/50°F). Summer pansies are best treated as biennials and sown in containers in summer for flowering from the following spring, although they can also be sown from late winter for flowers the same year. Winter pansies should be sown in summer. Take care to keep summer sowings cool.

V. × wittrockiana
Seed strains are usually ascribed to this complex hybrid group, which has emerged from cross-breeding a number of species. All are hardy/Z 4–9.

Summer pansies
'Jolly Joker' has intense orange and purple flowers. H and S 15–23cm (6–9in). **'Lilac Frost'** has glistening lilac flowers that are blotched centrally with rich purple. H and S 15–20cm (6–8in). **Majestic Giants Mixed** plants produce huge bicoloured flowers in a range of iridescent colours; early-flowering, they show greater tolerance to extremes of weather than other strains. H and S 15cm (6in). **'Padparadja'** has intense, solid orange flowers. H and S 15cm (6in). **'Velour Purple Wings'** makes compact mounds that are smothered with miniature flowers with purple and cream petals. The cream petals are edged with mauve and shade to yellow at the centre. H and S 18cm (7in).

Winter pansies
Plants belonging to the **Floral Dance Series** are reliable and produce flowers in a range of colours. Selections in single colours are available. H and S 15–23cm (6–9in). **Universal Mixed** plants are compact, producing both self-coloured and bicoloured flowers in a colour range including red, purple, yellow, apricot and white. H and S 15–20cm (6–8in).

ZINNIA

These half-hardy annuals, with their dahlia-like flowers, bring an exotic touch to the garden.

Zinnia haageana 'Profusion White'

Unusually among half-hardy annuals, they are best sown where they are to flower, since they resent root disturbance.
Cultivation Grow in any soil in sun. Seed can be sown in containers in spring, but it is better to sow them in situ from late spring.

Z. elegans
This Mexican species encompasses a number of seed strains. Tender/10–11. Plants of the **Cactus-flowered Group** have large double flowers, similar to those of a cactus-flowered dahlia, in a range of colours. H to 1m (3ft), S 30cm (1ft). The **Desert Sun Series** produces large, pleated flowers in primrose yellow, ivory white and golden-yellow, which are excellent for cutting. H 1m (3ft), S 30cm (1ft). **'Double Dwarf Mixed'** is a compact strain, with fully double flowers in white, salmon, pink, yellow and scarlet. H 20cm (8in), S 15cm (6in). **'Envy'** has semi-double, chartreuse green flowers. H 75cm (30in), S 30cm (12in). **'Envy Double'** is fully double.

Z. haageana
(syn. *Z. angustifolia*)
Mexican zinnia
Strains allotted to this species are somewhat more compact than those of *Z. elegans*. Half-hardy/Z 9–10. Plants raised from **Persian Carpet Mixed** produce double, bicoloured flowers in shades of golden yellow, maroon, purple, chocolate, pink and cream. They are seemingly impervious to weather extremes. H 38cm (15in), S 30cm (12in). **'Profusion White'** has white flowers. H 30cm (12in), S 10cm (4in).

Bulbs

Few groups of plants provide the gardener with such a range of brilliant colours as the bulbs, and nearly all are easy to grow. There is scarcely a moment in the year when they do not make a contribution, from the diminutive harbingers of spring that brighten up the garden from late winter, the bold tulips and daffodils that epitomize spring, to the exotic, slightly tender dahlias and gladioli that carry on the interest into autumn, with a host of others in between. Hyacinths and hippeastrums can be forced to flower in the dead of winter indoors, ensuring that you need never be without flowers.

Easy and reliable, these alliums raise their heads of almost geometric precision above the lower-growing perennials.

Growing bulbs

Bulbs are among the easiest plants to grow and so are an ideal starting point for newcomers to gardening. They need little more than planting and watering to get going and require very little maintenance thereafter.

Planting

As a rule, bulbs should be planted as soon as they are bought. Autumn- and spring-flowering types produce new roots in autumn and should be planted in late summer or early autumn. The main exceptions are tulips, which are best planted in late autumn. Plant bulbs in well-prepared, weed-free soil. If it is poor incorporate a sprinkling of slow-release fertilizer, such as bonemeal.

The depth of planting and spacing depends on the size of bulb. As a rule, all bulbs should be planted in a hole that is three times as deep as the bulb. For example a 5cm (2in) deep daffodil bulb will need a 15cm (6in) deep hole so that the bulb is covered by 10cm (4in) of soil. Similarly, a 1cm (½in) deep crocus corm will need to be planted 3cm (1½in) deep. Small bulbs should be about 2.5–5cm (1–2in) apart and larger bulbs 8–10cm (3–4in) apart.

Creating a natural effect

To get an instant effect you will need to plant bulbs quite thickly – say 70–140 per square metre (7–14 per square foot), depending on the size of bulb. Some bulbs, such as daffodils, spread mainly by offshoots from the bulb so that they form larger and larger clumps. Others, such as crocuses and chionodoxa, will seed themselves, so that after four or five years the original display will be transformed with the new plants.

If you want to create a natural-looking planting scheme it is important to plant in irregular clumps.

HOW TO PLANT BULBS

1 Fork over the ground before planting and, if the plants are to be left undisturbed for some years, try to incorporate plenty of organic material, such as rotted garden compost or manure. Many bulbs like well-drained soil but nevertheless benefit from plenty of organic material, which will hold moisture and nutrients.

2 Avoid adding quick-acting fertilizers in the autumn. Controlled-release fertilizers that provide nutrients according to the soil temperature can be used, but they are best employed in spring. Instead, rake a slow-acting fertilizer, such as bonemeal, which contains mainly phosphate, into the surface, or apply it to the planting holes.

3 Where there is space and the plants will benefit from planting in an informal group or cluster, dig out a hole about three times the depth of the bulbs and wide enough to take the well-spaced bulbs.

4 Space the bulbs so that they look like a natural clump, using the spacing recommended on the packet as a guide. Wide spacing will allow for growth and multiplication, but if you intend to lift the bulbs after flowering, closer spacing will create a bold display.

5 Draw the soil back over the bulbs, being careful not to dislodge them in the process. Firm the soil with the back of the rake rather than treading it down, which may damage the bulbs and compact the soil.

6 So that you do not disturb the bulbs when you are weeding, mark their position with canes. Don't forget to include a label.

If you are planting several varieties together, do not mix them up, but keep them in roughly separate clumps for the best effect. The easiest way to get a natural distribution of bulbs is to toss them gently on to the ground and plant them where they land. Individual bulbs can be planted using a cylindrical bulb planter. Push the planter vertically into the ground and remove a core of soil that is deep enough for the bulb being planted. After positioning the bulb replace the core and firm down. Clumps of bulbs are best planted by digging a trench or hole with a spade and planting in this.

Planting bulbs the correct way up

Most bulbs have an obvious top and bottom and present no problem. Others, especially tubers, can lack an obvious growing point. If in doubt, plant them on their side – the shoot will grow upwards and the roots down.

Some bulbs that do have an obvious top are planted on their side because the base tends to rot in wet soil, though these are rare exceptions. *Fritillaria imperialis* is sometimes planted in this way. It is always worth planting vulnerable bulbs on a bed of grit or sand to encourage good drainage around the base and prevent them from rotting.

Bulb planner

Type of bulb	planting time	depth	spacing	flowering time
Allium	early autumn	5–8cm (2–3in)	15–30cm (6–12in)	late spring to early summer
Anemone	early autumn	5cm (2in)	10cm (4in)	late winter to mid-spring
Arum	midsummer	15cm (6in)	10cm (4in)	mid- to late spring
Begonia	spring	2.5cm (1in)	23–30cm (9–12in)	summer
Chionodoxa	early autumn	2.5–5cm (1–2in)	8cm (3in)	late winter to mid-spring
Colchicum	late spring	8cm (3in)	10–15cm (4–6in)	autumn
Crocus, spring	late summer	5–8cm (2–3in)	10cm (4in)	spring
Crocus, autumn	midsummer	5–8cm (2–3in)	10cm (4in)	autumn
Cyclamen	late summer	2.5cm (1in)	15cm (6in)	autumn to spring
Eranthis	late summer	2.5–5cm (1–2in)	10cm (4in)	late winter to mid-spring
Erythronium	late summer	5–8cm (2–3in)	10cm (4in)	mid- to late spring
Fritillaria	early autumn	5–8cm (2–3in)	15–45cm (6–18in)	spring
Galanthus	late summer	8–10cm (3–4in)	10cm (4in)	late winter to mid-spring
Gladiolus	mid-spring	8–10cm (3–4in)	10–15cm (4–6in)	midsummer
Hyacinthus	early autumn	10cm (4in)	20cm (8in)	spring
Iris reticulata	autumn	8–10cm (3–4in)	10cm (4in)	midwinter to early spring
Leucojum	late summer	8–10cm (3–4in)	10–20cm (4–8in)	mid- to late spring
Lilium	mid-autumn	10–15cm (4–6in)	15–45cm (6–18in)	late spring to late summer
Muscari	late summer	5–8cm (2–3in)	10cm (4in)	spring
Narcissus	late summer	5–12cm (2–5in)	10–20cm (4–8in)	spring
Nerine	spring	2.5cm (1in)	15cm (6in)	late summer to early autumn
Ornithogalum	mid-autumn	5–8cm (2–3in)	10–15cm (4–6in)	spring
Puschkinia	early autumn	5–8cm (2–3in)	8cm (3in)	spring
Scilla	late summer	5–8cm (2–3in)	5–10cm (2–4in)	spring
Sternbergia	midsummer	8cm (3in)	12cm (5in)	autumn
Tigridia	late spring	5–8cm (2–3in)	15cm (6in)	late summer
Tulipa	late autumn	8–15cm (3–6in)	10–20cm (4–8in)	spring

Achimenes 'Prima Donna'

ACHIMENES
Hot water plant, cupid's bower

These tender plants are usually grown as houseplants. Nearly all plants sold commercially are hybrids, and they have short, trumpet-shaped flowers in shades of blue, peach, pink, red and orange and shiny, velvety leaves. The common name is misleading. When they are in growth the plants should be watered with barely tepid water, never hot water, which would kill them. The lax stems make them an excellent choice for hanging baskets. After they have died down the stunning bulbs, which look like miniature white pine cones, should be dried and stored over winter.

Cultivation These plants do best in containers in a light place but out of direct sun. Water them freely when in growth but keep them dry in winter at a temperature of 10°C (50°F).

A. hybrids
Hot water plants flower over a long period from early summer to autumn. There are many named varieties, including **'Blue Gown'**, which has blue flowers; **'Harry Williams'**, which has red flowers; **'Prima Donna'**, which has pink flowers; and **'Snow Princess'** with white flowers. H and S 30cm (12in) or more. Tender/Z 10.

ALLIUM
Ornamental onion

Only a few species of this large and important genus are grown in the flower garden. Some have the distinctive pungent, onion smell,

making them unsuitable for mass plantings. They combine well with old roses, and some, if grown in large quantities, will protect against aphids and fungal disease. Their bold, spherical heads of flowers make a strong statement, and they are the perfect foil for more flamboyant flowers. They look good dotted among lower growing perennials such as geraniums. The seedheads (which can be dried for winter decoration) are almost as attractive as the flowerheads. Small species can also be grown in rock gardens.

Cultivation Any well-drained soil in a sunny spot is suitable for alliums, although they will also tolerate semi-shade. Dead-head to prevent self-seeding.

A. cristophii
(syn. A. albopilosum, A. christophii)
Star of Persia

This species, originally from Turkey, has large flowerheads, up to 20cm (8in) across, of silver-purple, star-like flowers in late spring to early summer. These are attractive even after the flowers have faded. H 60cm (2ft), S 18cm (7in). Borderline hardy/Z 7–10.

A. giganteum
Giant onion

One of the tallest alliums, this dramatic plant, which is native to central Asia, has large purple flowerheads, up to 20cm (8in) across, carried at the top of the erect stems in late spring to early

Amaryllis belladonna

summer. H to 170cm (70in), S 15cm (6in). Hardy/Z 6–10.

A. hollandicum
(syn. A. aflatunense of gardens)

The species is native to central Asia. It bears globular heads, to 10cm (4in) across, of lilac-purple flowers from mid- to late spring. The blue-green leaves are also attractive. Plant in groups for the best display. H 1.2m (4ft), S 10cm (4in). **'Purple Sensation'** is a selection with deep purple flowers. H 1m (3ft), S 10cm (4in). Hardy/Z 4–10.

A. karataviense
This low-growing species from central Asia works well in containers as well as near the front a mixed border. It would be worth growing for its leaves alone, which are pewter-grey edged with maroon. The dull lilac-pink

flowers – interesting rather than beautiful – appear in late spring to early summer. H to 25cm (10in), S 10cm (4in). Hardy/Z 4–9.

A. moly
Golden garlic, lily leek

A species from southern Europe, suitable for a rock garden. It bears a profusion of yellow flowers in late spring to early summer. The grey-green leaves remain attractive over a long period. It is good for naturalizing in light shade and reliably damp soil. H to 30cm (12in), S 5cm (2in). Hardy/Z 3–9.

A. roseum
Rosy garlic

One of the most appealing alliums, the species is native to southern Europe and northern Africa. It has loose heads of scented pink flowers borne on sturdy stems in late spring to early summer. H 60cm (2ft), S 5cm (2in). Hardy/Z 8.

A. sphaerocepahlon
Round-headed leek

A good allium for a massed planting, this species, native to Europe, northern Africa and western Asia, bears almost pear-shaped heads of reddish-purple flowers in late spring and early summer. It combines especially well with hostas, *Alchemilla mollis* and ornamental grasses. H 1m (3ft), S 8cm (3in). Hardy/Z 6–10.

Allium karataviense

Allium moly

Allium roseum

Anemone blanda

AMARYLLIS

There is only one species in this South African genus, which is related to *Hippeastrum* and is usually sold as 'amaryllis'. The true amaryllis can be a star of the autumn garden, with its trumpet-like flowers, which are rather small in relation to the size of the overall plant. They look best grown in isolation, revelling in the comfort of a sheltered spot at the base of a warm wall, with nothing to compete with their beauty.
Cultivation Full sun is essential for these plants, which should be grown in a sheltered spot in fertile, well-drained soil. Plant with the neck of the bulb just above soil level. The flower stems may need staking. In cold areas, cover with a dry mulch of straw or similar material in winter.

A. belladonna
Belladonna lily, Jersey lily
The leaves appear in spring, then die down in early summer. About two months later stems appear, carrying fragrant, bright pink, trumpet-like flowers. H 75cm (30in), S 10cm (4in). Borderline hardy/Z 7–10.

ANEMONE
Windflower
The genus contains both spring-flowering corms as well as some valuable autumn perennials. A major claim to distinction is that the corms include some with red flowers, a colour in short supply in the garden until the tulips make their mark.
Cultivation Different species have different light requirements, but any soil type is acceptable, as long as it is well drained. *A. apennina* prefers dappled shade, ideally beneath deciduous trees. *A. blanda* prefers full sun, but will also grow (although it will flower less freely) in light shade. *A. coronaria* needs sun.

A. apennina
Blue anemone
This species from southern Europe bears starry blue flowers, sometimes tinged with pink, in early spring. H 15cm (6in), S 30cm (12in). Hardy/Z 6–9.

A. blanda
One of the most worthwhile species, this plant is found in south-eastern Europe. It has daisy-like flowers in white or shades of pink, blue and mauve in mid-spring. It is an excellent choice for carpeting large areas under deciduous trees. H and S 15cm (6in). Selections include 'Blue Shades', which has light to dark blue flowers; 'Pink Star', which has pink flowers; 'Radar', with deep mauve-pink flowers, shading to white towards the centre; and 'White Splendour', which has white flowers.

A. coronaria
This species, seldom grown in its typical form, has two main hybrid groups, De Caen (with single flowers) and St Brigid (with double flowers). They flower from late spring to late summer, depending on when they were planted. They are often sold in mixtures, but there are also several selected forms, including 'Die Braut' (syn. 'The Bride'; De Caen Group), which has green-centred, white flowers; 'Hollandia' (syn. 'His Excellency'; De Caen Group), which has white-centred, red flowers; 'Lord Lieutenant' (St Brigid Group), which has dark blue flowers; 'Mister Fokker' (De Caen Group), which has violet-blue flowers; 'Mount Everest' (St Brigid Group), which has white flowers; 'The Admiral' (St Brigid Group), which has purple-pink flowers; and 'The Governor' (De Caen Group), which has red flowers. H 30–40cm (12–15in), S 15cm (6in). Hardy/Z 8–10.

A. nemorosa
Wood anemone
A graceful plant, which is native to Europe, this is ideal for naturalizing beneath shrubs and trees, where it benefits from the shade. The white, cup-shaped flowers are borne in spring. H 15cm (6in), S 20cm (8in). Hardy/Z 4–8.

ARUM
Lords and ladies, cuckoo pint
These tuberous perennials are quiet but handsome plants for a woodland garden. Lords and ladies is a common hedgerow plant in northern Europe; the plant described is a treasured garden form. It has two seasons of interest: the leaves emerge in late autumn and are at their best by late winter, when they make a splendid foil for snowdrops. The plant then dies down to ground level, but spikes of juicy-looking (but poisonous) red berries appear in late summer.
Cultivation Arums will grow in any, preferably fairly moisture-retentive soil in partial shade.

A. italicum
As its name suggests, this is an Italian species, but it also found elsewhere in the Mediterranean. The dark green leaves have white veins. A greenish-white spathe encloses the spike of orange-red berries. H 40cm (16in), S 20cm (8in). The leaves of **A. italicum subsp. italicum 'Marmoratum'** (syn. 'Pictum') are beautifully marbled with cream and pink, appearing in autumn and lasting through the winter, dying back the following spring. Spikes of poisonous orange-red berries poke through the soil in autumn. Although frost flattens the leaves, they do stand up again as they thaw. It combines well with snowdrops. H to 45cm (18in), S 20cm (8in). Hardy/Z 7–9.

Anemone coronaria 'Die Braut'

Anemone nemorosa

Arum italicum subs. *italicum* 'Marmoratum'

Begonia × tuberhybrida 'Illumination Orange'

BEGONIA

This large genus contains about 900 species, including several annuals and a range of perennials that are usually grown as foliage houseplants. None of these plants are hardy, so in frost-prone climates they need to be lifted for overwintering or treated as annuals. Dwarf varieties make excellent bedding material for colour borders and are equally good in containers. Pendulous varieties are ideal subjects for a hanging basket. Some hybrid begonias have huge flowers and have been bred for enthusiasts. These, omitted here, must be grown in containers in controlled conditions under glass in order to give of their best.
Cultivation Tuberous begonias do best in a neutral soil or compost

Begonia × tuberhybrida 'Giant Flowered Pendula Yellow'

(soil mix) in light shade. Plants grown in containers should be lifted after the topgrowth has died back and stored dry in a frost-free place over winter. To coax them out of dormancy the following spring, repot the tubers into fresh compost, water and keep at a temperature of 16–18°C (61–64°F).

B. sutherlandii
This elegant, spreading species from South Africa is an ideal subject for a hanging basket and is perhaps best grown on its own with no competition from other plants. Its clear orange flowers are produced in succession throughout the summer. H 15–30cm (6–12in), S 30cm (12in). Half-hardy/Z 10.

B. × tuberhybrida
This vast hybrid group encompasses a range of different types and cultivars. They can be broadly divided into the Multiflora group (which are suitable for summer bedding) and the Pendula group (which have trailing stems and are suitable for hanging baskets). All are tender/Z 10. Flowers of the **Cascade Series** (Pendula) can be orange, pink, red or yellow. H and S to 30cm (12in). **'Giant Flowered Pendula Yellow'** (Pendula) has double yellow flowers. H and S to 20cm (8in). **'Helene Harms'** (Multiflora) has double yellow flowers. H and S to 45cm (18in). Flowers of the **Illumination Series** (Pendula) are pink or orange, **'Illumination Orange'** being a selected form. H 60cm (2ft), S 30cm (1ft). **'Madame Richard Galle'** (Multiflora) has double copper flowers. H and S 45cm (18in). Plants of the **Non Stop Series** (Multiflora) have double flowers in shades of orange, apricot, pink, yellow and red, and have a slightly more extended flowering period than the others. H and S 20cm (8in).

CAMASSIA
Quamash
This North American genus has not crossed the Atlantic very successfully, probably because it flowers at around the same time

Camassia leichtlinii

as bluebells, which most British gardeners seem to prefer. While nothing can match the blue of an English bluebell, camassias have a comparable distinction and should be more widely grown. They are best in drifts in light woodland or, as a prairie plant, in grass, but they can also be grown in borders.
Cultivation Any reliably moist garden soil is suitable, but these plants prefer humus-rich soil in sun that is not waterlogged in winter. They tolerate dappled shade but may flower less freely.

C. cusickii
This species flowers in late spring, its spikes of blue flowers combining well with *Dicentra spectabilis*. H 60–80cm (24–32in), S 10cm (4in). Borderline hardy/Z 3–8.

C. leichtlinii
This quamash readily forms compact groups. The star-like greyish-white or bluish purple flowers appear in late spring in tapering spikes. H 1m (3ft), S 10cm (4in). Borderline hardy/Z 5–9. Among selected forms are **'Alba'**, which has white flowers, and plants in the **Caerulea Group**, with flowers in shades of blue.

CANNA
Indian shot plant, Indian reed flower
These are exotic plants for the autumn garden. Even if they did not flower, they would be worth

Canna 'President'

growing for their large, smooth leaves, which often have a bronze cast. Use them with grasses, brilliant annuals and dahlias to bring the season to a close with a flourish. They are also excellent in large containers.
Cultivation Grow cannas in fertile soil in full sun. In cold climates cannas need to be bedded out. Bring the rhizomes into growth in containers in late winter or early spring and keep them in a frost-free greenhouse or conservatory. When there is no further risk of frost plant them out just deep enough to cover with soil. In autumn, cut back the topgrowth, dig up the rhizomes and store them dry in a frost-free place over winter.

C. hybrids
The cannas grown in gardens are hybrids, of which there are many. All the following have green leaves unless otherwise indicated. All are half-hardy/Z 7–10. **'Black Knight'** has dark red flowers and bronze leaves. H 1.8m (6ft), S 50cm (20in). **'City of Portland'** has yellow-edged, rose pink flowers. H 1m (3ft), S 50cm (20in). **'Ingeborg'** has salmon pink flowers and bronze leaves. H 60cm (2ft), S 50cm (20in). The free-flowering **'Lucifer'** has yellow-edged crimson flowers. H 60cm (2ft), S 50cm (20in). **'Orchid'** has pink flowers. H 60cm (2ft), S 50cm (20in). **'President'** has bright red flowers. H 1m (3ft), S 50cm (20in). The

Canna 'Roi Humbert'

flowers of **'Primrose Yellow'** are pale yellow. H 60cm (2ft), S 50cm (20in). **'Richard Wallace'** has canary yellow flowers. H 80cm (32in), S 50cm (20in). **'Roi Humbert'** has orange-red flowers and bronze leaves. H 80cm (32in), S 50cm (20in). **'Rosemond Coles'** has yellow-edged, bright red flowers. H 1.5m (5ft), S 50cm (20in). The orange flowers of **'Wyoming'** are frilled and have darker orange edges; the leaves are bronze. H 1.8m (6ft), S 50cm (20in).

CARDIOCRINUM
Giant lily
The name giant lily is well deserved from the point of view of the flowers, which certainly are lily-like, but the plant itself is unlike any lily, having rounded leaves and a pyramidal habit. They are not plants for the average garden. They need to stand in splendid isolation, or in small groups, in woodland clearings, where their scale and majesty can be best appreciated. Patience is needed: they take up to seven years to reach flowering size, when they die off, leaving seedlings behind. For a regular display you need to build up a colony of various ages.
Cultivation Cardiocrinums need fertile soil (ideally enriched with leaf mould) in light, dappled shade.

C. giganteum
This imposing plant produces stout stalks clothed with immense leaves that are smaller towards the top, giving a narrowly pyramidal outline. The trumpet-shaped summer flowers are greenish-white with maroon red throats. H to 3m (10ft), S 1m (3ft). Hardy/Z 7–9.

CHIONODOXA
Glory of the snow
This small genus provides some delightful plants for early spring, typically with starry blue flowers. Grow them in a rock garden or in a border, or under deciduous trees and shrubs.
Cultivation Chionodoxas will grow in any but waterlogged soil in sun or light shade.

C. forbesii
(syn. *C. luciliae of gardens*)
The lavender-blue flowers, with white centres, appear in early spring – sometimes earlier, after a

Cardiocrinum giganteum

Chionodoxa forbesii 'Pink Giant'

Colchicum 'The Giant'

mild winter. It is an excellent subject for naturalizing. H 15cm (6in), S 3cm (1in). Hardy/Z 3–9. There are several cultivars, including **'Alba'**, which has white flowers; and **'Pink Giant'**, which has slightly larger white-centred, pink flowers.

C. sardensis
This species is dwarfer than *C. forbesii*, but the deep blue flowers are more numerous. H 10cm (4in), S 4cm (1½in). Hardy/Z 5–9.

COLCHICUM
Autumn crocus, naked ladies
The flowers of colchicums are always a surprise when they appear in autumn – it is easy to forget that the corms are in the garden. The leaves, large and glossy, do not appear until the following spring (the best time to transplant them, if this is necessary). They are excellent in light woodland or planted around shrubs. In borders the leaves can be a nuisance in spring. Robust types are also excellent for naturalizing in grass.
Cultivation Grow in any good garden soil, ideally in light shade.

C. speciosum
This, the most widely grown member of the genus, produces

goblet-shaped, pink flowers in early autumn. H 25cm (10in), S 10cm (4in). Hardy/Z 4–9. **'Album'** has pure white flowers that are green at the base.

C. 'The Giant'
This is one of many hybrids, with the typical large, lilac-pink flowers. H to 20cm (8in), S 10cm (4in). Hardy/Z 4–9.

C. 'Waterlily'
This is a popular double form, with pinkish-purple flowers that, unfortunately, are not very weather-resistant. H 12cm (5in), S 10cm (4in). Hardy/Z 4–9.

Colchicum speciosum 'Album'

Crinum × powellii 'Album'

CRINUM
Swamp lily

This South African genus is similar to *Amaryllis*, and the plants enjoy similar conditions. In cold gardens, crinums need the hottest spot available, which will usually be at the base of a warm wall. They are best in splendid isolation, when the handsome, strap-shaped leaves and impressive trumpet-like flowers can be seen to advantage. Crinums take some years to adapt after planting, and by the time they are ready to flower, the bulbs will be almost as big as footballs. Left undisturbed, the display will improve year on year. They also do well in containers.
Cultivation Plant in fertile, humus-rich soil in full sun, with shelter from wind. In cold areas a dry mulch of straw in winter can help to protect the dormant bulbs from frost.

C. × powellii

This hybrid (of *C. bulbispermum* and *C. moorei*) is the plant most frequently offered for sale. In late summer to early autumn

Crocosmia 'Lucifer'

(sometimes earlier in favourable climates), it produces robust stems, topped with trumpet-like, pink flowers. H 1.2m (4ft), S 60cm (2ft). Borderline hardy/Z 7–10. 'Album', a distinguished selection, has white flowers. H 1m (3ft), S 60cm (2ft).

CROCOSMIA
Montbretia

This South African genus was not highly rated until Alan Bloom and others began to develop a range of hybrids, all with larger flowers than the plants previously seen in gardens, the most impressive of which, 'Lucifer', is an essential addition in any planting scheme. Excellent as they are as border plants, combining well with roses and annuals, they also look effective when grown in isolation in large groups, almost as a specimen.
Cultivation Crocosmias are tolerant of most garden soils in sun or light shade, but avoid sites that are too hot and dry.

C. × crocosmiiflora

The hybrid group includes many garden-worthy forms. '**Emily McKenzie**' has orange flowers with brown throats from midsummer to autumn. H 45cm (18in), S 8cm (3in). Also flowering from midsummer to autumn, '**Solfatare**', which is sometimes sold as *C.* 'Solfaterre', produces a succession of apricot-yellow flowers among its grassy, bronze-tinged leaves. H 60cm (2ft), S 8cm (3in).

C. 'Lucifer'

This superb plant produces brilliant tomato red flowers in late summer and pleated, fan-shaped leaves. H 1.2m (4ft), S 8cm (3in). Borderline hardy/ Z 7–9.

CROCUS

Essential as they are in the spring garden, it is worth remembering that this large genus also includes some autumn-flowering forms – although confusingly colchicums are often sold under the common name 'autumn crocus'. Their bowl-shaped flowers are distinctive, as are their narrow,

Crocus chrysanthus 'Blue Pearl'

striped leaves. Almost every flower colour but pink is available, and some are attractively striped. A few have stamens in a contrasting colour. Robust hybrids are splendid for naturalizing in lawns, and can create a stunning effect, either in the traditional mixture of colours, or with a more subtle selection of just one or two shades. They can also be grown in shallow pans, bowls and alpine troughs, which is perhaps the best way of displaying some of the more choice and delicate species. Established bulbs tend to flower earlier than new plantings.
Cultivation Grow the larger species and hybrids in a position in full sun in any garden soil (as long as it is not waterlogged). If crocuses are naturalized in lawns, wait until six weeks after flowering before mowing to allow time for the new cormlets to reach flowering size. Dwarf species are best in very free-draining soil or in shallow pans of gritty compost in an alpine house or bulb frame.

Early-flowering crocuses
C. ancyrensis

Each corm of this Turkish species produces three golden-yellow flowers in late winter. H 8cm (3in), S 5cm (2in). Hardy/Z 5–8. The selection '**Golden Bunch**' is more robust, with up to five flowers per corm. H 5cm (2in), S 4cm (1in).

C. chrysanthus

This species, from Greece and Turkey, is seldom grown in its straight form but is usually

represented in cultivation by its many selections, all flowering in late winter to early spring and including '**Advance**', yellow, with violet outer petals; '**Blue Pearl**', which has silver-blue flowers; '**E.A. Bowles**', which has golden-yellow flowers; '**Ladykiller**', which has slender, pure white flowers marked with purple; '**Snow Bunting**', pure white; and one of the most spectacular cultivars, '**Zwanenburg Bronze**', which has rich yellow flowers marked with purple-brown. H 8cm (3in), S 5cm (2in). Hardy/Z 3–8.

C. sieberi

Flowering in late winter to early spring, this species from the Balkans and Crete has yellow-centred, light blue flowers with striking bright orange pistils. H 8cm (3in), S 5cm (2in). Among the worthwhile forms are the golden-throated, white '**Albus**' (syn. 'Bowles' White'), which flowers in early spring; '**Firefly**', which has unusual violet-red flowers; and the eye-catching *C. sieberi* subsp. *sublimis* '**Tricolor**', which has flowers banded in the centre with purple, white and yellow. Hardy/Z 3–8.

C. tommasinianus

One of the best-loved species, this crocus, from the Balkans, Bulgaria, Hungary and Siberia, is also one of the best for naturalizing, producing gleaming lavender flowers in late winter. H 10cm (4in), S 2.5cm (1in). The different selections, which are

Crocus tommasinianus

Crocus sieberi subsp. *sublimis* 'Tricolor'

among the earliest crocuses to flower, are the cause of some confusion within the nursery trade. **'Ruby Giant'** has large, rich purplish-red flowers; **'Whitewell Purple'** also has purplish-red flowers, but with silvery mauve lining inside and more slender than those of 'Ruby Giant'. Hardy/Z 3–8.

C. vernus
The species, as found in Italy, Austria and Eastern Europe, is usually represented in gardens by its many selections, all of which are excellent for naturalizing and flower in late winter to early spring. These include **'Jeanne d'Arc'**, which has pure white flowers; **'Pickwick'**, which has greyish-white flowers, striped with violet; and **'Remembrance'**, which has violet flowers with a silvery sheen. H 10cm (4in), S 8cm (3in). Hardy/Z 3–8.

Crocus vernus 'Remembrance'

Autumn-flowering crocuses
C. banaticus
An unusual crocus from Central Europe, this has lilac flowers in early autumn, which look effective in drifts near the front of a border. It needs soil that stays moist in summer. H 10cm (4in), S 5cm (2in). Hardy/Z 3–8.

C. ochroleucus
This species from the Middle East has slender, creamy white flowers. It is excellent for naturalizing in grass or under deciduous shrubs and is one of the easiest of the late species to grow. H 5cm (2in), S 2.5cm (1in). Hardy/Z 3–8.

C. pulchellus
A species native to the Balkans and Turkey with pale lilac-blue flowers. A vigorous crocus that likes dry soil in full sun. H 12cm (5in), S 4cm (1½in). **'Zephyr'** has larger flowers. Hardy/Z 3–8.

CYCLAMEN
Sowbread
This delightful genus is native to the Mediterranean. The flowers are unique and distinctive, with their swept-back petals. Some cyclamen are not hardy and have been used to produce a range of houseplants with larger flowers. The hardy species are invaluable in the garden, as they belong to a select group of plants that thrive in dry shade and are therefore excellent for planting beneath trees, where in time they will build up large colonies. The leaves are usually beautifully marked. Make sure that any plants you buy are seed raised; wild populations have been decimated through over-collection.
Cultivation Hardy cyclamen prefer moderately fertile, moist but well-drained soil in partial shade, but they will tolerate drier soils. An annual mulch of leaf mould is beneficial. *C. persicum* hybrids grown as houseplants should be kept out of direct sunlight when in full growth. When watering, avoid wetting the upper surface of the tuber, which can collect water and rot. In winter keep the plants dry and place the pots in full light.

C. coum
This species flowers from late winter to mid-spring, in a variety of colours, from purple-violet to pink and white. H 8cm (3in), S 10cm (4in). Hardy/Z 5–9.

C. hederifolium
(syn. *C. neapolitanum*)
The name indicates that the leaves are ivy-like. The fact that they remain green when many other plants are below ground makes this a valuable plant for winter interest. The flowers, which may be deep pink, pale pink or pinkish-white, appear in late summer to mid-autumn. H 10cm (4in), S 15cm (6in). Hardy/Z 5–9.

C. persicum
This species is the parent of a large number of hybrids that are often sold unnamed. The scented flowers range in colour from white to a glowing cerise red and appear in winter and spring. Some combine two colours on the frilly petals. H and S to 15cm (6in). Tender/Z 9–10.

DAHLIA
These exotic-looking flowers are now enjoying something of a revival. They are the ideal plant for adding a splash of colour to the autumn garden, with their perfectly formed, almost geometric flowers. Flower colours include white, all shades of pink, red, orange, yellow and a warm rosy purple. Some combine more than one colour. For maximum impact,

Cyclamen coum

Dahlia 'Small World'

plant dahlias in groups. Tall varieties are excellent for the back of a border.

Dahlias have been extensively hybridized, resulting in a range of flower shapes classified as described below.
Cultivation Dahlias need rich soil (although they do reasonably well in any ordinary, well-drained soil) in full sun. Pinch out the growing tips for bushiness and deadhead to keep the flowers coming. Tall varieties, particularly those with very large flowers, need staking. In cold areas the tubers should be lifted after the topgrowth has been blackened by frost, then dried off and stored over winter for planting out again the following spring. Alternatively, treat them as annuals and plant fresh tubers each year. For earlier flowers, start them into growth in containers under glass six weeks before planting out.

Cyclamen hederifolium

Dahlia 'Ellen Huston'

All the following dahlias are half-hardy/all zones.

Single-flowered dahlias (Division 1)

One or two rows of petals surround a central disc. Mostly dwarf, these dahlias are suitable for bedding. **'Ellen Huston'** has orange-red flowers and contrasting purple-tinged foliage. H and S 30cm (12in). **'Moonfire'** has single, deep gold flowers with vermilion centres and dark bronze-green foliage. H 75cm (30in), S 30cm (12in). **'Tally Ho'** has red flowers with yellow centres and dark copper foliage. H and S 60cm (2ft).

Anemone-flowered dahlias (Division 2)

The flowers are double, with one or more rings of outer petals surrounding a central group of tubular florets. Those of **'Paso Doble'** have white outer petals and yellow centres. H 1m (3ft), S 60cm (2ft). **'Scarlet Comet'** has vivid red flowers with upright central petals. H 1.2m (4ft), S 60cm (2ft).

Collerette dahlias (Division 3)

The flowers have two rings of outer florets around a central group of disc florets.

Dahlia 'Hillcrest Regal'

'Chimborazo' has flowers with a yellow-tipped collar. H 1.2m (4ft), S 60cm (2ft). **'Hillcrest Regal'** has maroon flowers with a white-tipped collar. H 1.2m (4ft), S 60cm (2ft).

Waterlily dahlias (Division 4)

The flowers classified large, medium, small or miniature, are fully double and flattened. **'Figurine'** has small, pink and white flowers. H 1.2m (4ft), S 60cm (2ft). **'Glorie van Heemstede'** has small, orange-yellow flowers. H 1.2m (4ft or more, S 60cm (2ft). **'Lismore Willie'** has small, pale gold flowers. H 1.2m (4ft), S 60cm (2ft). **'Porcelain'** has small, white flowers flushed with lilac-pink. H 1.2m (4ft), S 60cm (2ft).

Decorative dahlias (Division 5)

The flowers, classified as giant, large, medium, small or miniature, are fully double, and the tips of the petals are bluntly pointed. **'Alva's Supreme'** has giant, soft yellow flowers. H 1.2m (4ft) or more, S 60cm (2ft). **'Charlie Two'** has medium, light yellow flowers. H 1.2m (4ft), S 60cm (2ft). **'David Howard'** has miniature, rich orange flowers and copper-tinged foliage. H 1m (3ft) or more, S 60cm (2ft). **'Fire Mountain'** has miniature, bright red flowers and very dark green foliage. H 1m (3ft) or more, S 60cm (2ft). **'Hamari Gold'** has giant, golden-bronze flowers. H 1.2m (4ft), S 60cm (2ft). **'Karenglen'** has miniature, orange-red flowers. H 1m (3ft), S 60cm (2ft). **'Kenora Valentine'** has large, brilliant red flowers. H 1.2m (4ft), S 60cm (2ft). **'Kidd's Climax'** has giant, yellow-flushed pink flowers. H 1m (3ft) or more, S 60cm (2ft). **'Phill's Pink'** has small, warm orange-pink flowers, the petals yellow at the base. H 1m (3ft), S 60cm (2ft). **'Skipley Spot'** has small, red flowers with white-tipped petals. H 1m (3ft), S 60cm (2ft).

Ball dahlias (Division 6)

The flowers, small or miniature, are fully double and globe-shaped. **'Cornel'** has small, rich red

Dahlia 'Figurine'

flowers. H 1.2m (4ft), S 60cm (2ft). **'Jomanda'** has miniature, terracotta-red flowers. H 1m (3ft) or more, S 60cm (2ft).

Pompon dahlias (Division 7)

The flowers are fully double and globe-shaped with petals that are round or blunt at the tips. **'Minley Carol'** has orange flowers with a hint of red at the tips of the petals. H 1m (3ft) or more, S 60cm (2ft). **'Small World'** (syn. 'Bowen') is one of the best white dahlias. The flowers are sometimes flecked with purple. H 1m (3ft) or more, S 60cm (2ft). **'Willo's Surprise'** has wine red flowers. H 1m (3ft) or more, S 60cm (2ft).

Cactus dahlias (Division 8)

The flowers, classified as giant, large, medium, small or miniature, are fully double and have rolled, pointed petals. **'Doris Day'** has small, cardinal red flowers. H 1m (3ft) or more, S 60cm (2ft). **'Kiwi Gloria'** has small, lilac-pink and white flowers. H 1m (3ft) or more, S 60cm (2ft).

Semi-cactus dahlias (Division 9)

As for cactus dahlias, but the petals are rolled to only half their length. **'Belle of the Ball'** has large, lavender-pink flowers. H 1.2m (4ft), S 60cm (2ft). **'Eastwood Moonlight'** has medium, pale yellow flowers. H 1m (3ft) or more, S 60cm (2ft). **'Fidalgo Climax'** has large, bright yellow flowers. H 1.2m (4ft), S 60cm (2ft). **'Hamari Accord'** has large, clear yellow flowers. H 1.2m (4ft), S 60cm (2ft). **'Hayley Jane'** has small, white flowers, the petals tipped with purple. H 1.2m (4ft) or more, S 60cm (2ft). **'Kenora Challenger'**

Dahlia 'Alva's Supreme'

has large, pure white flowers. H 1.2m (4ft), S 60cm (2ft). **'Kenora Sunset'** has medium, orange-red flowers with yellow centres. H 1.2m (4ft), S 60cm (2ft). **'Lemon Elegans'** has small, pure yellow flowers. H 1.2m (4ft), S 60cm (2ft). **'Match'** has small, white flowers, the petals tipped with purple. H 1.2m (4ft), S 60cm (2ft). **'Nargold'** has medium orange and gold flowers, with ragged petals. H 1.2m (4ft), S 60cm (2ft). **'Pink Pastelle'** has medium, bright pink flowers, with white centres. H 1.2m (4ft), S 60cm (2ft). **'Piper's Pink'** has small, glowing pink flowers. H and S 60cm (2ft). **'So Dainty'** has miniature, orange-bronze flowers. H 1m (3ft) or more, S 60cm (2ft). **'Tahiti Sunrise'** has medium, yellow flowers, the petals tipped with red. H 1.2m (4ft), S 60cm (2ft). **'Weston Pirate'** has miniature, dark red flowers. H 1m (3ft), S 60cm (2ft). **'White Moonlight'** has medium, white flowers. H 1.2m (4ft), S 60cm (2ft).

Miscellaneous (Division 10)

This designation covers a wide range of hybrids that are sometimes defined further as peony-flowered, orchid-flowered, mignon, gallery and so on, not all

Dahlia 'Jomanda'

Dahlia 'Art Deco'

Eranthis hyemalis

Erythronium dens-canis

Eucomis bicolor

of which are universally accepted. **'Art Deco'** (dwarf bedding) has orange flowers. H and S 25–30cm (10–12in). **'Bishop of Llandaff'** has semi-double bright red flowers with yellow centres and blackish-red foliage. H 60cm (2ft) or more, S 45cm (18in). **'Fascination'** (dwarf bedding) has pinkish-purple flowers and dark bronze foliage. H 60cm (2ft), S 45cm (18in). **'Rembrandt'** (dwarf bedding) has pink flowers, the petals tipped with darker pink. H and S 25–30cm (10–12in). **'Renoir'** (dwarf bedding) has deep pink flowers, more open than those of 'Rembrandt'. H and S 25–30cm (10–12in).

ERANTHIS
Winter aconite
These are one of the earliest bulbs to come into flower. They are robust enough to penetrate a light covering of snow, which is a charming effect when it occurs. Like snowdrops, they transplant best when putting on growth after flowering, so when buying them, look for plants 'in the green' rather than dormant tubers. They are excellent when planted to

carpet large areas beneath deciduous trees. The flowers, surrounded by a characteristic 'ruff' of green leaves, open only when the sun is shining.
Cultivation Grow in any well-drained soil, ideally humus-rich, in sun or light shade.

E. hyemalis
(syn. *Aconitum hyemale*)
The species has bright green leaves, forming a ruff beneath the lemon-yellow flowers. H 8cm (3in), S 5cm (2in). Hardy/Z 4–9. Plants in the **Cilica Group** (syn. *Aconitum cylicum*) have rather larger flowers thatn those of the species, and the leaves of the ruff are smaller. H 10cm (4in), S 5cm (2in).

ERYTHRONIUM
Dog's tooth violet
To those who grow them, these are one of the delights of the spring garden, although their presence is fleeting. The flowers, with their upswept petals, are of unique charm, and the leaves of some forms are attractively mottled. Grow them in clumps around deciduous trees and shrubs or on lightly shaded rock gardens.
Cultivation They will grow in most soils enriched with organic matter, and moisture retentive without being boggy. They prefer a cool spot, out of sun in summer: in the shade of deciduous trees is ideal. They must not be allowed to dry out. Plant them as soon after you buy them as possible and cover them with a mulch in dry summers.

E. californicum
The species is usually represented in cultivation by **'White Beauty'** (syn. *E. revolutum* 'White Beauty'),

which has large white flowers with brownish-yellow throats in mid- to late spring. The leaves are flecked with brown. H 20–25cm (8–10in), S 25cm (10in). Hardy/Z 3–9.

E. dens-canis
European dog's tooth violet
The beautiful species produces one flower, which may be white, pink or lilac, on each stem in early to mid-spring. H and S 25cm (10in). Hardy/Z 3–9. **'Rose Queen'** has pink flowers. H and S 25cm (10in).

E. 'Pagoda'
Probably the most popular of all the dog's tooth violets, 'Pagoda' has nodding, yellow flowers in late spring. The glossy, faintly mottled leaves are green. H 40cm (16in), S 15cm (6in). Hardy/Z 4–9.

EUCOMIS
Pineapple plant
So-called because of the pineapple-like flowers, which have a characteristic tuft of green leaves at the top of the spike, these South African species do best in a sheltered spot (such as by a warm wall) and also thrive in containers. The flowers are attractive to bees.
Cultivation Grow in full sun in moderately fertile, well-drained soil. Protect in winter with a mulch of straw or other similar dry material.

E. bicolor
This species produces spikes of green flowers from mid- to late summer among the strap-shaped leaves. H 30–60cm (1–2ft), S 20cm (8in). **'Alba'** has white flowers. Borderline hardy/Z 8–10.

E. comosa
(syn. *E. punctata*)
A species with tall, narrow spikes of white flowers that are edged with purple. H 75cm (30in), S 20cm (8in). Borderline hardy/Z 8–10.

Dahlia 'Hayley Jane'

Erythronium 'Pagoda'

Fritillaria imperialis 'The Premier'

Fritillaria meleagris

FRITILLARIA
Fritillary

This is a variable genus, containing species that provide garden plants fit for a number of purposes. The imposing crown imperial is good for adding height to spring borders, while the snake's head fritillary is excellent for naturalizing in meadows or by the streamside. Others are connoisseurs' plants, needing special conditions but providing ample reward with their subtly coloured flowers. Only a few of the nearly 100 species are widely grown, all with pendent, bell-like flowers.
Cultivation Most fritillaries do well in any well-drained soil in sun. *F. meleagris* does best in heavier, moisture-retentive soil in sun or light shade but will tolerate ordinary soil. Bulbs of *F. imperialis* are prone to rotting. Planting them on their sides will help to prevent water collecting on the hollow upper surface.

F. imperialis
Crown imperial

These majestic plants are unmistakable. The yellow, orange-red or red flowers hang down from the tops of erect, sturdy stems in late spring. Plant the bare bulbs (which are unpleasantly scented) as soon after purchase as possible. H 1.2m (4ft) or more, S 30cm (1ft). Selections include 'Lutea', which has yellow flowers; 'Rubra', vermilion-red; and 'The Premier', which has orange-red flowers. Hardy/Z 5–9.

F. meleagris
Snake's head fritillary

This species is often found growing wild in damp European

meadows. The flowers, which come in late spring, are appealingly chequered with dull purple. In the right conditions this species will self-seed. H 30cm (12in), S 5cm (2in). *F. meleagris* **var. unicolor subvar. alba** has white flowers that are delicately touched with green. Hardy/Z 3–8.

F. michailovskyi

Also flowering in late spring, this species has fascinating bell-like flowers that are a dusky reddish-purple edged with yellow. Grow in a shady rock garden or an alpine trough. H 20cm (8in), S 5cm (2in). Hardy/Z 5–8.

GALANTHUS
Snowdrop

Few plants have the charm of the snowdrop or are as welcome. They are usually among the first flowers to appear in the gardening year. Each flower has six petals, the outer three longer than the inner ones. Unusually among bulbs, snowdrops seem to prefer slightly damp soil. They are delightful in drifts in light woodland, or pushing through ivy.
Cultivation Most snowdrops do best in reliably moist soil, in a spot where they are in sun when in growth but lightly shaded when dormant; beneath deciduous trees and shrubs is usually an ideal spot.

G. elwesii

This species from Turkey and the Balkans is less well known than *G. nivalis* but possibly superior. It is a larger plant, with bright green, strap-shaped leaves and flowers with large green spots on the inner petals. H to 25cm (10in), S 8cm (3in). Hardy/Z 3–9.

G. nivalis

The best-known of the snowdrops and one that will naturalize very easily. The bell-shaped, pure white flowers hang downwards, the outer petals flaring outwards to reveal the green markings on the inner ones. H and S 10cm (4in). 'Flore Pleno', the double form, is no less charming. Hardy/Z 3–9.

GALTONIA
Cape hyacinth, summer hyacinth

These elegant plants, valued for their late season, provide a welcome freshness to summer borders where they are allowed to rise above annuals or late-flowering perennials. The flowers open in succession on the flower spike, from bottom to top, providing interest over a number of weeks.
Cultivation Galtonias need fertile, well-drained soil in a sunny spot.

G. candicans

The most popular species, this bears spikes of fragrant white flowers in late summer to early autumn. H 1–1.2m (3–4ft), S 10cm (4in). Hardy/Z 7–10.

G. viridiflora

The species is similar to *G. candicans* but has green flowers. H 1m (3ft), S 10cm (4in). Half-hardy/Z 7–9.

GLADIOLUS

Nowadays a less popular flower with gardeners than formerly, the gladiolus is still an excellent florist's flower. The ease with which it hybridizes has led to a huge number of selected forms.

The spikes can be picked while still in bud, and the flowers will open indoors. They do not combine well with other plants but can be used in a colour border in large groups. Otherwise, grow them in a picking border exclusively to provide flowers for the house. Shorter-growing forms are also effective in containers.
Cultivation Hardy gladioli will grow in any well-drained soil in full sun. The large-flowered hybrids need fertile soil that does not dry out in summer. Where these will not survive the winter, lift the corms in autumn and dry them off. Snap off the old corm and store the new one in a dry, frost-free place over winter for planting out again the following spring. Tall varieties need staking.

G. communis subsp. byzantinus
(syn. G. byzantinus)

The exception to all other gladioli, this elegant species flowers in late spring. The rich magenta flowers (typical of gladioli but much smaller) are produced in long spikes. A superb plant for naturalizing, it is also effective in borders and large rock gardens. H 1m (3ft), S 8cm (3in). Borderline hardy/Z 7–10.

G. hybrids

Gladiolus hybrids, of which there are a vast number, are usually classified according to flower size: giant, large, medium, small and miniature. Butterfly gladioli are small-flowered, often with a contrasting patch of colour on the lower petals. Primulinus gladioli have funnel-shaped

Galtonia candicans

Gladiolus communis subsp. *byzantinus*

Gladiolus 'Seraphin'

Hippeastrum 'Christmas Star'

Hyacinthus 'Amethyst'

flowers that are less densely packed on the spike than with the other types. All flower from midsummer to early autumn and are half-hardy/Z 7–10. **'Aristocrat'** (medium) is late, with purple flowers. H 1m (3ft), S 10cm (4in). **'Bluebird'** (small) is early, with rich violet-blue flowers. H 1m (3ft), S 10cm (4in). The greenish-yellow flowers of **'Green Woodpecker'** (butterfly) are blotched with red. H 1.5m (5ft), S 12cm (5in). **'Lady Godiva'** (primulinus) is white. H 60cm (2ft), S 10cm (4in). **'Leonore'** (primulinus) has bright yellow flowers. H 1m (3ft), S 10cm (4in). The salmon pink and yellow flowers of **'Mykonos'** (butterfly) are marked with red. H 1m (3ft), S 10cm (4in). **'Peter Pears'** (large) is soft apricot-orange. H 1.2m (4ft), S 18cm (7in). **'Seraphin'** (butterfly) has muffled pink flowers with white throats. H 70cm (28in), S 10cm (4in). **'The Bride'** (miniature) is pure white. H 1m (3ft), S 10cm (4in). **'Trader Horn'** (giant) has deep, rich scarlet flowers. H 1.2m (4ft), S 18 cm (7in).

HIPPEASTRUM
Confusingly, these are usually sold under the name 'amaryllis'. Few of the species are grown, but there are a growing number of hybrids, all with huge, showy flowers, intended for growing exclusively as houseplants. They are often sold in packs with pots and compost (soil mix) for the Christmas gift market. Large bulbs produce more flowers (up to five) on each stem than smaller ones.

Cultivation Use any proprietary compost, with added grit (both for drainage and weight because these plants can be top-heavy). Plant with the neck of the bulb above the surface of the compost. Keep them well-watered and stand them in full light, but not directly next to a window. Stake the flower stem if necessary.

H. hybrids
There are many cultivars, with a wide range of flower forms and colours. All are tender/Z 10. **'Apple Blossom'** has white flowers with pink-edged petals. H 50cm (20in), S 30cm (12in). **'Christmas Star'** is an attractive, compact form with white flowers that are edged and striped with bright red. H to 45cm (18in), S 30cm (12in). **'Florida'** has bright red flowers. H to 60cm (2ft), S 30cm (12in). **'Snow Queen'** is one of several white-flowered amaryllis, others being **'White Dazzler'** and **'White Lady'**. H to 60cm (2ft), S 30cm (12in).

Hippeastrum 'Florida'

HYACINTHOIDES
Bluebell
This genus includes the well-known English bluebell, as well as the rather coarse Spanish species. Bluebells are excellent for colonizing areas beneath deciduous trees.
Cultivation Grow in any reasonable garden soil in light shade.

H. hispanica
(syn. *Scilla campanulata*)
Spanish bluebell
A rather more robust species than the English bluebell (with which it will hybridize), this sends up erect stems with blue, bell-shaped flowers in spring. H 60cm (2ft), S 10cm (4in). Hardy/Z 4–9.

H. non-scripta
English bluebell
Broadly similar to the Spanish bluebell, this species has daintier, somewhat darker blue flowers, which are also more tubular. They are borne in late spring. There are a number of pink and white forms. H to 60cm (2ft), S 8cm (3in). Hardy/Z 6–9.

HYACINTHUS
Hyacinth
Nothing can match the scent of hyacinths. In addition, they have one of the widest colour ranges of all the bulb genera, including the elusive blue. Only the hybrids are cultivated. Planted in blocks in beds, they are a little stiff and formal, and they do not integrate well with other plants. It is better to tuck them into odd corners and allow the scent to hit you as you wander around the garden. Otherwise, they are good in bowls and can be grown as houseplants. 'Forced' bulbs are sold from autumn onwards, and these will flower in the middle of winter, but all can be grown indoors initially. Planted out in the garden after flowering, they will take a season or two to recover. The more compact forms are best for growing outdoors; larger ones are top-heavy and are best kept inside.
Cultivation Outdoors, grow in any well-drained soil in full sun. If treated as annuals, they can be planted in light shade. Indoors, grow in bowls of special bulb fibre. Bulbs for forcing should be

planted up and placed in a cool, dark place (such as a dry cellar or garage) for 8–10 weeks, then brought into a light, warm room for flowering 3–4 weeks later. Alternatively, they can be grown in special glass hyacinth vases that allow the roots to be in water while keeping the actual bulb dry.

H. hybrids
The following flower naturally in mid-spring but can be forced to flower at other times. All are hardy/Z 6–9. **'Amethyst'** has lilac-blue flowers; **'Anna Marie'** is bright pink; **'Blue Jacket'** is an arresting deep blue; **'Carnegie'** has pure white flowers; **'City of Haarlem'** is bright yellow; **'Gipsy Queen'** is a subtle salmon orange; the double flowers of **'Hollyhock'** are deep red; **'Jan Bos'** is carmine red; the well known **'L'Innocence'** is pure white; **'Ostara'** has deep violet-blue flowers; and **'Pink Pearl'** has pink flowers. H 20–30cm (8–12in), S 8cm (3in).

Hyacinthus 'City of Haarlem'

Iris reticulata 'George'

IRIS

Irises form a large genus that includes true bulbs (in the generally accepted sense of the term) as well as perennials (so-called rhizomatous irises are treated as perennials in this book). Some have very specific cultivation needs. Early-flowering species seldom last long in the garden and are best treated as annuals. So-called 'Dutch irises' are grown commercially for the cut flower market. Bulbous irises are excellent in borders, rock gardens and containers.
Cultivation Bulbous irises need a preferably well-drained, alkaline soil, in full sun.

I. bucharica

This species, native to central Asia, has fragrant, golden-yellow and white flowers in mid-spring, blotched with either green, brown or violet. It needs protection from winter wet and is probably best grown in an alpine house. H 40cm (16in). Hardy/Z 4–9.

I. danfordiae

This delightful dwarf species from Turkey, valued for its bright yellow flowers, blooms in late winter. It will tolerate some shade. H 10cm (4in). Hardy/Z 6–9.

I. reticulata

This dainty species from the Caucasus is one of the first bulbous plants to flower in the gardening calendar, producing its rich violet-blue, yellow-splashed flowers in late winter. It is excellent in rock gardens and shallow pans but unfortunately is not reliably perennial, so it is advisable to plant fresh stocks annually. H 15cm (6in). Hardy/Z 6–9. Selections include **'George'**,

which has deep purple flowers; **'Harmony'**, with deep blue flowers; **'Joyce'**, which has sky blue and orange flowers; and **'J.S. Dijt'**, with purple-violet flowers.

Xiphium irises

This large group, consisting mainly of robust hybrids that are easy to grow, includes irises sometimes referred to as 'Dutch irises', 'English irises' and 'Spanish irises'. They make excellent border plants that flower in late spring or early summer, but they are forced to flower at any time for the cut flower market. They are often sold as mixed colours, but there are several named selections, including **'Apollo'**, with yellow and white flowers; **'Casablanca'**, with white flowers; **'Imperator'**, which have blue and orange flowers; **'Professor Blaauw'**, deep blue; **'Symphony'**, with yellow and white flowers; and **'Telstar'**, deep blue. H 60–65cm (24–26in). Hardy/Z 5–8.

LEUCOJUM
Snowflake

These neglected bulbs look like large snowdrops, but differ in having six white petals of equal length, each one spotted with yellow-green at the tip. These plants appreciate damp soil and are at their most attractive when planted on the banks of a natural stream. They can also be grown in borders and rock gardens.
Cultivation The snowflakes described here need fertile soil that does not dry out and a position in full sun or light shade.

L. aestivum
Summer snowflake

This is the most commonly grown species. Despite the name,

it flowers in mid-spring, producing green-tipped white flowers and glossy green leaves. H 40cm (16in), S 8cm (3in). Hardy/Z 4–9.

L. vernum
Spring snowflake

The flowering period of this often coincides with the snowdrops (late winter to early spring). They need a fertile soil and are best left undisturbed after planting. H 35cm (14in). Hardy/Z 4–8.

LILIUM
Lily

This huge genus is also one of the most varied in terms of cultivation: there are lilies for sun, for shade, acid or alkaline soils. Lilies work well in mixed summer borders, appreciating the shade at their roots that the neighbouring plants provide. They are also excellent in pots. A few are delightful in woodland, but building up colonies of good size can take several years.
Cultivation All the lilies described here need well-drained soil and are better off where their flowers will be in sun while their roots are shaded. A few will tolerate light overhead shade. Most prefer acid to neutral soil, although some tolerate alkaline soil, with a few even preferring it. Many modern hybrids have been bred to thrive whatever the pH. Individual requirements are specified in the entries below.

Asiatic hybrids (Division I)

Derived from Asiatic species and hybrids, these are sturdy stem-rooting lilies. There are three subdivisions: 1a, with upward-facing flowers; 1b, with outward-facing flowers; and 1c, with

Lilium 'Concorde'

pendent flowers. All are hardy/Z 4–8. **'Admiration'** (1a) has large, unscented, creamy yellow flowers spotted with maroon in early to midsummer. H to 40cm (16in). **'Bronwen North'** (1c) is striking with slightly scented, pale mauve-pink flowers heavily spotted and lined with purple in early summer. H to 1m (3ft). **'Concorde'** (1a), an excellent border plant, has unscented, lemon-yellow flowers, greenish at the base, that open from early to midsummer. H to 1m (3ft). **'Connecticut King'** (1a) is a popular hybrid, with unscented, rich deep yellow flowers in early summer. H to 1m (3ft). **'Côte d'Azur'** (1a) produces unscented, rich pink flowers in early to midsummer. H to 1m (3ft). **'Eros'** (1c) has nodding, fragrant, turkscap flowers in midsummer. The sepals are pinkish orange spotted with maroon. H to 1.2m (4ft). **'Karen North'** (1c) bears lightly scented turkscap flowers in midsummer. The sepals are orange-pink, lightly spotted with darker pink. H to 1.4m (55in). **'Mont Blanc'** (1a) produces unscented, brown-spotted, white flowers in early to midsummer. H to 70cm (28in). **'Orange Pixie'** (1a) has unscented, bright orange flowers in summer that are spotted with

Leucojum aestivum

Lilium 'Bronwen North'

Lilium 'Orange Pixie'

Lilium 'Roma'

chocolate-maroon. H to 40cm (16in). **'Peggy North'** (1c) is a good border lily, with lightly scented turkscap flowers in mid-summer. The sepals are glowing orange spotted with dark brown. H to 1.5m (5ft). **'Roma'** (1a) has fragrant creamy white flowers, lightly spotted with maroon, which open in early to midsummer. H to 1.2m (4ft).

Martagon hybrids (Division 2)
Derived mainly from *L. martagon* and *L. hansonii*, these are hardy, mainly stem-rooting lilies with turkscap flowers, suitable for light shade or woodland. All are hardy/Z 4–8. **'Mrs R.O. Backhouse'**, a famous lily, is one of the oldest still in cultivation. It has unscented, turkscap flowers that hang from the stems in early to midsummer. The sepals are orange-yellow with maroon spotting and are flushed pink on the outside. H 1.3m (52in).

Candidum hybrids (Division 3)
Derived from *L. chalcedonicum*, *L. candidum* and other European species (excluding *L. martagon*), this is a small group of lilies with sometimes scented, turkscap flowers. They are usually not stem-rooting. *L. × testaceum* (Nankeen lily) is a lime-tolerant

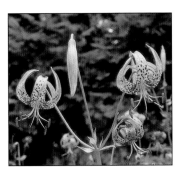

Lilium Bellingham Group

hybrid bearing fragrant, turkscap flowers in early to midsummer. The sepals are pale apricot-pink lightly spotted with red. H 1.2m (4ft). Hardy/Z 5–8.

American hybrids (Division 4)
Derived from American species, these are rhizomatous lilies, with sometimes scented, usually turkscap flowers. They are not stem-rooting. **Bellingham Group** have occasionally fragrant turkscap flowers that can vary in colour from yellow to orange and orange-red, all spotted deep brown and appearing in early and midsummer. They are excellent for naturalizing in light shade and need acid soil, preferably reliably moist. H to 1.5m (5ft). **'Shuksan'** is a selected form, with lightly scented, tangerine-yellow flowers tipped with red and spotted with black or reddish-brown. H to 1.2m (4ft). Hardy/Z 4–8.

Longiflorum hybrids (Division 5)
Derived from *L. formosanum* and *L. longiflorum*, this is a small but growing group of lilies with fragrant, trumpet- or funnel-shaped flowers, usually grown for the cut flower market.

Trumpet and Aurelian hybrids (Division 6)
Derived from Asiatic species (excluding *L. auratum*, *L. japonicum*, *L. rubellum* and *L. speciosum*), these are mostly hardy, fragrant, stem-rooting lilies. There are four subdivisions: 6a, with trumpet-shaped flowers; 6b, with usually outward-facing, bowl-shaped flowers; 6c, with shallowly bowl-shaped flowers that often open flat; and 6d, with sepals that are distinctly recurved. The lilies described are borderline hardy/Z 4–8. In mid- and late summer the beautiful lilies in the **African Queen Group** (6a) have heavily scented, tangerine-apricot flowers that are veined with deep purple on the outside. H 2m (6ft). **'White Henryi'** (6d) has large, fragrant flowers in midsummer that open flat. The sepals are white, flushed deep orange at the base and with rust-red papillae. H to 1.5m (5ft).

Lilium African Queen Group

Oriental hybrids (Division 7)
Derived from species from the Far East, these are late-flowering lilies, often with scented flowers. Most are lime-hating and need sun or partial shade. There are four subdivisions: 7a, with trumpet-shaped flowers; 7b, with bowl-shaped flowers; 7c, with flat flowers; and 7d, with sepals that are distinctly recurved. All are hardy/Z 4–8. **'Acapulco'** (7d) has fragrant, rich pink flowers with recurving sepals. H to 1m (3ft). **'Belle Epoque'** (7b), which flowers from midsummer to early autumn, has white to soft pink flowers, each sepal centrally banded with cream. H to 1m (3ft). **'Casa Blanca'** (7b) has heavily scented, pure white flowers in mid- to late summer. H to 1.2m (4ft). **'Little Joy'** (7d), bred for container growing, is a sturdy dwarf, with unscented flowers with recurved, pink to soft red sepals, spotted with dark maroon. H to 35cm (14in). From midsummer to early autumn **'Royal Class'** (7b) produces fragrant flowers, the sepals varying in colour from white to soft pink, with a central yellow band and prominent papillae. H to 1m (3ft). **'Star Gazer'** (7c) is a popular lily, albeit lime-hating. From midsummer it produces rich

Lilium 'Acapulco'

Lilium 'Royal Class'

crimson-pink, unscented flowers that are spotted with darker pink. H to 1.5m (5ft).

Other hybrids (Division 8)
This group includes all hybrids not accommodated by the other groups. **'Moneymaker'** produces up to six, sweetly scented, clear pink flowers in midsummer. H to 1m (3ft). Hardy/Z 4–8.

Species (Division 9)
This group includes all true species and their forms.

L. auratum
Golden-rayed lily
This species from Japan has the largest flowers of any lily. The heavily scented flowers open in late summer to autumn; the sepals are white, usually spotted with crimson, and banded with yellow and with fleshy papillae. It needs acid soil. H to 1.5m (5ft). Hardy/Z 5–8.

L. candidum
Madonna lily
This is a species from the Balkans and eastern Mediterranean with fragrant, trumpet-shaped, pure white flowers in summer. Grow in neutral to alkaline soil and plant the bulbs shallowly. H to 2m (6ft). Hardy/Z 4–9.

Lilium 'Moneymaker'

Lilium regale

Lilium speciosum var. *album*

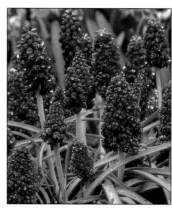

Muscari armeniacum 'Blue Spike'

L. formosanum

This elegant but slightly tender species is native to Taiwan. In late summer and early autumn fragrant, trumpet-shaped, white flowers open from buds that are strongly flushed with wine purple. It needs moist, acid soil. H to 1.5m (5ft). Borderline hardy/Z 5. The naturally occurring variant *L. formosanum* var. *pricei* is hardier and much smaller. H to 30cm (12in).

L. henryi

This Chinese species is clump-forming and easy to grow. In late summer elegant stems carry hanging, lightly scented, orange, turkscap flowers, spotted darker. It is best in neutral to alkaline soil in light shade. H to 3m (10ft). Hardy/Z 4–9.

L. martagon
Martagon lily, common turkscap lily

This species occurs in a range from northwest Europe to northwest Asia. The turkscap flowers, slightly unpleasant to smell, hang from the stems in early to midsummer. They are dull pink, spotted with maroon. It does well in almost any well-drained soil in sun or light shade. H to 2m (6ft). The naturally occurring *L. martagon* var. *album* is a desirable white form. Hardy/Z 4–8.

L. regale
Regal lily

An essential plant in any garden, this species is found growing wild in western China. Opening in midsummer, its richly scented,

white flowers have yellow bases and are heavily stained purple on the outside. It tolerates most well-drained soils. H to 2m (6ft). Hardy/Z 4–9. *L. regale* var. *album* has pure white flowers with golden yellow anthers.

L. speciosum

This attractive species from China, Japan and Taiwan needs moist, acid soil, preferably in light shade. The pale pink or white, fragrant, turkscap flowers are produced in late summer. H to 2m (6ft). There are a number of selected forms, including *L. speciosum* var. *album*, which has white flowers with prominent papillae; '**Krätzeri**', which has white sepals striped green on the back; and '**Uchida**', which has brilliant crimson flowers, spotted with green or darker red and tipped with white. Hardy/Z 5–8.

MUSCARI
Grape hyacinth

These flowers do indeed resemble miniature hyacinths, and their shape and deep purple-blue colour are also evocative of tiny grape bunches. They self-seed freely, making them a weed in some gardens, but can be of of value for their unassuming charm. They are seen at their best when planted in large, river-like drifts among shrubs and trees.
Cultivation Grow in any well-drained soil in sun or light shade.

M. armeniacum

This is the most commonly grown species, with clusters of dull blue, bell-like flowers in spring. Try it in conjunction with

the yellow-flowered *Doronicum orientale*. H to 20cm (8in), S 5cm (2in). Hardy/Z 2–9. Selected forms include '**Blue Spike**', which has double flowers; and '**Fantasy Creation**', which has flowers that fade to green. H to 20cm (8in), S 5cm (2in).

M. botryoides

The straight species is rarely cultivated, but the selection '**Album**' is becoming more popular. It has spikes of white flowers (less compact than those of *M. armeniacum*) in spring. Plant the bulbs in quantities, and close together, for the best display. H 20cm (8in), S 5cm (2in). Hardy/Z 3–9.

NARCISSUS
Daffodil

Spring would not be spring without daffodils, probably the largest of the bulb genera, with their distinctive central cups or trumpets. They have one of the longest flowering seasons of almost any bulb, with a few appearing as early as midwinter. Almost without exception, the daffodils grown in gardens today are artificial hybrids. The number of these is so vast that they are usefully categorized in a number of divisions (see right). Daffodils look best when planted en masse, in grass, on banks or beneath deciduous trees and shrubs. Smaller species and hybrids are excellent in sunny rock gardens or alpine troughs.
Cultivation Daffodils are tolerant bulbs that will grow in any reasonable garden soil so long as it is well drained. They should be

in sun when in growth, so if planting beneath deciduous trees, choose varieties that die down before the tree is in full leaf. Deadhead after flowering, where practicable, to ensure good flowering in subsequent seasons.

Trumpet daffodils (Division 1)

The trumpet is the same length as, or longer than, the petals. All are hardy/Z 3–9. The classic '**King Alfred**' is a popular, sturdy hybrid, with bright yellow flowers in mid-spring. H 35cm (14in).

Large-cupped daffodils (Division 2)

The cup is longer than one-third of, but less than the length of, the petals. All are hardy/Z 3–9. '**Carlton**' has soft yellow flowers with large cups with frilly edges in mid-spring. It is good for naturalizing. H 45cm (18in). One of the best-loved white daffodils, '**Ice Follies**' has flowers, opening in early to mid-spring, with contrasting lemon-yellow coronas that fade to creamy white. It is excellent for naturalizing, especially where strong yellows are not wanted. H 40cm (16in). The strongly coloured '**Pinza**' has rich yellow petals and deep red cups in mid-spring. It is an effective contrast to *Muscari armeniacum*. H 35cm (14in). The vigorous '**Rainbow**', which flowers in late spring, is an unusual daffodil with white petals surrounding a pink cup. H 45cm (18in). '**Saint Patrick's Day**' is an eye-catching daffodil, flowering in mid-spring, with lime green coronas surrounded by creamy-white petals. H 35cm (14in).

Narcissus 'Carlton'

Small-cupped daffodils (Division 3)

The cup is less than one-third the length of the petals. All are hardy/Z 3–9. **'Merlin'** has pure white petals and pale yellow cups. H 45cm (18in). **'Verona'** has white petals and a cream cup that fades to white. H 45cm (18in).

Double daffodils (Division 4)

The petals or the cup (or both) are doubled, sometimes leading to a muddled appearance. All are hardy/Z 3–9. One of the best-known, **'Rip van Winkle'** has bright yellow flowers in early spring. H 25cm (10in). **'White Lion'** has unusual flowers, with white outer petals and pale lemon-yellow central segments. Flowering in mid-spring, it is a good choice for naturalizing. H 40cm (16in). The fragrant **'Yellow Cheerfulness'** has golden-yellow flowers in mid-spring. It is a good border daffodil. H 45cm (18in).

Triandrus daffodils (Division 5)

Derived from *N. triandrus*, with usually between two and six flowers on each stem. All are hardy/Z 3–9. **'Hawera'** has dainty, canary yellow flowers in mid- to late spring. It is excellent in pots and can be brought indoors when in flower. H 25cm (10in). **'Thalia'** is technically a dwarf but is taller than most. It produces shining white flowers in mid-spring, combining well with *Fritillaria meleagris*. H 30cm (12in).

Cyclamineus daffodils (Division 6)

Derived from *N. cyclamineus*, these

Narcissus 'Jetfire'

have solitary flowers with characteristically swept-back petals. They are usually dwarf. All are hardy/Z 3–9. As its name suggests, **'February Gold'** produces bright yellow flowers in late winter. It is excellent in containers, windowboxes and in spring borders with primroses. H 30cm (12in). **'Jetfire'**, which flowers in early spring, has orange cups and rich yellow petals that flex back. It is a good contrast to *Muscari armeniacum*. H 20cm (8in). The vigorous **'Little Witch'** has bright yellow flowers. H 20cm (8in). **'Peeping Tom'** is sturdy, with golden-yellow flowers that have long trumpets and swept-back petals in early spring. It is an excellent border daffodil. H 25cm (10in).

Jonquilla daffodils (Division 7)

These have from one to five, usually fragrant, flowers on each stem. All are hardy/Z 3–9. **'Quail'** has appealing, clear yellow flowers in mid-spring. H 30cm (12in). **'Suzy'** is a strongly scented daffodil, which flowers

in mid-spring. Yellow petals surround flattened orange cups. H 40cm (16in).

Tazetta daffodils (Division 8)

These have from three to twenty flowers on each stem. Some are half-hardy but the following are both hardy/Z 3–9. The dainty **'Minnow'**, which flowers in early spring, has three to five flowers on each stem, with rounded, creamy-white petals and short primrose-yellow cups. H 18cm (7in). The fragrant **'Silver Chimes'** produces its silver-white flowers in mid- to late spring. It works well with *Fritillaria meleagris*. H 30cm (12in).

Poeticus daffodils (Division 9)

Related to *N. poeticus*, these have white petals and very shallow cups and are fragrant. They are usually late flowering. All are hardy/Z 3–9. One of the last to flower in late spring, **'Actaea'** has glistening white petals surrounding a brilliant orange corona. H 45cm (18in).

Species (Division 10)

The plants in this group are species and wild variants, few of which are suitable for general garden use.
N. bulbocodium (hoop-petticoat daffodil) is a charming species from southern Europe and northern Africa. It has broad, funnel-like cups and pointed petals in mid-spring. Tricky to grow, it needs a site that is moist in spring and dry in summer, so is often easiest in an alpine house. H 10–15cm (4–6in). Hardy/Z 7–9.

N. cyclamineus is a distinctive species from Spain and Portugal. The bright yellow flowers, produced in early spring, have swept-back petals (like a cyclamen) and long, narrow cups. H 15–20cm (6–8in). Hardy/Z 3–9.
N. poeticus var. *recurvus* (old pheasant's eye) is fragrant and flowers in late spring. It has distinctive, glistening white petals and, short red-edged, yellow cups. It is a parent of **'Actaea'** and is excellent for naturalizing in grass. H 35cm (14in). Hardy/Z 3–9.

Split-corona daffodils (Division 11)

The flowers in this group are usually solitary with cups that are split for more than half their length. All are hardy/Z 3–9. **'Chanterelle'** has white petals and yellow cups. H 45cm (18in). **'Orangery'** has white petals and orange cups. H 45cm (18in).

Miscellaneous (Division 12)

Daffodils that do not fit easily into any of the above categories. The following are hardy/Z 3–9. **'Jumblie'** is a reliable dwarf for early spring display. Each stem carries several golden-yellow cups whose petals flex back slightly. It is a good choice for a hanging basket. H 20cm (8in). In early to mid-spring **'Quince'** has pale yellow petals that sweep back and surround darker yellow cups with frilly edges. H 15cm (6in). The popular **'Tête-à-Tête'** produces reliable crops of bright yellow flowers in early spring. It is good for a hanging basket or windowbox. H 15cm (6in).

Narcissus 'Rip van Winkle'

Narcissus 'Suzy'

Narcissus 'Actaea'

Narcissus bulbocodium

Nectaroscordum siculum

NECTAROSCORDUM

The small genus is related to *Allium*, but the flowers are distinctive. It is a quiet, elegant plant that combines well with the neater growing old roses.
Cultivation Grow in any reasonable, well-drained soil in sun or light shade.

N. siculum
(syn. *Allium siculum*)
This species from the eastern Mediterranean has pale greenish-cream flowers that hang from the tops of erect stems in summer; the outsides are flushed with plum red. H to 1.2m (4ft), S 10cm (4in). Hardy/Z 7–10.

NERINE
Guernsey lily
A well-established clump of nerines will be a focus of attention when the flowers appear in autumn. Each is trumpet-shaped, but the petals curve sharply backwards, giving a most elegant appearance. Usually a clear

Nerine bowdenii

pink, they look as if they have been lightly dusted with sugar.
Cultivation Nerines need a hot spot in well-drained soil. Plant the dormant bulbs with the necks just above soil level and leave them undisturbed unless they become very congested and stop flowering well.

N. bowdenii
The most commonly grown species, this has flowers that appear at the end of the growing season in late summer to autumn, when the foliage (which emerges in spring) has all but died down. H 45cm (18in) or more, S 8cm (3in). Hardy/Z 8–10. 'Alba' has white flowers, occasionally tinged with pink. H 45cm (18in) or more, S 8cm (3in).

ORNITHOGALUM
Star of Bethlehem
This is a large genus of about 80 species, which are found through Africa, Asia and Europe. Not all are hardy, but the species described are easy to grow. Hardy species naturalize readily. In cold areas, the less hardy species can be grown in containers or treated as annuals and planted in borders in spring. All make long-lasting cut flowers.
Cultivation Grow in well-drained soil in sun or light shade.

O. arabicum
This species produces cup-shaped, fragrant white flowers in early summer. H 30–80cm (12–32in), S 8cm (3in). Half-hardy/Z 7–10.

O. nutans
From 10 to 20 starry, white flowers, striped with green on the outside, hang from the stems in early to mid-spring. This does best in woodland. H 30–40cm (12–16in), S 5cm (2cm). Hardy/Z 6–10.

O. thyrsoides
Chincherinchee
This popular species has dense spikes of cup-shaped, white flowers from early spring to summer (depending on the planting time). H to 70cm (28in), S 10cm (4in). Half-hardy/Z 7–10.

Ornithogalum nutans

O. umbellatum
Later flowering than *O. nutans*, this has starry flowers that open only when the sun is shining, closing during dull weather and showing the green exteriors of their petals. It is excellent for naturalizing. H 20cm (8in), S 10cm (4in). Hardy/Z 7–10.

SCILLA
Squill
This is a large genus, although some of its species have now been transferred to *Hyacinthoides*. The species described is the best-known. It combines well with *Chionodoxa* (glory of the snow) in borders, rock gardens and under deciduous trees and shrubs.
Cultivation Grow in well-drained soil in sun or partial shade.

S. siberica
Siberian squill
This species, from central Russia, produces nodding, star- to bell-shaped, blue flowers in early spring. H 15cm (6in), S 5cm (2in). Among the selections are 'Alba', a rare white form; and 'Spring Beauty', which has larger flowers and is more robust. H to 20cm (8in), S 5cm (2in). Hardy/Z 1–8.

TIGRIDIA
Tiger flower, peacock flower
These exotic and distinctive flowers for late summer combine well with dahlias and cannas, and are also suitable for growing in containers. Treat them as annuals in cold areas, planting the bulbs only when all danger of frost has passed.

Tigridia pavonia

Cultivation Grow in well-drained, fertile soil in full sun. Alternatively, plant in containers of well-drained compost (soil mix).

T. pavonia
This is the species most generally grown. It produces several flowers on each spike, in shades of white, cream, yellow, pink or red, each lasting for one day only. The flowers are conspicuously spotted. Single-colour selections are seldom available. H 45–60cm (18–24in), S 10cm (4in). Tender/Z 8–10.

TULIPA
Tulip
Highly prized by many, but tulips are unlikely to achieve again the degree of popularity they enjoyed in the 17th century, when Tulipomania swept western Europe, bankrupting many. So vast is the number of hybrids, that the genus is split into divisions (see right).

All tulips can be grown in containers. Some of the species are dwarf, modest plants that are best in rock gardens, but the hybrids are more versatile. They should be grown en masse, the strikingly marked ones in isolation, but the self-coloureds combine well with a range of spring-flowering plants, including pulmonarias, winter pansies and polyanthus. Pink tulips with blue forget-me-nots is a classic cottage-garden combination, which also works well in containers. Tulips provide a memorable display, but most are

Tulipa 'Oranje Nassau'

Tulipa 'Golden Melody'

Tulipa 'Striped Bellona'

Tulipa 'Esther'

hard work from the gardener's point of view because they cannot simply be left in situ to flower every year – they need lifting. Many prefer to treat them as annual bedding plants, discarding them after flowering and buying in new stock each autumn – making it possible to try out new varieties. Growing tulips is an addictive but expensive hobby.

Cultivation Tulips do well in any ordinary garden soil, provided it is well drained. An open site in full sun is desirable, but some shelter from strong winds is advisable for taller varieties. Most of the hybrids, although perennial, do best if not left in the ground permanently. They should be lifted after they have died back, then cleaned and dried off for storage in a cool, well-ventilated place over summer. In autumn, replant the larger bulbs where they are to flower. Small bulbs will not flower but can be grown on in a nursery bed until they reach flowering size.

Single early tulips (Division 1)

The cup-shaped flowers are borne in early to mid-spring. These tulips are suitable for growing in borders or in mixed bedding. All are hardy/Z 3–8. **'Apricot Beauty'** has salmon-pink flowers. H 45cm (18in). **'Brilliant Star'** has scarlet flowers. H 30cm (12in). **'Yokohama'**, one of the best yellows, has lemon-yellow flowers. H 35cm (14in).

Double early tulips (Division 2)

These tulips have double, bowl-shaped flowers in mid-spring. They are suitable for bedding. All are hardy/Z 3–8. **'Carlton'** has blood-red flowers. H 40cm (16in). **'Monte Carlo'** has sulphur-yellow flowers. H 30cm (12in). **'Oranje Nassau'** is deep orange. H 25cm (10in). **'Schoonoord'** has pure white flowers. H 25cm (10cm). **'Stockholm'** is bright red. H 30cm (12in). **'Willem van Oranje'** has orange flowers, flushed with copper red. H 25cm (10in). **'Willemsoord'** has red flowers, edged with white. H 25cm (10in).

Triumph tulips (Division 3)

The single, cup-shaped flowers are produced from mid- to late spring. They are good for bedding and are rain resistant. All are hardy/Z 3–8. **'Abu Hassan'** has purple-brown flowers edged with yellow. H 50cm (20in). **'Attila'** has purple-violet flowers. H 50cm (20in). **'Barcelona'** has fuchsia-purple flowers. H 50cm (20in). **'Blue Ribbon'** has lilac-purple flowers. H 50cm (20in). **'Couleur Cardinal'** has violet-red

flowers. 35cm (14in). **'Don Quichotte'** is deep pink. H 50cm (20in). The violet flowers of **'Dreaming Maid'** are edged with white. H 55cm (22in). **'Garden Party'** has white and carmine red flowers. H 40cm (16in). **'Golden Melody'** has golden-yellow flowers. H 55cm (22in). **'Lustige Witwe'** (syn. 'Merry Widow') has red flowers, edged with white. H 40cm (16in). The yellow flowers of **'New Design'** fade to pinkish white. H 50cm (20in). **'Passionale'** has purple flowers. H 45cm (18in). **'Pax'** is pure white. H 45cm (18in). **'Prinses Irene'** has orange and red flowers. H 35cm (14in). **'Silver Dollar'** has yellow flowers. H 55cm (22in). **'Striped Bellona'** has yellow flowers striped with red. H 50cm (20in).

Darwin hybrids (Division 4)

The large, single, oval flowers are carried at the tops of tall, sturdy stems, making them excellent for cutting. (These should not be

confused with Darwin tulips, now included in division 5.) All are hardy/Z 3–8. **'Ad Rem'** has deep orange flowers. H 60cm (2ft). **'Apeldoorn'** has brilliant vermilion red flowers. H 55cm (22in). **'Golden Apeldoorn'** has lemon-yellow flowers. H 55cm (22in). **'Parade'** has bright red flowers. H 60cm (2ft).

Single late tulips (Division 5)

The flowers are cup- or goblet-shaped and are borne in late spring. (Darwin, Breeder and Cottage tulips belong to this group.) All are hardy/Z 3–8. **'Avignon'** has bright red flowers. H 50cm (20in). **'Electra'** has magenta flowers. H 25cm (10in). **'Esther'** has light magenta flowers. H 50cm (20in). **'Menton'** has rose-red flowers with pale orange stripes. H 65cm (26in). **'Pink Lady'** has pink flowers. H 50cm (20in). **'Queen of Night'** has purple-black flowers. H 60cm (2ft). **'Sorbet'** is pinkish-white. H 60cm (2ft).

Tulipa 'Attila'

Tulipa 'Apeldoorn'

Tulipa 'Queen of Night'

Tulipa 'Ballerina'

Tulipa 'West Point'

Tulipa 'Fantasy'

Lily-flowered tulips (Division 6)

The petals of the slender flowers are often pointed and curve backwards. They are late-flowering tulips and rather susceptible to wind damage. All are hardy/Z 3–8. **'Aladdin'** has deep red flowers edged with yellow. H 55cm (22in). **'Ballerina'** has blood-red flowers. H 55cm (22in). **'Mariette'** is pure pink. H 55cm (22in). **'Mona Lisa'** has yellow streaked with red flowers. H 55cm (22in). **'West Point'** has primrose-yellow flowers that look good with forget-me-nots. H 50cm (20in). **'White Triumphator'** has pure white flowers. H 60cm (2ft).

Fringed tulips (Division 7)

The petals of the cup-shaped flowers are fringed at the edges (sometimes in a different colour). The flowers appear in late spring. All are hardy/Z 3–8. **'Crystal**

Beauty' has rose-pink flowers with an orange fringe. H 55cm (22in). **'Red Wing'** has rich red flowers. H 50cm (20in).

Viridiflora tulips (Division 8)

The flowers, which are produced in late spring, are touched with varying amounts of green. All are hardy/Z 3–8. **'Artist'** has deep orange and green flowers. H 30cm (12in). **'Groenland'** has pink and green flowers. H 55cm (22in). **'Spring Green'** has creamy white flowers with broad green stripes. H 50cm (20in).

Rembrandt tulips (Division 9)

The cup-shaped flowers, borne in late spring, are dramatically variegated with contrasting colours, usually brown, bronze, black, red, pink or purple on a white, yellow or red ground. (These are the tulips depicted in Dutch old master paintings. Unfortunately, since the breaking

of the flower colour is caused by a virus, few are nowadays produced commercially. The obsolete Bizarre and Bijbloemen tulips belonged to this division.) All are hardy/Z 3–8. **'Gala Beauty'** has red and yellow streaked flowers. H 60cm (2ft). **'Jack Laan'** has purple flowers shaded with brown and feathered with white and yellow. H 55cm (22in).

Parrot tulips (Division 10)

The cup-shaped flowers, borne in mid- to late spring, have twisted petals, which are irregularly cut and evenly banded with other colours. The flowers gradually open flat, exposing black centres and golden stamens. These tulips are sensitive to cold, wet weather and do best in a sheltered spot. These are sports of tulips from other divisions. All are hardy/Z 3–8. **'Black Parrot'** has violet-black flowers. H 50cm (20in). **'Blue Parrot'** is mauve-blue. H 55cm (22in). **'Estella Rijnveld'** has red and creamy white flowers. H 50cm (20in). **'Fantasy'** has pink flowers crested with green and irregularly crimped petals. H 55cm (22in). **'Texas Flame'** has yellow and red flowers. H 45cm (18in).

Double late tulips (Division 11)

Sometimes called peony-flowered tulips, these flower in late spring. They have fully double, bowl-shaped flowers and should be planted in a sheltered spot because they do not stand up well to bad weather. They do well in

areas with cold winters and late springs. All are hardy/Z 3–8. **'Allegretto'** has red flowers edged with yellow. H 35cm (14in). The pink flowers of **'Angelique'** are edged with white. H 45cm (18in). **'Casablanca'** has white flowers. H 45cm (18in).

Kaufmanniana tulips (Division 12)

These small, sturdy tulips are usually very early, often with bicoloured flowers and sometimes with spotted foliage. The flowers open flat in sunshine, hence the name 'waterlily tulips'. All are hardy/Z 3–8. **'Chopin'** has yellow flowers streaked with red and grey-green foliage mottled with brown. H 25cm (10in). **'Giuseppe Verdi'** has carmine-red flowers edged with yellow and mottled foliage. H 30cm (12in). **'Gluck'** has carmine-red flowers edged with bright yellow and spotted foliage. H 20cm (8in).

Tulipa 'Mona Lisa'

Tulipa 'Spring Green'

Tulipa 'Blue Parrot'

Tulipa 'Chopin'

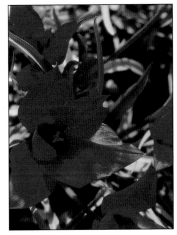

Tulipa linifolia

The salmon-pink flowers of 'Shakespeare' are flushed with orange and yellow. H 25cm (10in). 'Stresa' has currant-red and yellow flowers and spotted foliage. H 25cm (10in).

Fosteriana tulips (Division 13)
The group includes *T. fosteriana* and hybrids developed from it. They are similar to the Kauffmanniana and Greigii tulips but have larger, slender flowers. The leaves are sometimes striped. They are suitable for naturalizing. The group includes many red tulips. All are hardy/Z 3–8. 'Madame Lefeber' has bright red flowers. H 40cm (16in). 'Orange Emperor' has bright orange flowers with a yellow base. H 40cm (16in). 'Purissima' (syn. 'White Emperor') is pure white. H 45cm (18in).

Greigii tulips (Division 14)
The group includes *T. greigii* and hybrids developed from it. They

have blue-grey leaves, mottled to varying degrees with brownish purple. The flowers open wide in full sun. They are early flowering and good for naturalizing. All are hardy/Z 3–8. 'Ali Baba' has deep pink flowers and spotted foliage. H 30cm (12in). 'Compostella' has red flowers. H 30cm (12in). 'Ontario' has magenta-pink flowers and spotted foliage. H 30cm (12in). 'Toronto' has red flowers. H 30cm (12in).

Miscellaneous (Division 15)
The group includes the species, selected forms and hybrids that are not in the other divisions. All are hardy/Z 3–8.

T. clusiana var. *chrysantha* (syn. *T. chrysantha*, *T. stellata* var. *chrysantha*)
The species, which is from northern Afghanistan, has yellow flowers that open flat, like stars, in mid-spring. H 30–35cm (12–14in).

'Cynthia' has cream flowers, flushed with coral-red and edged with green.

T. linifolia
Native to Bukhara and the Pamir Alai mountains, this easy-to-grow species has fluorescent red flowers in late spring. H 20cm (8in).

T. praestans
A multi-flowered species from Central Asia, this is an excellent subject for naturalizing. It has orange-red flowers in early to mid-spring. H 20–25cm (8–10in). There are several cultivars, including 'Fusilier', which is a luminous vermilion red; and 'Unicum', which has bright red flowers and yellow-edged leaves.

T. saxatilis
This species, which is native to Crete, appreciates very well-drained soil. The flowers, which open wide in early spring, are soft lilac-pink with yellow centres and are lightly scented. H 30–40cm (12–16in).

T. tarda
Native to Central Asia, this is one of the best species for ordinary garden use. The star-shaped flowers, with yellow, white-tipped petals, appear in early spring. It naturalizes easily. H 12–15cm (5–6in).

T. turkestanica
This Turkish species is one of the first to bloom, the flowers appearing in late winter in a good year. The white flowers have bright yellow centres. H 25–30cm (10–12in).

ZANTEDESCHIA
Arum lily
South Africa is home to many fine bulbous plants, but few are as ravishing as this one, with its bold, glossy leaves and flowers of breathtaking purity. Planted en masse, arum lilies can be a breathtaking sight. For bulbs, they have a long flowering season. In cold gardens, the shelter of a warm wall will offer protection for many, but some selections are hardy enough to be grown in the

open border. Arum lilies can also be planted as an aquatic, but although plants undoubtedly look spectacular reflected in water, they are susceptible to rot. A number of tender hybrids have been bred for growing in containers under glass in cold areas.
Cultivation Arum lilies need soil that does not dry out in the growing season and a position in full sun. In cold areas, provide winter protection in the form of a mulch of straw or other dry material. When grown as an aquatic, plant in plastic baskets to a depth of 15–30cm (6–12in). Make sure that plants in containers do not dry out in winter.

Z. aethiopica
The best known species, this is also the hardiest, particularly in the form 'Crowborough'. This produces pure white, funnel-shaped spathes on long stems, from early to midsummer among the glossy green leaves. H 85cm (33in), S 60cm (2ft). Borderline hardy/Z 8–10. 'Green Goddess' has spathes splashed with green and is more susceptible to frost. Borderline hardy/Z 8–10.

Z. hybrids
Among the many hybrids are 'Black-eyed Beauty', which has deep creamy-yellow spathes, marked with black inside; 'Cameo', which has apricot-coloured spathes; 'Mango', with orange spathes; and 'Solfaterre', which has yellow and black spathes. H 30–40cm (12–16in), S 15–20cm (6–8in). Tender/Z 9–10.

Tulipa 'Shakespeare'

Tulipa saxatilis

Zantedeschia aethiopica 'Crowborough'

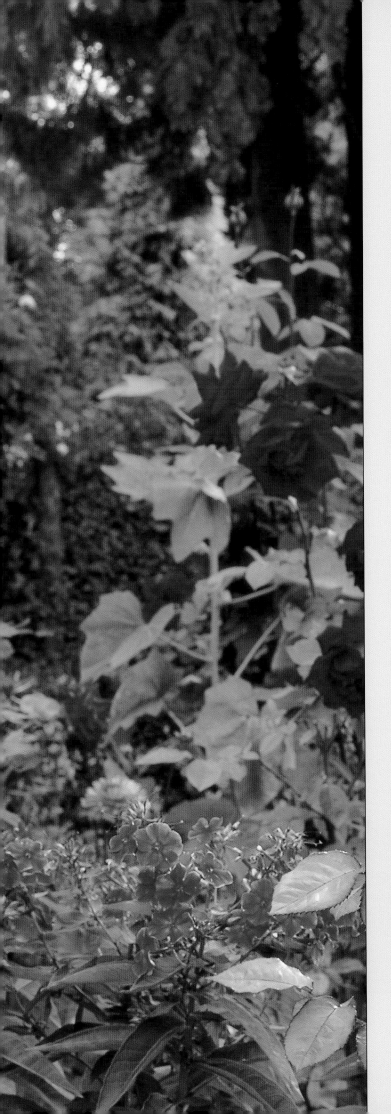

Roses

As a garden plant, the rose is unrivalled. Few other plants have attracted so much attention from breeders and down the ages they have epitomized the summer garden. From the uncomplicated charm of the species to the sophistication of the hybrid teas, there is a rose for virtually every purpose, as hedging, to give weight and substance to borders, as specimens or to provide cut flowers. The climbers provide magnificent cover for walls and pergolas, while nowadays the range has been extended to include tough, compact, disease-resistant plants that are excellent as ground cover or for growing in containers.

Elegant hybrid tea roses are esssential plants for any cottage garden scheme, here combining well with phlox and other border perennials.

Growing roses

Roses are a breed apart. No other plant genus has been so extensively hybridized to produce the wide range of plants that we enjoy in gardens today.

Buying roses

Roses are sold as bare-root plants or in containers. The former are lifted from the open ground when dormant, and the roots are shaken free of soil. They are often sold by mail order and a huge range is available, including rare varieties.

Roses sold in containers are lifted from the field, potted up and grown on. They are available at garden centres throughout the growing season but are more expensive than bare-root plants. However, they often establish more quickly.

When buying a containerized rose, choose one that is growing evenly, showing no sign of disease or pest attack. The presence of moss or lichens on the surface of the potting mix suggests nutrient exhaustion, or that the plant has been waterlogged. Slide the plant from its container and check the root system. If the roots are tightly packed around the pot, reject it.

Cultivating roses

Roses will grow in all soil types apart from soil that is permanently waterlogged. It is often stated that roses prefer heavy clay soils, but this is only because clay tends to retain nutrients well. Light, sandy soil will also support roses if improved with organic matter prior to planting.

'Chicago Peace' is a large-flowered modern rose with lightly scented flowers. The flowers are produced from summer to autumn.

Roses generally prefer an open site in full sun, with shelter from strong, drying winds. Rugosa roses tolerate some degree of shade, but flowering is less profuse. No rose thrives in deep shade.

Roses benefit from an annual mulch of organic matter in autumn or spring. This improves soil fertility and structure and conserves moisture.

All roses benefit from additional feeding during the growing season, even if you mulch annually. Organic and inorganic fertilizers are available, some specially formulated for roses. Some are in powder or granular form, to be forked in round the plant; others are liquid feeds applied as a root drench from a watering can or sprayed on as a foliar feed. Foliar feeds are advantageous if you need to give a rose a boost after a disease or pest attack, since the nutrients are immediately available to the plant. Fertilizers must be applied according to the manufacturer's instructions.

Planting roses

Prior to planting, prepare the site by digging it over. Remove all weeds and dig in organic matter. If the soil is very heavy, add grit.

PLANTING A CONTAINER-GROWN ROSE

1 Fork over the site to break up and aerate the soil. Remove all weeds and fork in organic matter at about the rate of one bucketful per square metre (yard). Then, dig a hole about twice the width and depth of the pot.

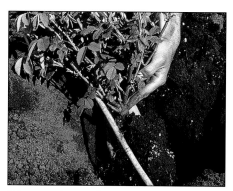

2 Remove the rose from its pot, trim any damaged roots, and place it in the hole. Check the depth with a cane laid across the hole. The graft union should be about 2.5cm (1in) below soil level.

3 Backfill with soil and firm in. Fork in rose fertilizer around the base of the plant, then water in thoroughly.

4 Mulch with more organic matter to reduce water evaporation from around the base of the plant.

Bare-root roses should be planted as soon after receipt as possible, preferably during a mild spell. If the ground is frozen or waterlogged, they can be stored unopened for up to six weeks in a cool, dark, frost-free place. Remove the packaging and cut back twiggy growth. Lightly trim the roots, then soak the rose for up to one hour in a bucket of water.

Containerized roses can be planted at any time of year except when the ground is frozen or during periods of drought. If you cannot plant immediately, keep the rose in a sheltered place and water it regularly.

Dig a hole large enough to take the root system comfortably (bare-root), or twice the width and depth of the pot (containerized). Fork in a handful of bonemeal, ensuring you wear gloves, and a little organic matter at the base of the hole. Set the rose in position and check the planting depth. The graft union (where the top-growth meets the rootstock) should be just below soil level. Ease containerized roses out of their pots and gently loosen the roots.

Backfill with the excavated soil. Firm in lightly with your foot, fork a little fertilizer around the base of the plant and water well. Apply a mulch of organic matter in a ring around the base to conserve moisture, and lightly prune the top-growth, if necessary. Water freely during the first season after planting to ensure rapid establishment. In later years, provided you mulch, watering should not be necessary.

Pruning roses

Rose pruning is important for two main reasons. The first is that, left unpruned, the plant will get big and straggly, with a bare base; the second is that the stems will bear flowers for only a few years before becoming exhausted. Pruning tackles both problems, keeping the plant small and the shoots young and vigorous.

The same basic rules apply when rose pruning as for any other shrub, so use sharp, clean blades and a pair of thornproof gloves. There are different approaches to pruning depending on the type of rose. This

Rose classification

The classification of roses represents an attempt to bring some order to a vast and diverse range of plants.

Wild roses
Old roses
Bourbon roses
Centifolia roses
China roses
Damask roses
Gallica roses
Hybrid perpetuals
Scotch roses

Modern roses
Climbing roses
Floribunda or cluster-flowered roses
Ground-cover roses
Hybrid tea or large-flowered roses
Miniature roses
Patio or dwarf cluster-flowered bush roses
Polyanthas
Rambler roses
Rugosa roses
Shrub roses

goes beyond the scope of this book, so consult a specialist reference book for detailed advice on pruning specific rose types.

HOW TO PRUNE ROSES

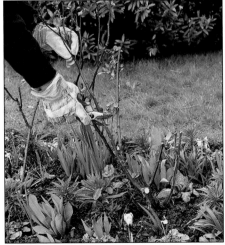

1 Moderate pruning is the most appropriate for established large-flowered roses. Cut back all the main stems by about half, or to within 20–25cm (8–10in) of the ground. Cut to an outward-facing bud to keep the centre of the bush open, with no congestion.

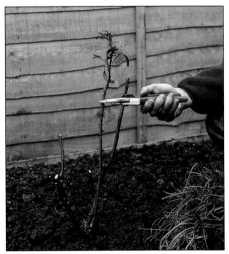

2 You can treat cluster-flowered roses in the same way, but if you prune some shoots severely and others lightly, flowering may be spread over a longer period. Prune the oldest shoots back close to the base, but those that grew last year by about one-third only.

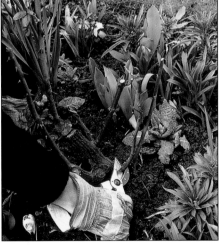

3 Whichever type of rose you are pruning, cut back any dead or diseased shoots to healthy wood. Also remove any very thin, spindly shoots, cutting either to their point of origin or to two or three buds from the base of the shoot.

'Agnes'

An upright, healthy rugosa of undoubted distinction, this bears double, scented, pale yellow flowers in summer, with only a few following in autumn. It combines the toughness of the rugosas with an old-rose look to the flowers. H 2m (6ft), S 1.2m (4ft). Hardy/Z 2–9.

R. × alba 'Alba Maxima'
(syn. R. × alba 'Maxima')

This alba rose dates from the 15th century, or even earlier, and is sometimes assumed to be the white rose of York. It is also a beauty, with untidy, double, very fragrant flowers that are tinged pink on opening in summer, then fade to creamy white. Red hips follow. It is also known as the great white rose, the Jacobite rose or the Cheshire rose. H 2.1m (7ft), S 1.5m (5ft). Hardy/Z 4–9.

R. × alba 'Alba Semiplena'
(syn. 'Semiplena')

An alba rose, this has been grown in gardens since the 16th century or before. It is a graceful shrub with clusters of semi-double, very fragrant, milky white flowers in summer. These open flat to display prominent golden stamens, with red hips making a second display in autumn. 'Alba Semiplena' is usually held to be the white rose of York, competing for that title with R. × alba 'Alba Maxima'. H 2.1m (7ft), S 1.5m (5ft). Hardy/Z 4–9.

'Alba Meidiland'
(syn. 'Meiflopan')

This is a groundcover rose, and unusually for a rose in this group, the pure white, fully double flowers are good for cutting. H 1m (3ft), S 1.2m (4ft). Hardy/Z 4–9.

'Albéric Barbier'

This vigorous rambling rose is a good choice for brightening up a shady wall or a dull tree. In early to midsummer, masses of double, rosette, creamy white, scented flowers cover the plant. To compensate for the lack of further flowers, the glossy leaves often hang on through the winter. H 5m (16ft), S 3m (10ft). Hardy/Z 4–9.

'Albertine'

A vigorous rambling rose, this has fully double, light pink flowers, which appear in a single flush in midsummer, opening from copper-tinted buds; they become untidy as they age. The rich, distinctive scent of this rose has assured its continuing popularity, despite its all too obvious drawbacks: its talon-like thorns and propensity to mildew. Thinning the growth after flowering to improve air circulation can help the latter problem. H 5m (16ft), S 4m (12ft). Hardy/Z 4–9.

'Alec's Red'
(syn. 'Cored')

This is a bushy hybrid tea with fully double, heavily scented, rich red flowers that open from pointed buds throughout summer and into autumn. A versatile rose,

Rosa 'Alec's Red'

it is suitable for cutting, bedding and as a hedge, but blackspot can be a problem. H 1m (3ft), S 60cm (2ft). Hardy/Z 4–9.

'Alexander'
(syn. 'Harlex')

An upright hybrid tea, this has double, luminous red flowers opening from pointed buds from summer to autumn. The leaves are glossy dark green and show good resistance to disease. The flowers are produced on long stems, which means that this is a good rose for cutting as well as for planting as a tight hedge with little sideways spread. H to 2m (6ft), S 75cm (2ft 6in). Hardy/Z 4–9.

'Allgold'

A compact floribunda and an ideal bedding rose, this bears a succession of double, lightly scented, bright yellow flowers from summer to autumn. H 75cm (2ft 6in), S 50cm (20in). Hardy/Z 5–9.

'Aloha'

This climbing rose bears a succession of cupped, fully double, sweetly scented, light pink flowers from summer to autumn. The leaves are dark green, leathery and healthy. This is a rain-resistant variety, which is also good in a container. H 3m (10ft), S 2.5m (8ft). Hardy/Z 4–9.

Rosa × alba 'Alba Semiplena'

Rosa 'Albertine'

Rosa 'Anna Ford'

Rosa 'Apricot Nectar'

Rosa 'Avon'

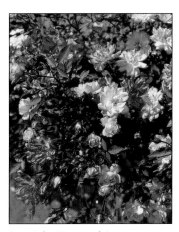

Rosa 'Baby Masquerade'

'Amber Queen'
(syn. 'Harroony', 'Prinz Eugen van Savoyen')
A neat-growing floribunda, this rose bears clusters of fully double, heavily scented, rich amber-yellow flowers, which open from rounded buds. Its compact habit makes it a good choice for bedding, hedges and containers. H and S 50cm (20in). Hardy/Z 4–9.

'Anna Ford'
(syn. 'Harpiccolo')
This is a dense, low-growing patio rose. The warm orange-red flowers, produced freely from summer to autumn, open flat from pointed buds to reveal yellow centres. One of the earliest of its type, this remains a popular bedding or container rose. H 45cm (18in), S 38cm (15in). Hardy/Z 4–9.

'Anne Harkness'
(syn. 'Harkaramel')
An upright, branching floribunda, this bears large clusters of pointed, urn-shaped, double, soft buff-yellow flowers from late summer to autumn. Spectacular when in full flower, This is a disease-resistant rose that is suitable for bedding, hedging and cutting. H 1.2m (4ft), S 60cm (2ft). Hardy/Z 4–9.

'Apricot Nectar'
This bushy floribunda bears tight clusters of large, fully double, sweetly scented, pinkish-buff-apricot flowers from summer to autumn. It is a good hedging rose, but it can be susceptible to mildew from midsummer. H 80cm (32in), S 65cm (26in). Hardy/Z 4–9.

'Arthur Bell'
An upright, branching floribunda, this bears clusters of semi-double to double, bright yellow flowers that pale as they age. The scent is outstanding for a rose of this type. This is a versatile rose, suitable for bedding, hedging and containers; the autumn flowering is especially good, making it a good companion for annuals and late-flowering perennials and bulbs. H to 1m (3ft), S 60cm (2ft). Hardy/Z 4–9.

'Avon'
(syn. 'Fairy Lights', 'Poulmulti', 'Sunnyside')
From summer to autumn this compact, spreading groundcover rose bears clusters of small, semi-double, fragrant, pinkish-white flowers, which open flat to reveal golden stamens. Besides its obvious uses for massed planting and as a low hedge, this rose can also be grown successfully in containers. H 30cm (1ft), S 1m (3ft). Hardy/Z 4–9.

'Baby Masquerade'
(syn. 'Baby Carnival', 'Tanba', 'Tanbakede')
Many people believe that this miniature rose is more attractive than its full-sized equivalent. From summer to autumn it carries clusters of tiny, double, rosette-shaped flowers, which open yellow and fade to pink then to deeper red, so that all the colours are present at any one time. The rose is probably seen at its best when grown as a miniature standard. H and S 40cm (16in). Hardy/Z 4–9.

Rosa 'Anne Harkness'

Rosa 'Arthur Bell'

'Belle de Crécy'

The quartered-rosette, sweetly scented flowers of this gallica rose are produced in abundance in midsummer. They open rich purple-pink then fade to a greyish pale pink. It has a laxer habit than most other gallicas and its arching stems may require some support; alternatively, simply allow them to trail into neighbouring shrubs. It does not flower as well in poor, light soil. H 1.2m (4ft), S 1m (3ft). Hardy/Z 5.

'Blairii Number Two'

In midsummer, this strangely named bourbon, first raised in 1845, carries an abundance of large, cupped, fully double, sweetly scented flowers, which are pale silvery pink with deeper pink centres. However, unlike some other bourbon roses, it produces only a few further blooms in autumn, if any. Untrained, it will grow into an arching shrub about 2.1m (7ft) high and across. Its vigour and flexible canes make it suitable for growing as a pyramid, on a pergola or against a wall, where it can reach 5m (16ft). H 4m (12ft), S 2m (6ft). Hardy/Z 4–9.

'Blue Moon'
(syn. 'Blue Monday', 'Mainzer Fastnacht', 'Sissi', 'Tannacht')

An intriguing hybrid tea, this is not one of the best overall, but is worth growing for the individual

Rosa 'Belle de Crécy'

Rosa 'Blue Moon'

Rosa 'Buff Beauty'

flowers. Borne in summer and autumn, they are not blue, as the name implies, but silvery lilac, a colour associated with the old roses. However, the flower form is modern: high-centred and shapely. It is also one of the most sweetly scented of modern roses. 'Blue Moon' needs careful placing in the garden because of its curious colouring; it is perhaps best grown in isolation under glass. H 1m (3ft), S 60cm (2ft). Hardy/Z 4–9. The climbing form is also worth considering, but it needs good cultivation and a site where the flowers will not be bleached by too much sun.

'Bobbie James'

One of the most vigorous of ramblers, this rose looks like its wild antecedents. In summer it is covered with clusters of small, white, semi-double flowers that are also sweetly scented. It is a

good choice for growing into a large tree, and although it would be just as dramatic over a large pergola, its vigour could cause problems. H 10m (33ft), S 6m (20ft). Hardy/Z 5–9.

'Buff Beauty'

This is an excellent modern shrub rose or hybrid musk. The name refers to the colour of the cupped, fully double, sweetly scented flowers, which are pale buff-apricot, fading to creamy white in hot sun. They are carried in clusters in two distinct flushes, the autumn flowering being less profuse than the summer. 'Buff Beauty' can be used for hedging but needs the support of horizontal wires, since the canes are often bent down low by the weight of the flowers. Mildew may be a problem in late summer but need not deter you from growing this rose. H and S 1.5m (5ft). Hardy/Z 6–9.

'Cardinal de Richelieu'

This grandly named gallica – and one of the most sumptuous – was produced in 1840. It makes a

compact bush and will exceed its usual size if the flexible stems are supported. The clusters of scented, dark maroon flowers appear in midsummer; the petals are velvety in texture and reflex as the flowers age to form a ball shape. The stems are well-covered with healthy, dark green leaves. This rose needs fertile, well-drained soil and regular thinning of the old wood to give of its best. H 1m (3ft), S 1.2m (4ft). Hardy/Z 4–9.

'Cécile Brünner'

Sometimes identified as the sweetheart rose or Maltese rose, this is a dainty, airy cultivar, which is classified as either a China rose or a polyantha. It flowers over a long period from early summer to mid-autumn, when clusters of elegant, pointed buds open to urn-shaped, delicately scented, pale pink flowers, which become more untidy as as they age. H and S 1m (3ft). Hardy/Z 5–9. A climbing form is available, which is less restrained and easily reaches 6m (20ft) in all

Rosa 'Blairii Number Two'

Rosa 'Cardinal de Richelieu'

Rosa 'Cécile Brünner'

Rosa 'Céleste'

Rosa 'Charles de Mills'

Rosa 'Chinatown'

Rosa 'Complicata'

directions; it is ideal for growing into a tree. The white-flowered bush form 'White Cécile Brünner' is rare.

'Céleste'
(syn. *R.* × *alba* 'Celestial')
The date of the introduction of this Alba rose is unrecorded, but it is certainly a very old cultivar, perhaps dating back to ancient times. The semi-double, sweetly scented, shell-pink flowers, with petals that seem almost transparent, are borne in summer and open flat to reveal prominent golden stamens. Red hips succeed them in autumn. H and S 2m (6ft). Hardy/Z 4–9.

R. × *centifolia* 'Cristata'
(syn. 'Chapeau de Napoléon', 'Crested Moss')
This distinguished centifolia rose is sometimes included among the moss roses, though incorrectly, since only the calyces and not the stems are mossed. It makes a graceful, slender-stemmed shrub. In summer it produces drooping, cupped, fully double, richly scented, deep silvery-pink flowers that open flat and are sometimes quartered. The alternative name, 'Chapeau de Napoléon' (Napoleon's hat), refers to the unopened buds, which look like a tricorn hat. H 1.5m (5ft), S 1.2m (4ft). Hardy/Z 4–9.

'Charles de Mills'
(syn. 'Bizarre Triomphant')
This is a gallica rose of unknown origin. The fully double, quartered-rosette, moderately scented, rich crimson flowers, which appear in summer, fade with grey and purple tones as they mature. The

abundant foliage is matt dark green. It makes a compact shrub, but the slender stems may need staking to support the large flowers as they open. H 1.2m (4ft), S 1m (3ft). Hardy/Z 4–9.

'Chinatown'
(syn. 'Ville de Chine')
A floribunda rose, this is probably unmatched for size and overall vigour; indeed, it is sometimes justifiably classified as a shrub rose. The fragrant clusters of fully double, bright golden-yellow flowers are freely produced throughout summer and into autumn among glossy dark green leaves. It is ideal grown at the back of a border as a backdrop for smaller plants, as a hedge or as a specimen plant. H 1.5m (5ft), S 1m (3ft). Hardy/Z 5–9.

'City of London'
(syn. 'Harukfore')
A spreading floribunda, this shows some of the characteristics of one of its parents, 'New Dawn', notably its continuity (it flowers from summer to autumn), its scent and its appealing soft pink colour. More versatile than some other members of this group, if it is pruned fairly hard it can be used for bedding, but with minimum pruning it can also be treated as a specimen or trained as a short climber. It also associates well with old roses. H to 2m (6ft), S to 1.2m (4ft). Hardy/Z 4–9.

'Compassion'
From summer to autumn this climbing rose produces shapely, rounded, fully double, sweetly scented, warm apricot-pink flowers. It is an excellent choice

for a pillar or a sturdy garden fruit tree. H 3m (10ft), S 2.5m (8ft). Hardy/Z 4–9.

'Complicata'
(syn. *R. gallica* 'Complicata')
Although this is a gallica rose, it has few of the characteristics normally associated with the group and is of uncertain origin, its pedigree possibly including the vigorous species *R. canina*. Its name also implies double flowers; in fact, they are single but are produced in abundance all along the arching canes in summer. Bright porcelain pink, they are sweetly scented and open wide to reveal white centres and golden stamens. Unusually for a gallica, the matt greyish-green leaves are rather pointed. 'Complicata' tolerates light, sandy soils and can be used as a rambler among trees and shrubs in a wild garden

or it can be trained on a pillar; H and S 2.5m (8ft) if supported, probably more as a climber. Hardy/Z 4–9.

'Constance Spry'
(syn. 'Autance')
This was one of the first of David Austin's 'English' roses, and it is still one of the best, although it flowers once only, in midsummer. The large, cupped, fully double, peony-like flowers of this shrub rose are rich pink and heavily scented. It can also be grown as a climber on a pillar or against a wall, where it will tolerate some shade. Even as a shrub it is best given some support or pruned hard to keep it compact. Untrained, it will grow into a large, lax shrub. H and S to 2m (6ft), though the spread can sometimes exceed the height. Hardy/Z 4–9.

Rosa 'Constance Spry'

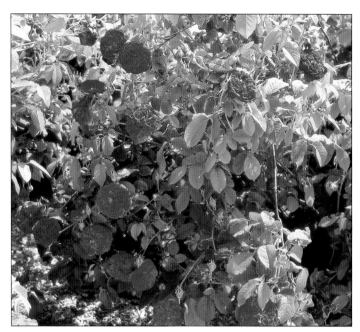

Rosa 'Duc de Guiche'

'Danse du Feu'

A stiffly branched climbing rose that, as far as the flower colour – luminous red – is concerned has not been surpassed, and it has retained its place in catalogues in spite of its tendency towards blackspot. The rounded, double flowers appear from summer to autumn, but the scent is not strong. H and S 2.5m (8ft). Hardy/Z 4–9.

'Desprez à Fleurs Jaunes'
(syn. 'Jaune Desprez')

This exquisite, vigorous climbing rose, introduced in 1830, should be planted more widely. The double flowers, borne throughout summer, are an unusual creamy buff-yellow and are also sweetly scented. The lax, flexible canes make this an excellent choice for training against a wall, preferably a sunny one. H and S 5m (16ft). Hardy/Z 6–9.

'Du Maître d'Ecole'

The date of origin of this gallica rose is in dispute, but some authorities say it was introduced in 1840. It makes a compact plant, and in summer the weight of blossom makes the stems arch over. The fragrant, fully double, quartered-rosette, carmine-pink flowers open flat and fade to lilac-pink and grey. H and S 1m (3ft). Hardy/Z 4–9.

'Dublin Bay'
(syn. 'Macdub')

A valuable red climber, this has almost fluorescent flowers. Double and lightly scented, they are carried in clusters from summer to autumn among glossy, healthy leaves. It is a good choice if space is limited, in a border on a tripod, for instance, since the growth tends to be upright. H and S 2.2m (7ft). Hardy/Z 4–9.

'Duc de Guiche'

The fully double, highly scented flowers of this outstanding gallica change colour as they age. Rich crimson initially, they develop purple veining before finally flushing purple. H and S 1.2m (4ft). Hardy/Z 4–8.

'Duchesse de Montebello'

This spreading gallica was bred before 1829. The open-cupped, fully double, sweetly fragrant flowers are soft blush pink. The foliage is light green. It is one of the daintiest and neatest growing of the gallicas. H and S 1.2m (4ft). Hardy/Z 4–8.

'Elina'
(syn. 'Dicjana', 'Peaudouce')

A bushy hybrid tea, this has fully double, lightly scented, creamy white flowers, which open to reveal lemon-yellow flushed centres. The flowering season lasts from summer to autumn. A versatile rose and easy to grow, it is generally healthy and can be used for bedding and cutting. H 1m (3ft), S 75cm (2ft 6in). Hardy/Z 4–9.

'Escapade'
(syn. 'Harpade')

This elegant floribunda has a freely branching habit, and it is also something of a novelty in being an outstanding garden plant. The semi-double, sweetly scented flowers, which are borne in clusters throughout summer into autumn, are of unusual coloration: they are soft lilac-pink, opening flat to reveal white centres and golden stamens. Unlike some other roses, it blends easily with other plants; it occasionally produces pure white flowers within the cluster, which adds to its charm. Shiny, light green foliage is borne in abundance. H to 1.2m (4ft), S 60cm (2ft). Hardy/Z 4–9.

Rosa 'Fantin-Latour'

'Fantin-Latour'

A centifolia rose, this makes a handsome, vase-shaped shrub, which is ideal as a specimen. The many-petalled, cup-shaped flowers are delicately scented. They are blush-pink and are borne in profusion over a long period in summer, their petals reflexing to reveal a green button eye. 'Fantin-Latour' was named in honour of the French painter, admired for his flower pieces, some of which include roses. Spraying against mildew may be necessary in summer. H and S to 2.2m (7ft). Hardy/Z 4–9.

'Félicité Parmentier'

This compact Alba rose bears a single crop of cup-shaped, highly scented, quartered, pale blush-pink flowers, which open from primrose yellow buds in midsummer. The densely packed petals fade to almost white in hot sun and reflex to form a ball

Rosa 'Du Maître d'Ecole'

Rosa 'Duchesse de Montebello'

Rosa 'Escapade'

Rosa 'Félicité Parmentier'

shape. The leaves are healthy and grey-green. One of the daintiest of its type, this is suitable for the smallest garden. H and S 1.2m (4ft). Hardy/Z 4–9.

'Fred Loads'

A strongly upright floribunda, this rose is ideal for the back of a border. Its generous clusters of semi-double, pleasantly scented, soft orange-vermilion flowers are produced from summer to autumn, making it invaluable for a long display in a mixed planting. Hard pruning can keep it in bounds, or it can be used for hedging. The flowers last well in water. H 2m (6ft), S 1m (3ft). Hardy/Z 5–9.

'Fru Dagmar Hastrup'
(syn. 'Frau Dagmar Hartopp')

This compact, spreading rugosa rose bears single, pale pink

summer flowers, which open almost flat to reveal prominent golden stamens; large, tomato-red hips develop in autumn as a second, sparser flush appears. This makes an excellent low hedge and can also be used for ground cover, possibly in light woodland. H 1m (3ft), S 1.2m (4ft). Hardy/Z 3–9.

'Frühlingsgold'

A Scotch hybrid rose, sometimes classified as a modern shrub rose, this makes a vigorous shrub, each arching cane reaching up to 2.2m (7ft) in length. The large, cupped, semi-double, fragrant, primrose-yellow flowers cover the stems in late spring to early summer, opening flat from long, pointed buds to display golden stamens. Its toughness and thorniness suggest that it might be used as a barrier plant at the end of the garden rather than in the border. H 2.5m (8ft), S 2.2m (7ft). Hardy/Z 4–8.

R. gallica var. *officinalis*
(syn. *R. officinalis*)

This is a bushy gallica rose, which has been recorded in gardens since the 13th century. In summer it produces an abundance of large, semi-double, sweetly fragrant, light crimson flowers, which open flat and reveal golden stamens. Rich in historical association both as the red rose of Lancaster and the medieval apothecary's rose, this remains a superb garden plant in its own right. H and S 1.2m (4ft). Hardy/Z 5–9.

Rosa 'Graham Thomas'

R. gallica 'Versicolor'

An eye-catching gallica rose, this old rose was first recorded in the 16th century but is probably much older. The lightly scented flowers, produced in midsummer, are semi-double, opening flat to reveal golden stamens. The pale pink petals are dramatically splashed and striped with red and crimson. The common name, Rosa Mundi, reputedly commemorates Fair Rosamund, the mistress of Henry II of England. H and S 1.2m (4ft). Hardy/Z 5–9.

'Gentle Touch'
(syn. 'Diclulu')

Neat and upright, this patio rose bears clusters of double, slightly fragrant, pale salmon-pink flowers, opening from urn-shaped buds, from summer to autumn. In addition to its suitability for containers and as groundcover, 'Gentle Touch' is excellent as a cut flower. H and S 40cm (16in). Hardy/Z 4–9.

'Gloire de Dijon'

One of the oldest climbing roses still in cultivation, this was introduced in 1853 and is usually one of the first climbers to flower. The striking, fully double, fragrant, quartered-rosette, buff-apricot flowers are produced over a long period from late spring to late summer. Its early flowering makes it susceptible to frosts, so grow it against a warm wall in cold areas. H 5m (16ft), S 4m (13ft). Hardy/Z 5–9.

'Golden Showers'

This climbing rose is a perennial favourite for many gardeners. It produces clusters of double, lightly scented, yellow flowers from summer to autumn. The flowers lack distinction, having few petals, but the reliability of this rose in a variety of situations, including light shade, has ensured its longevity. H 3m (10ft), S 2m (6ft). Hardy/Z 4–9.

'Graham Thomas'

A vigorous modern shrub or 'English' rose, this is one of the best of its type, combining the flower form of the old roses with a decidedly modern colour – rich orange-yellow – and a long season that lasts from summer to autumn. The rose is named in honour of the great rosarian, Graham Stuart Thomas. H and S 1.2m (4ft). Hardy/Z 4–9.

Rosa 'Frühlingsgold'

Rosa gallica var. *officinalis*

Rosa 'Gruss an Aachen'

Rosa 'Ingrid Bergman'

Rosa 'Just Joey'

'Gruss an Aachen'

Bred around 1909, this rose is variously described as a floribunda or a polyantha, but it has the air of an old rose. The shapely, deeply cupped, fully double, delicately scented flowers, which are carried in clusters from early summer to autumn, are tinged with pink on opening then fade to creamy white. A long flowering season and low habit of growth make 'Gruss an Aachen' an outstanding bedding rose. H and S 1m (3ft). Hardy/Z 4–9.

'Handel'

A vigorous climber, branching stiffly from the base, this bears double, urn-shaped, only lightly scented flowers from midsummer to autumn. These have cream petals, which are edged with pink, creating an unusual effect. With hard pruning it can be grown as a shrub; in any case its stiff canes make it a reluctant climber. Fan the stems against a wall or spiral them up a pillar. Blackspot may be a problem. H 3m (10ft), S 2.2m (7ft). Hardy/Z 4–9.

'Iceberg'
(syn. 'Fée des Neiges', 'Korbin', 'Schneewittchen')

One of the most successful roses ever produced, this deservedly popular floribunda has retained its place in the catalogues ever since its introduction in 1958. The double, ivory-white, lightly scented flowers open from tapering, pink-flushed buds and are produced in two very distinct flushes, with, unusually, the later, autumn display surpassing the summer one. An outstanding rose of its type, it can be used for bedding, hedging or cutting, but is best, with minimum pruning, as a specimen. H to 1.5m (5ft), S 1m (3ft). Hardy/Z 4–9. The climbing form, **'Climbing Iceberg'**, is equally valuable in the garden, suited to fences or trees.

'Ingrid Bergman'
(syn. 'Poulman')

This upright, branching hybrid tea bears fully double, only lightly scented, deep red flowers from summer to autumn. Good for cutting, bedding and in containers, this is one of the best roses in its colour range. H 75cm (2ft 6in), spread 60cm (2ft). Hardy/Z 4–9.

'Ispahan'

A compact damask rose, this was first recorded in 1832 but is quite probably much older and is possibly Persian in origin. Large clusters of cupped, loosely double, reflexing, richly scented, pink flowers appear throughout summer. The grey-green foliage is attractive. 'Ispahan' has a longer flowering season than most other damasks and is in bloom for up to six weeks. H 1.2–1.5m (4–5ft), S 1–1.2m (3–4ft). Hardy/Z 4–9.

'Just Joey'

The charm of the individual flowers makes this upright hybrid tea rose worth growing. Opening from long, shapely buds, throughout summer, the flowers are a warm coppery orange-pink with slightly ruffled petals, developing creamy buff tints as they age. Disease-resistance is another virtue. H 75cm (2ft 6in), S 60cm (2ft). Hardy/Z 4–9.

'Königin von Dänemark'
(syn. 'Queen of Denmark', 'Belle Courtisane')

This tall, elegant alba is thought by many to be one of the loveliest of all old roses. The luminous pink, fully double, quartered-rosette and richly scented flowers are borne in summer, and fade to rose-pink as they mature,. It also has one of the longest flowering seasons, up to six weeks, and the flowers have good resistance to wet weather. H to 1.5m (5ft), S 1.2m (4ft). Hardy/Z 4–9.

'Korresia'
(syn. 'Friesia', 'Sunsprite')

A neat, upright floribunda, this bears clusters of shapely buds, opening to fragrant, bright golden-yellow flowers, from summer to autumn. It can be used for bedding and for cut flowers; it is similar to 'Allgold' but has bigger flowers. H 75cm (30in), S 60cm (2ft). Hardy/Z 4–9.

'Laura Ford'

This miniature climber is unusual in that its dainty yellow double flowers are also scented. Borne from summer to autumn, they appear in clusters among small, shiny, dark green leaves. A good choice for a small garden, this rose is also suitable for growing in a container. H to 2.2m (7ft), S 1.2m (4ft). Hardy/Z 4–9.

'Madame Alfred Carrière'

This reliable, free-flowering, climbing rose was introduced

Rosa 'Iceberg'

Rosa 'Ispahan'

Rosa 'Königin von Dänemark'

Rosa 'Korresia'

Rosa 'Madame Hardy'

Rosa 'Madame Isaac Pereire'

in 1879. It bears creamy white, double, cupped, fragrant flowers from summer to autumn on almost thornless stems. Although the flowers are not of individual beauty, its many virtues – length of season, health, tolerance of shade – make this one of the best choices for growing against a house wall. H 5m (16ft), S 3m (10ft). Hardy/Z 5–9.

'Madame Grégoire Staechelin'
(syn. 'Spanish Beauty')
The sight of this vigorous climbing rose in full flower in early summer is unforgettable. The fully double, sweetly scented, warm pink flowers hang in clusters on arching stems. There is no repeat flowering. The large, showy hips redden in autumn, but not reliably. H 6m (20ft), S 4m (13ft). Hardy/Z 4–9.

'Madame Hardy'
An undoubted queen among roses, this damask dates from 1867. The fully double, quartered-rosette, strongly scented, white flowers are borne in profusion in summer, the petals reflexing to reveal a green button eye. It is generally considered to be one of the most sumptuous of old roses, though the flowers may be spoilt by rain. H and S 1.5m (5ft). Hardy/Z 4–9.

'Madame Isaac Pereire'
A bourbon rose, introduced in 1881, this retains its place in the catalogues on account of its strong scent, which is all but unsurpassed in a genus noted for exactly that attribute. The flower colour is also of note: a luminous, deep cerise pink. Produced throughout summer and into autumn, the flowers open as quartered-rosettes but become muddled as they mature, especially those of the first flush. A tendency towards mildew is its only drawback. H 2.5m (8ft), S 2m (6ft), possibly more if grown as a climber. Hardy/Z 4–9.

'Margaret Merril'
(syn. 'Harkuly')
An upright floribunda, this bears clusters of large, shapely, double, sweetly scented, pure white flowers from summer to autumn. In addition to its versatility in the garden, it can also be grown in

containers and is useful as a cut flower. Blackspot can be a problem, but the rose is worth persevering with for its delicious scent. H 1m (3ft), S 60cm (2ft). Hardy/Z 4–9.

'Marguerite Hilling'
(syn. 'Pink Nevada')
A sport of the popular 'Nevada', this shrub rose is similar in all respects apart from the colour of its semi-double flowers, which are pale pink and smother the arching canes in early summer. Healthy and vigorous, it makes an excellent specimen. H and S to 2.2m (7ft). Hardy/Z 4–9.

'Mermaid'
This beautiful climber is vigorous once established, but it can take some years to do this. The flowers are produced spasmodically from midsummer until autumn, with a handful later. The elegant, pointed buds open to reveal single, pale yellow, fragrant saucers with prominent golden stamens that

persist after the petals have dropped. The leaves are glossy and can be evergreen; the stems are viciously thorny. Tolerant of some shade, 'Mermaid' may be cut back by hard frost, so appreciates some shelter. H and S 6m (20ft). Hardy/Z 4–9.

'Mountbatten'
(syn. 'Harmantelle')
The clusters of mimosa yellow flowers are beautifully set off by the glossy dark green leaves on this shrub rose. With minimum pruning this makes an excellent specimen. H to 1.5m (5ft), S to 1m (3ft). Hardy/Z 4–9.

'Mrs Oakley Fisher'
This rather spindly hybrid tea has claims to attention on account of its unusual flowers. Not only are they subtle in colour – soft apricot-yellow flowers fading to pale buff yellow – but they are deliciously fragrant and, unusually for a rose in this group, single. H and S 1m (3ft). Hardy/Z 6–9.

Rosa 'Laura Ford'

Rosa 'Margaret Merril'

Rosa 'Mountbatten'

Rosa 'Orange Sunblaze'

'Nevada'

This vigorous shrub rose, which tolerates some shade, puts on a great show in early summer, when its arching, blackish canes are smothered in semi-double, creamy white flowers; their elusive fragrance seems to hang on the air. A few flowers are occasionally produced later in the season. It is best with light pruning. H and S to 3m (10ft). Hardy/Z 4–9.

'New Dawn'

This vigorous, healthy rambler is valued for its late flowering. From midsummer there is a great profusion of deliciously fragrant, silvery pink, semi-double flowers, which continue until well into autumn. Its thorny stems and occasional stiffness of habit need to be taken into consideration when planting. H and S to 5m (16ft). Hardy/Z 4–9.

'Nozomi'

This was one of the first ground-cover roses to be bred and is still one of the best, producing clusters

Rosa 'Pascali'

of single, only lightly scented, very pale pink to white flowers in midsummer. The trailing stems, which are covered in glossy dark green leaves, will root where they touch the ground. To maintain the creeping habit, cut back upward-growing shoots in winter. It can also be treated as a miniature climber. H 45cm (18in), S to 1.5m (5ft). Hardy/Z 4–9.

R. × *odorata* 'Mutabilis' (syn. *R. chinensis* 'Mutabilis')

A China rose, of uncertain age and parentage, this was evidently grown in China for many years before its introduction to Europe in 1894. The single flowers, produced over a long period from mid-spring to autumn, are unusual: flame orange in bud, they open to coppery yellow then fade to pink, the pink deepening to purple as they age. None too hardy, this rose is best grown in the shelter of a warm wall, where it can reach a height of 3m (10ft) with a spread of 2m (6ft). In the border it can also be trained on a tripod. H 1.2m (4ft), S 1m (3ft). Borderline hardy/Z 7–9.

R. × *odorata* 'Pallida'

Introduced to Europe around 1752 but undoubtedly much older, this China rose has one of the longest flowering seasons of all roses. From summer until the first winter frosts it produces double, cupped, sweetly fragrant, clear pink flowers amid elegant, pointed leaves. None too hardy, in some areas it will need growing against a warm wall to give of its best. It can also be trained as a climber. It is sometimes known as the old blush China rose or Parsons' pink China rose. H 1–3m (3–10ft), S 2m (6ft). Borderline hardy/Z 7–9.

'Orange Sunblaze' (syn. 'Meijikatar', 'Orange Meillandina', 'Sunblaze')

A neat and dainty miniature rose, this bears fully double, only lightly scented, bright vermilion-orange flowers from summer to autumn. It is an excellent choice where space is limited or for a container. H and S 30cm (12in). Hardy/Z 4–9. There is also a

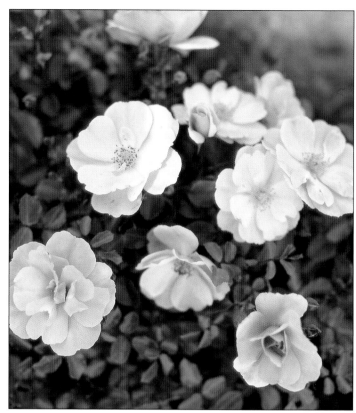

Rosa 'Queen Mother'

climbing form, 'Climbing Orange Sunblaze' (syn. 'Meiji Katarsar'), which produces a dazzling display when grown on a sunny wall.

'Pascali'

This is one of the few pure white hybrid teas (albeit lightly touched with creamy buff). Shapely double, only lightly scented flowers are displayed from early summer into autumn. The rain-resistance of the flowers is unsurpassed in this colour range; they are also exceptionally long-lasting when cut. H 1m (3ft), S 75cm (2ft

6in). Hardy/Z 4–9. **'Climbing Pascali'**, a climbing form, shares the same qualities.

'Peace' (syn. 'Gioia', 'Gloria Dei', 'Madame A. Meilland')

One of the most popular hybrid teas ever produced, this rose is surely worthy of revival. The large, fully double, only lightly scented flowers are pale yellow with pink flushes, and they appear from midsummer to autumn. Its present lack of popularity is due to its supposed coarseness – that

Rosa 'Peace'

Rosa 'Président de Sèze'

Rosa 'Roseraie de l'Haÿ'

is, it is a vigorous, spreading, bushy rose that makes a fine specimen with light pruning. H 1.5m (5ft), S 1m (3ft). Hardy/Z 4–9.

'Président de Sèze'

Richly scented, large, quartered flowers appear on this sturdy gallica rose in summer. The centre petals are rich magenta-purple, the colour fading across the flower to soft lilac-pink, almost white, at the edges. The leaves are larger than is usual for a gallica rose. A well-grown specimen is a stunning sight when in full bloom. H 1.2m (4ft), S 1m (3ft). Hardy/Z 4–9.

'Queen Mother'
(syn. 'Korquemu')

This spreading patio rose deserves its popularity. The dainty buds open to semi-double, clear pink flowers from summer to autumn. It does well in a container and is sometimes available as a weeping standard. H 45cm (18in), S 60cm (2ft). Hardy/Z 4–9.

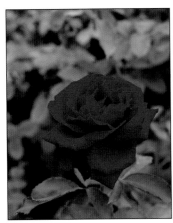

Rosa 'Royal William'

'Rambling Rector'

A vigorous rambling rose, this is covered with clusters of small, semi-double, fragrant, white flowers in summer. Small red hips follow in autumn. It is suitable for growing into a large tree, and a mature rose in full flower is an impressive sight, but it is not a rose suited to every garden. H and S 6m (20ft). Hardy/Z 5–9.

'Roseraie de l'Haÿ'

Despite its reluctance to produce the characteristic autumn hips, this is one of the best of the rugosa roses. Its value rests on its strongly scented, velvety, wine-red flowers, which open to reveal creamy stamens. The blooms are produced in abundance from summer to autumn. The wrinkled leaves redden in autumn. Dense and spreading, 'Roseraie de l'Haÿ' makes an excellent hedge and can also be planted in light woodland. H 2m (6ft), S 1.2m (4ft). Hardy/Z 4–9.

'Royal William'
(syn. 'Duftzauber '84', 'Fragrant Charm '84', 'Korzaun')

An upright hybrid tea, this rose is valued for its succession of large, fully double, fragrant, deep crimson flowers. The graceful blooms are carried on long stems from summer to autumn. This rose is excellent planted en masse for a stunning effect, or it can be grown to provide flowers for cutting. H 1m (3ft), S 75cm (2ft 6in). Hardy/Z 4–9.

'Savoy Hotel'
(syn. 'Harvintage', 'Integrity')

This bushy hybrid tea has strong stems that carry large, shapely, fully double, fragrant, light clear pink flowers from summer to autumn and with good repeat-flowering. It is a versatile rose, which provides excellent material for cutting, as long as you keep it well fed. H 1m (3ft), S 60cm (2ft). Hardy/Z 4–8.

'Schneezwerg'
(syn. 'Snow Dwarf')

A rugosa rose introduced in 1912, this has a dense, spreading habit. The anemone-like, semi-double, white flowers open flat to

Rosa 'Savoy Hotel'

reveal golden stamens. They are followed by small, orange-red, tomato-shaped hips. Although its flowers are unremarkable, this rose is perhaps at its best in autumn; the foliage does not change colour, but the flowers continue to appear alongside the reddening hips. In order to get the best of both worlds, therefore, deadhead selectively in summer. H 1.2m (4ft), S 1.5m (5ft). Hardy/Z 3–9.

'Sexy Rexy'
(syn. 'Heckenzauber', 'Macrexy')

This is an outstanding floribunda, of upright habit. It produces clusters of shapely, fully double, palest coral-pink flowers throughout summer and autumn. These are shown off by plentiful

Rosa 'Schneezwerg'

dark, glossy leaves. It is a versatile rose good for general garden use, growing in containers and for providing cut flowers. H and S 60cm (2ft). Hardy/Z 4–9.

'Sombreuil'

A distinctive and unusual rose, this is generally classified as a climbing tea, although it is not particularly vigorous, nor are its flowers tea-like, lacking a high centre. Borne from summer to autumn, the sweetly scented blooms are flat, quartered rosettes, creamy white in colour and acquiring pink tinges as they age. Wet weather will ruin them. H and S to 2.4m (8ft) when grown as a climber with support, but smaller if allowed to grow as a lax shrub. Hardy/Z 5–9.

Rosa 'Sexy Rexy'

Rosa 'Stanwell Perpetual'

'Southampton'
(syn. 'Susan Ann')
This is an excellent floribunda, with an upright, branching habit and shiny, dark green leaves. Clusters of large, double, soft apricot-orange flowers, which are flushed with scarlet, are carried from early summer into autumn; the petals are wavy-edged. The scent is not especially strong. H 1m (3ft), S 60cm (2ft). Hardy/Z 4–9.

'Souvenir de la Malmaison'
This beautiful, dense, spreading bourbon rose, produced in 1843, commemorates the famous garden created by Empress Josephine at Malmaison, although it is not clear whether it was actually grown there. Repeat-flowering throughout the summer, it bears very fragrant, fully double, soft pink flowers, which open to a quartered-rosette shape as they fade to blush-white. One major drawback is that the silk-textured

flowers may be spoilt by wet weather. H and S 1.5m (5ft). Hardy/Z 4–9.

'Stanwell Perpetual'
This Scotch rose, raised in 1838, forms a dense, prickly shrub. The double, sweetly scented, attractive blush pink to white flowers open flat and are produced almost continuously throughout summer among the grey-green leaves. Tolerant of poor soil and some shade, this rose is ideal for growing in light woodland; it also makes a good hedge. H and S 1.5m (5ft). Hardy/Z 5–9.

'Sweet Dream'
(syn. 'Fryminicot')
One of the best of the patio roses, this produces an abundance of fully double, lightly scented, soft apricot-orange flowers from midsummer to autumn. It is usually well covered with glossy, healthy foliage. A good edging plant, 'Sweet Dream' is also

suitable for growing in a container. H 40cm (16in), S 35cm (14in). Hardy/Z 4–9.

'Tango'
(syn. 'Macfirwal', 'Rock 'n' Roll', 'Stretch Johnson')
This upright floribunda is chiefly of interest to flower arrangers. From summer to autumn it produces clusters of semi-double flowers of some distinction: the petals, frilled at the edges, are orange-red with white rims, yellow at the base and on the reverse. H 75cm (2ft 6in), spread 60cm (2ft). Hardy/Z 4–8.

'The Fairy'
A dainty floribunda or polyantha, this has a dense, mounding habit and is well worth considering if you are planning an autumn border. It flowers later than almost any other rose, the clusters of small, double, light pink flowers appearing only from midsummer, but then continuing in profusion until the onset of winter. H and S 60cm (2ft). Hardy/Z 4–9.

'The Queen Elizabeth'
(syn. 'Queen Elizabeth', 'The Queen Elizabeth Rose')
This is one of the best of all the floribundas, but not especially characteristic of the group. Its vigour and strongly vertical habit really make it unsuitable for most of the purposes for which the floribundas were developed. It is best used at the back of a border or as a tall, informal hedge. Its fully double, china pink flowers, which are freely carried from summer to autumn, last well when cut. H 2.2m (7ft), S 1m (3ft);

Rosa 'The Queen Elizabeth'

with minimal pruning it will easily top 3m (10ft). Hardy/Z 4–9. The climbing form, **'Climbing the Queen Elizabeth'**, is also well worth growing.

'Troika'
(syn. 'Royal Dane')
An outstanding hybrid tea, this has an upright, branching habit. The display of large, shapely, double, lightly scented, copper-orange flowers, sometimes veined scarlet, continues throughout summer and into autumn. Disease- and weather-resistant, this is a good choice for a massed planting and also provides good cut flowers. H 1m (3ft), S 75cm (2ft 6in). Hardy/Z 4–9.

'Tuscany Superb'
(syn. 'Double Velvet')
This erect gallica rose was raised before 1837. The large, semi-double, lightly scented, deep crimson flowers are produced in midsummer. They open flat, showing golden stamens, then fade to purple. Tolerant of poor

Rosa 'Souvenir de la Malmaison'

Rosa 'Sweet Dream'

Rosa 'The Fairy'

Rosa 'Tuscany Superb'

Rosa 'Veilchenblau'

Rosa 'Whisky Mac'

Rosa 'William Lobb'

soil, this is one of the few old roses that is suitable for hedging. It is not too thorny. H 1.5m (5ft), S 1m (3ft). Hardy/Z 4–9.

'Veilchenblau' (syn. 'Blue Rambler', 'Violet Blue')

A vigorous rambling rose, this was introduced in 1909. In midsummer it bears clusters of sweetly scented, semi-double, violet-pink flowers with yellow stamens; the flowers fade to an unusual purplish grey as they mature. The leaves are glossy and light green. More modest than most ramblers, this rose is suitable for a small garden and is best grown with some shelter from the midday sun. H and S 4m (13ft). Hardy/Z 4–9.

'Whisky Mac' (syn. 'Tanky', 'Whisky')

This famous hybrid tea has retained its popularity despite its propensity to die-back and fungal diseases. Its appeal lies in the unusual colouring of its sumptuous double flowers, which are a rich golden-orange of unrivalled intensity, and with a fragrance to match. Since it needs almost constant attention, this is really a plant for dedicated rose-growers only. H 75cm (2ft 6in), S 60cm (2ft). Hardy/Z 4–9.

'White Bells'

A dense, spreading groundcover rose, this bears a single, but abundant, crop of small, fully double, white flowers in summer. It is shade-tolerant, and thus useful for difficult areas of the

garden, but overall perhaps not as good as some other groundcover roses. H 60cm (2ft), S 1.2m (4ft). Hardy/Z 5–9.

'White Cockade'

This is one of the few white climbing roses. The perfectly shaped, fully double flowers appear almost continuously from summer to autumn, and the absence of a strong scent in no way detracts from its overall merit. Slow-growing, it is a good choice for growing in a container or on a short pillar. H 2.2m (7ft), S 1.5m (5ft). Hardy/Z 4–9.

'White Grootendorst'

A vigorous rugosa rose, with a dense, spreading habit, this produces clusters of small, double, scentless, white flowers, particularly notable for the frilly edges of the petals, which look like carnations. Like most of the rugosas, it tolerates some shade and poor soil, making it ideal for a wild garden. H 1.2m (4ft), S 1m (3ft). Hardy/Z 3–8.

'William Lobb' (syn. 'Duchesse d'Istrie')

This rather sprawling moss rose is worth growing for its sumptuous rosette flowers. Richly scented, they open magenta-purple in midsummer from heavily mossed buds, then pass through a remarkable range of tones before fading to a subtle violet-grey. The ungainly habit makes it unsuitable as a specimen. Instead, try it wrapped around a tripod or as a short climber on a pillar or against a wall. H and S 2m (6ft). Hardy/Z 4–9.

R. xanthina 'Canary Bird'

This wild rose is usually one of the first to flower in the garden, offering a burst of welcome colour in late spring. The single, cupped, scented, canary yellow flowers have prominent stamens. In a good year there will be a second, though lesser, flush of flowers in autumn. It makes an attractive arching shrub, although it is sometimes available as a grafted standard, when it makes a fine specimen. H and S 2.2m (7ft). Hardy/Z 5–9.

'Yellow Doll'

This spreading miniature rose has double, slightly scented, bright yellow flowers, which are produced singly or in clusters from summer to autumn. Rather unusually for a miniature, it is good for cutting; it can also be forced under glass for early flowers. It will tolerate harsh weather conditions. H and S to 30cm (12in). Hardy/Z 3–8.

'Yesterday' (syn. 'Tapis d'Orient')

A floribunda or polyantha rose, this has an elegant, open, spreading habit and a long flowering season, from summer to autumn. The clusters of semi-

double, fragrant, deep lilac-pink flowers open flat to reveal paler centres and golden stamens. It is good for cutting and, given lighter pruning than usual, makes an attractive specimen. H and S 1m (3ft). Hardy/Z 4–9.

'Zéphirine Drouhin'

This climbing rose is notable for its thornless stems, making it a good choice for an archway or pergola or for framing a doorway. In summer and autumn it produces clusters of double, cupped to flat, fragrant, magenta flowers. It can be prone to mildew. H 3m (10ft), S 2m (6ft). Hardy/Z 4–9. **'Kathleen Harrop'** is a pale pink sport.

Rosa 'Yesterday'

Alpines

Alpines are among the gems of the plant kingdom. Small but beautifully formed, they can be found producing their jewel-like blooms from the last days of winter to late autumn, providing a wealth of interest through the seasons. Since the majority are neat and compact-growing, alpines are eminently suited to gardens of restricted size, and are ideal for growing in troughs and containers, or, where space allows, in a dedicated rock garden or raised bed; but many can also be grown in mixed borders alongside bigger plants.

A rock garden is one of the most attractive ways of growing alpines. Here carpets of alpines create a tapestry of form and vivid colour.

Growing alpines in a rock garden

Like ponds or watercourses, rock gardens benefit from an open site. If planned well, they can each enhance the other. In a level garden the soil excavated during pond installation can be used to form the base.

Building a rock garden

When you build a rock garden, aim as far as possible to create as natural-looking outcrop, otherwise it will take on the appearance of a rock-encrusted heap of soil. The most important ingredient is the rocks, which are more likely to "gel" as a rocky outcrop if they are of the same natural stone. Choose a type of rock that has clear strata lines running through it and an attractive texture and colour. Limestone and sandstone are perhaps the best rock types, but it is possible to create an attractive feature from other types of rock.

You will need a range of sizes of rock – anything from 15kg (33lb) to 100kg (well over 200lb) – so make sure you have help to manoeuvre the larger stones. If you live near a quarry, use this as your source, otherwise suppliers can be found in local directories, and a limited selection of rocks is offered at some garden centres.

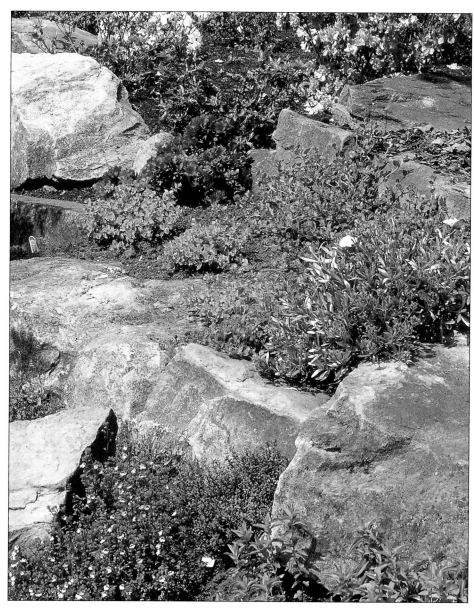

Rock gardens are perfect for growing a selection of alpine plants.

HOW TO BUILD A ROCK GARDEN

1 The base of the rock garden is a good place to dispose of rubble and subsoil excavated if you have dug out a pond.

2 Use a special soil mixture for the top 15–23cm (6–9in), especially if soil excavated from a pond is used. Mix equal parts of soil, coarse grit and peat (or peat substitute) and spread evenly over the mound.

3 Lay the first rocks at the base, making sure that the strata run in the same direction, and add more soil mixture around them.

Designing a rock garden

The design should suit the situation. On sloping ground you can build a natural-looking outcrop or a series of terraces or a combination of the two for a very large rockery. On a level site a more acute outcrop, with strata lines at a 45 degree angle, can work well, or choose a series of flattish stones to create a pavement effect with horizontal strata lines.

Careful planning is essential. Mark out the site using string and improve drainage if necessary – if you have heavy soil this may mean digging a hole 30cm (12in) deep, half-filling it with rubble and covering it with a layer of sharp sand before topping with good-quality, free-draining topsoil mixture.

Building a rockery on a slope

If practicable start at the bottom of the slope and build in layers. Choose the best-looking stone to start building your rockery and position it in the middle so that the strata lines angle gently back into the ground. About one-third of the stone will be underground, so you will have to scoop out a hole to accommodate it. Then add stones either side so that the strata lines

HOW TO PLANT A ROCK GARDEN

1 Position the plants while still in their pots so that you can see how they look and adjust if necessary. Alpines are a good choice of plant for a rock garden.

2 Use a trowel to take out a hole a little larger than the rootball. You can buy narrow trowels that are particularly useful for planting in the crevices between rocks.

3 Make sure that the plant is at the correct depth, then trickle gritty soil around the roots and firm it well.

4 Finish off by covering the exposed surface with more grit to improve drainage and protect leaves from splashing mud.

fall away at exactly the same angle. Make sure that each stone is set firm before positioning the next by ramming soil around the rock. Repeat the process for each layer of the rockery, then fill any gaps with a

free-draining mixture consisting of equal parts of good quality topsoil, peat (or peat substitute) and coarse grit. Then plant and mulch the surface with stone chippings to match the rocks used in the rockery.

4 Lever the next row of rocks into position. Using rollers and levers is the best way to move heavy rocks around.

5 As each layer is built up, add more of the soil mixture and consolidate it around each of the rocks in turn.

6 Make sure that the sides slope inwards and make the top reasonably flat rather than building it into a pinnacle. Position the plants, then cover the exposed soil with a layer of stone chippings.

Androsace sempervivoides

Aquilegia alpina

Aquilegia flabellata

ALCHEMILLA

This large genus contains many plants that are too large for the rock garden, but the species described here are neater and less prone to self-seeding than the familiar *Alchemilla mollis*.
Cultivation Grow in fertile, well-drained soil in sun or semi-shade.

A. alpina
Alpine lady's mantle
The dark green, deeply lobed leaves form mats, surmounted by tiny, yellow-green flowers in summer. H to 10cm (4cm), S 45cm (18in). Hardy/Z 3–7.

A. conjuncta
The lobed leaves are blue-green. Clusters of tiny yellow-green flowers are borne in summer and autumn. H to 40cm (16in), S 30cm (12in). Hardy/Z 4–8.

ANDROSACE

This genus of about 100 species includes many mat-forming perennials that are ideal for rock gardens or alpine troughs.
Cultivation Grow in gritty, well-drained but reliably moist soil in sun.

A. carnea
The species from the Pyrenees and Alps has rosettes of evergreen, hairy leaves and, in spring, clusters of small, yellow-eyed, pink flowers. H to 5cm (2in), S to 15cm (6in). Hardy/Z 4–7.
A. carnea subsp. *laggeri* has pinkish-red flowers and is more densely tufted. H to 5cm (2in), S to 15cm (6in).

A. sempervivoides
(**syn.** *A. mucronifolia* of gardens)
This evergreen, mat-forming species, native to the western Himalayas, has small, neatly formed, deep-green rosettes, which produce further rosettes on short, strawberry-like runners. The clusters of small, mauve-pink to mid-pink flowers are held above the rosettes on short stalks. H 5–7.5cm (2–3in), S 15–30cm (6–12in). Hardy/Z 4–7.

AQUILEGIA
Columbine
The genus is best known for the herbaceous perennials grown in the border, but it also includes a number of species suitable for the rock garden.
Cultivation Grow in gritty but fertile, well-drained soil in full sun.

A. alpina
(**syn.** *A. montana*)
Alpine columbine
Too tall for all but the largest rock gardens, this has pretty blue flowers in late spring and blue-green, ferny foliage. H 45cm (18in), S to 30cm (12in). Hardy/Z 4–7.

A. flabellata
(**syn.** *A. akitensis*)
This delightful little alpine columbine has neat, grey-green, divided foliage. The typical flowers are purple-blue with white tips to the petals. They are borne in late spring and early summer and will seed around in the garden. H 40–50cm (16–20in), S 15–20cm (6–8in). Hardy/Z

4–9. *A. flabellata* var. *pumila* f. *alba* (**syn.** *A. flabellata* 'Nana Alba') has up to three white flowers on each stem. H and S 10–15cm (4–6in). Hardy/Z 3–9.

ARABIS
Rock cress
The genus contains more than 100 species of annuals and evergreen perennials with white or purple, four-petalled flowers.
Cultivation These plants need well-drained soil and a warm position in full sun.

A. alpina subsp. caucasica
(**syn.** *A. caucasica*)
The common arabis of gardens comes from the Balkans and western Asia. It is a mat-forming evergreen with close, rather coarse rosettes of greyish-green leaves and bears clusters of white flowers in spring and early summer. H to 15cm (6in), S 50cm (20in). Hardy/Z 4–8. Selected forms

include '**Flore-Pleno**', which has double, pure white flowers; and '**Variegata**', which has leaves variegated with creamy yellow. H 15–25cm (6–10in), S 20–40cm (8–16in). Hardy/Z 4–8.

ARMERIA
Sea pink, thrift
The genus of evergreen perennials and subshrubs is distributed across Europe, northern Africa and North America. All species produce the little spherical flowerheads.
Cultivation Grow in well-drained soil that is not too rich, in a position in full sun.

A. maritima
(**syn.** *A. vulgaris*)
The familiar, tough, evergreen hummocks of slender, deep green leaves bear long-stalked heads of pink to reddish-purple flowers in summer. H and S 15–25cm (6–10in). Hardy/Z 4–7.
'**Vindictive**' has large, rich pink flowerheads. H to 15cm (6in), S 25cm (10in). Hardy/Z 4–7.

AUBRIETA

These evergreen perennials are popular and reliable garden plants, ideal for sunny walls, scree beds and all manner of crevices. The forms grown in gardens are derived from *A. deltoidea*.
Cultivation Grow in well-drained, neutral to alkaline soil in sun. Shear over after flowering to maintain a neat shape.

A. deltoidea
This species is the familiar aubrieta of gardens, which is

Arabis alpina subsp. caucasica

Armeria maritima

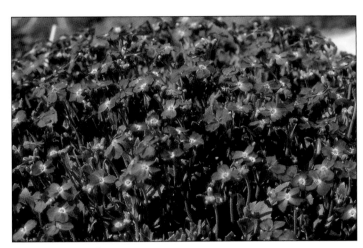

Aubrieta 'Doctor Mules'

native to south-eastern Europe. It is an evergreen, mat-forming plant with close, deep green or grey-green foliage in lax rosettes. The clusters of reddish-purple, violet, mauve or pink flowers are borne in spring and intermittently through summer. H 10–15cm (4–6in), S 15–50cm (6–20in). Hardy/Z 5–7. Among the many named forms are 'Argenteovariegata' (syn. *A. albomarginata*), which has single, silver-pink flowers and leaves variegated with cream; 'Doctor Mules', which has deep purple flowers; and 'Joy', which has single, mauve flowers.

AURINIA

The evergreen perennials in the genus are found in mountainous areas throughout southern and central Europe. The small yellow or white flowers have four petals.
Cultivation Grow in a position in full sun in moderately fertile soil.

Plants will benefit from being sheared over after flowering to keep them neat.

A. saxatilis
(syn. *Alyssum saxatile*)
Gold dust
The familiar yellow alyssum of gardens is a subshrub with large tufts of greyish- or whitish-green leaves. In spring and through summer the plants produce sprays of tiny, yellow flowers. H 20–30cm (8–12in), S 30–50cm (12–20in). Hardy/Z 4–7.

BALLOTA

This genus includes shrubs and perennials. The species described here is a compact subshrub for a sunny spot in a scree garden or in a Mediterranean planting.
Cultivation This needs well-drained soil, which need not be fertile. Grow in full sun and clip back in spring to keep plants neat.

B. acetabulosa
The grey-green leaves, the main attraction, are borne in pairs along the upright stems. Tiny purple-pink flowers appear in summer. H and S to 60cm (24in). Hardy/Z 5–9.

CAMPANULA
Bellflower
In addition to the many border perennials in this large genus, there are many species that can be grown in the rock garden.
Cultivation Campanulas should be grown in fertile, well-drained soil, ideally neutral to alkaline. Grow in a position in full sun.

Aurinia saxatilis

Campanula carpatica

C. 'Birch Hybrid'
This prostrate, evergreen hybrid has mauve-blue, bell-shaped flowers in summer. H to 10cm (4in), S 50cm (20in). Hardy/Z 4–7.

C. carpatica
This widely grown, herbaceous plant, originally from the Carpathian mountains, forms small tufts with numerous, bright green, oval, sharply toothed leaves. The upright, broadly bell-shaped flowers are violet, purple, blue or white and are borne in summer and autumn. H 15cm (6in), S 30–45cm (12–18in). Hardy/Z 4–7.

C. cochleariifolia
(syn. *C. bellardii, C. pusilla*)
Fairies' thimbles
This dainty little bellflower, native to the mountains of Europe, forms spreading mats by means of underground rhizomes. The small leaves are bright, lustrous green, and the thin stems bear several small, nodding bells in blue, lilac, lavender or, occasionally, white. H 8–13cm (3–5in), S 15–40cm (6–16in). Hardy/Z 5–7.

C. portenschlagiana
Dalmatian bellflower
An excellent plant from Croatia for rock crevices or for colonizing old walls. The tufts of small leaves are bright green, and in early summer the numerous branched stems bear a profusion of lilac-blue, rather narrow, bell-shaped flowers. H 15–25cm (6–10in), S 15–50cm (6–20in). Hardy/Z 4–7.

C. saxatilis
The spreading species, found in rocky areas of Crete, has round leaves that form rosettes. In summer pale blue, tubular flowers are borne in spikes. H to 8cm (3in), S to 20cm (8in). Hardy/Z 5–8.

CERASTIUM

The species described, a vigorous, mat-forming plant, can be invasive, and the genus, in fact, includes some weeds. The popular perennial *C. tomentosum* is too vigorous and invasive for a rock garden and should be confined to areas of poor soil where nothing else will grow, or allowed to cascade over a wall or bank.
Cultivation Grow in full sun in gritty, well-drained soil.

C. alpinum
Alpine chickweed
The grey-green, evergreen leaves of this European species form compact mats above which clusters of small white flowers are borne in late spring to early summer. H 10cm (4in), S 30cm (12in). Hardy Z 3–8.

Campanula portenschlagiana

Campanula 'Birch Hybrid'

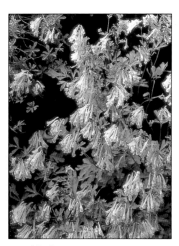

Corydalis flexuosa

CORYDALIS

There are some 300 species in the genus, including many attractive annuals and biennials and some perennials, suitable for shady, woodland gardens and herbaceous borders.
Cultivation Grow in a semi-shaded spot in moist, humus-rich but well-drained soil.

C. flexuosa

This widely available herbaceous perennial is native to China. The tufts of grey-green or bright green, fern-like, dissected leaves are present through most of the year except high summer. The sprays of blue or lilac-blue, spurred flowers are borne on wiry stems in spring and early summer. H 30cm (12in), S 20–50cm (8–20in). Hardy/Z 5–8.

C. lutea
(syn. *Pseudofumaria lutea*)
This tufted, evergreen perennial has rather fleshy, grey-green,

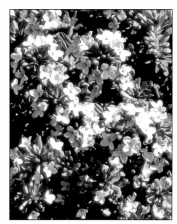

Daphne cneorum

dissected leaves. The pale stems bear small sprays of yellow, spurred flowers from spring until autumn. An excellent plant for crevices, it often self-sows profusely in the garden. H and S to 30cm (12in). Hardy/Z 5–8.

DAPHNE

The genus is possibly best known for its wonderfully fragrant shrubs, but it also includes some delightful small species, suitable for rock and scree gardens and alpine troughs. All parts of the plants are poisonous.
Cultivation Daphnes need moist but well-drained, fertile soil and a position in sun or partial shade.

D. alpina

This upright, deciduous, twiggy shrub with elliptical, greyish leaves bears clusters of fragrant white flowers in late spring and early summer. H and S 40cm (16in). Hardy/Z 6–8.

D. arbuscula

This very small, extremely slow-growing, twiggy, evergreen shrub has narrow, rather leathery, shiny, deep green leaves. The clusters of fragrant pink flowers appear in late spring. This is an excellent trough plant. H and S 15cm (6in). Hardy/Z 5–7.

D. blagayana

The trailing stems of this mat-forming, usually evergreen shrub can root where they touch the ground. Clusters of sweet-smelling, white flowers appear in spring. H 10cm (4in), S 30cm (12in) or more.

D. cneorum
(syn. *D. odorata*)
Garland flower
This branching and trailing evergreen shrub has fragrant pink flowers in spring and, occasionally, a second flush in autumn. The dark green leaves are greyish on the underside. H 20cm (8in), S 1m (3ft). Hardy/Z 5–8. 'Eximia' is a vigorous cultivar, with narrow, grey-green leaves and small clusters of deep rose pink, sweetly fragrant flowers in late spring. H 20cm (8in), S 1m (3ft).

D. sericea Collina Group
(syn. *D. collina*)
Plants sold under this name are dense-growing, with elliptical, rather bristly, grey-green leaves. Pale to mid-pink flowers are borne in dense clusters in late spring and early summer. H and S 60cm (24in). Hardy/Z 7–8.

DIANTHUS
Pink
This huge genus includes many perennials as well as annuals and biennials. There are also several members of the genus that are ideally suited to raised beds, rock and scree gardens and to alpine troughs.
Cultivation Grow in fertile but gritty, well-drained soil (ideally neutral to alkaline) in full sun.

D. alpinus
Alpine pink
This delightful pink, which is native to the eastern Alps, forms a small, evergreen mat of deep green, narrow, blunt-tipped leaves. The relatively large, fringed flowers are pink to cerise or purplish-pink, with generous speckling above. H 10cm (4in), S 20cm (8in). Hardy/Z 5–8.
'Joan's Blood' has very dark flowers with almost black centres. H 10cm (4in), S 20cm (8in).

D. deltoides
Maiden pink
This variable species, native to Europe and western Asia, is a mat-forming, evergreen perennial with numerous narrow, deep green leaves that are often flushed with

Dianthus deltoides

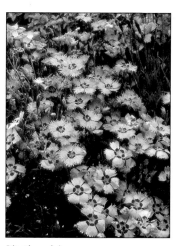

Dianthus alpinus

bronze or purple. The spreading, branched stems bear numerous small, fringed flowers in pink, cerise, crimson or white in summer and autumn. H 15–25cm (6–10in), S 30–50cm (12–20in). Hardy/Z 5–8.

DODECATHEON
American cowslip, shooting star
The perennial species that comprise this genus are native to North America, where they are found in meadows and woodland. They have cyclamen-like flowers, with swept-back petals.
Cultivation Grow in well-drained, reliably moist and fertile soil in sun or partial shade.

D. pulchellum
(syn. *D. radicatum*)
The dark green, oval leaves form rosettes above which the deep pink flowers are borne in mid- to late spring. H 35cm (14in), S 15cm (6in). Hardy/Z 3–8.

ERIGERON
Fleabane
This genus, which includes annuals and biennials, is best known for the perennial hybrids that bring colour to the summer border, but a number of species are suitable for rock gardens.
Cultivation Grow in well-drained but reliably moist soil in sun.

E. alpinus
Alpine fleabane
This species, native to central and southern Europe, has narrow, grey-green, hairy leaves. Yellow-centred, mauve, daisy-like flowers

are borne from mid- to late summer. H 25cm (10in), S 20cm (8in). Hardy/Z 5–8.

E. glaucus
Beach aster
This evergreen, leafy sub-shrub is native to western North America. It has rather coarse, pale bluish-green, oval leaves, and in summer numerous pale violet to lavender flowerheads are produced, each with an egg-yolk yellow centre. H to 50cm (20in), S 45–90cm (18–36in). Hardy/Z 5–8.

ERINUS
The two semi-evergreen or evergreen species that comprise this genus are native to rocky areas in central and southern Europe and northern Africa. Only the species described is in general cultivation.
Cultivation Grow in well-drained soil in sun or partial shade.

E. alpinus
Fairy foxglove
This species is found in rocky places in central and southern Europe, where it forms small, evergreen tufts. The neatly toothed foliage is mainly borne in small rosettes, and from late spring to summer the rosy-purple or white flowers are clustered at the ends of short leafy stems. H 15cm (6in), S 20cm (8in). Hardy/Z 4–7.

EURYOPS
Although there are about 100 species in the genus, only a few are widely grown. The species

Euryops acraeus

described is not reliably hardy and needs a sheltered position in a rock garden or raised bed.
Cultivation Grow in fairly rich, well-drained soil in full sun. Shear after flowering to keep plants neat.

E. acraeus
(syn. E. evansii of gardens)
This compact evergreen shrub, which is native to South Africa, has crowded, narrow, silver-grey leaves. The daisy-like flowers are acid-yellow and appear in summer. H and S 40cm (16in). Borderline hardy/Z 9–10.

GENTIANA
Gentian
The genus contains about 400 species of annuals, biennials and perennials, which may be evergreen, semi-evergreen or herbaceous. Some require the specialized cultural conditions best provided in an alpine house, but many other species are suitable for growing in a rock or scree garden or an alpine trough.
Cultivation Grow in moist but well-drained soil. Most summer-flowering gentians need a position in full sun and prefer neutral to alkaline soil; most autumn-flowering gentians need acid soil and shelter from hot sun.

G. acaulis
(syn. G. excisa, G. kochiana)
Trumpet gentian
One of the most beautiful of alpine plants, the species is from the mountains of central and southern Europe. It forms dense mats of evergreen, leathery leaves.

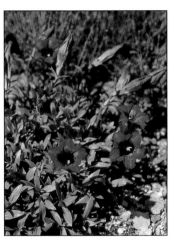
Gentiana acaulis

In spring, and sometimes also in autumn, large, bell-shaped flowers in rich kingfisher-blue appear. H 10cm (4in), S 40cm (16in). Hardy/Z 4–7.

G. asclepiadea
Willow gentian
This herbaceous perennial is from the mountains of southern and central Europe. In mid- to late summer it bears beautiful, trumpet-shaped, rich blue flowers. The narrow leaves are mid-green. H 75cm (30in) or more, S 45cm (18in). Hardy/Z 6–9.

G. septemfida
This herbaceous species is from the mountains of western Asia. It forms discreet tufts with spreading stems, which bear pairs of elliptical, deep green leaves. One or several deep blue, bell-shaped flowers are borne at the stem tips in late summer and autumn. H 10–25cm (4–10in), S 20–40cm (8–16in). Hardy/Z 6–8.

G. sino-ornata
Autumn gentian
This, the finest autumn-flowering gentian, comes from western China. It is a herbaceous perennial, forming small tufts of narrow, sharply pointed, deep green, rather glossy leaves. The solitary, deep blue, green- and purple-striped, bell-shaped flowers are held on the ends of the spreading stems. It needs humus-rich, acid soil. H 10–15cm (4–6in), S 15–25cm (6–10in). Hardy/Z 5–7.

G. verna
Spring gentian, star gentian
This evergreen perennial species from mountainous areas across Europe is one of the great delights of the alpine garden. It forms small tufts of bright green, oval foliage. The rich-blue, white-centred flowers appear in spring to early summer. H 8cm (3in), S 10–20cm (4–8in). Hardy/Z 4–7.

GERANIUM
Cranesbill
The large genus includes many perennials, but the dainty species described below are ideal for rock gardens and alpine troughs.
Cultivation Grow in any well-drained soil in full sun.

G. cinereum
The species, which is native to the Pyrenees, is an evergreen or semi-evergreen perennial with rounded, lobed, grey-green leaves. The paired, saucer-shaped flowers are pink with an elaborate network of purple veins and are produced in late spring and summer. H 15cm (6in), S 25cm (10in). Hardy/Z 4–9. **'Ballerina'** has grey leaves and purplish flowers with dark red-purple eyes.

G. dalmaticum
This clump-forming, evergreen perennial from the western Balkans has rounded, deeply lobed, glossy green leaves. The flowers, borne in masses in early and midsummer, are a rich pink with orange-red anthers. H 15cm (6in), S 50cm (20in). Hardy/Z 5–8.

Erinus alpinus

Geranium cinereum 'Ballerina'

GYPSOPHILA

The genus is best known for *G. paniculata*, which produces the familiar sprays of tiny white flowers, but the species described is a mat-forming plant, ideal for a rock or scree garden.
Cultivation Grow in well-drained, preferably alkaline soil in full sun.

G. repens

This mat-forming, semi-evergreen perennial is native to central and southern Europe. It has grey-green leaves and, in summer, clouds of tiny white, pink or purplish-pink flowers. H 20cm (8in), S 50cm (20in). Hardy/Z 4–7. 'Dorothy Teacher' is a neat cultivar, with pale pink flowers. H 5cm (2in), S 40cm (16in). 'Fratensis' has narrow, grey-green leaves, and the spreading stems bear sprays of small pink flowers. H 8cm (5in), S 30cm (12in).

G. tenuifolia
(syn. *G. gracilescens*)

This low-growing, hummock-forming, evergreen alpine is native to the Caucasus. It has a mass of grass-like, mid-green foliage, and the small white or pale pink flowers are borne aloft on delicate wiry stems in summer. H 10–15cm (4–6in), S 15–25cm (6–10in). Hardy/Z 5–9.

IBERIS
Candytuft

These easy-to-grow plants are ideal for sunny rock gardens or walls.
Cultivation Grow in any moist, well-drained soil, preferably neutral to alkaline, in sun.

I. saxatilis

This evergreen species from southern Europe has dark green leaves and clusters of small white (occasionally purplish) flowers in summer. H 15cm (6in), S 20cm (8in). Hardy/Z 4–8.

I. sempervirens
(syn. *I. commutata*)

A useful plant, this spreading, evergreen subshrub from southern Europe has dark green leaves carrying dense heads of brilliant white flowers in late spring and early summer. H 30cm (12in), S 60cm (24in). Hardy/Z 5–9.

Gypsophila repens 'Fratensis'

LEONTOPODIUM
Edelweiss

The genus contains species from the mountains of Europe and Asia. The insignificant flowers are surrounded by long, narrow bracts. Although some species require the specialized conditions of an alpine house, the species described will grow in rock gardens and raised beds.
Cultivation Grow in very well-drained, slightly alkaline soil in full sun. Protect from winter wet.

L. alpinum

This is the edelweiss of the European mountains. It is a small, short-lived, tufted perennial with narrow, greyish, felted foliage. The small, button-flowerheads are clustered and surrounded by white, woolly bracts, giving a daisy-like appearance. H and S 15cm (6in). Hardy/Z 4–6. 'Mignon', which is more mat-forming, has dark green leaves and smaller flowerheads than the species. H 10cm (4in), S 30cm (12in).

Leontopodium alpinum

Iberis sempervirens

LEWISIA

This genus of hardy perennials from North America form rosettes of strap-shaped leaves and showy, colourful flowers. Because they resent winter wet, they are often grown in alpine houses. Where they can be sheltered, they are ideal for rock gardens or walls.
Cultivation Grow in neutral to acid soil in light shade. Good drainage is essential.

L. cotyledon

This evergreen perennial is the most tolerant of the genus, and has spoon-shaped leaves, which form a tight rosette. The flowers, usually pinkish-purple but sometimes white, yellow or pinkish-yellow, are borne in clusters on upright stems. H 30cm (12in), S 25cm (10in). Hardy/Z 6–7. **Cotyledon Hybrids** have funnel-shaped flowers in shades of pink, magenta, orange and yellow. H to 30cm (12in), S to 40cm (16in). Flower colours of plants in the **Sunset Group** are in the yellow to red range.

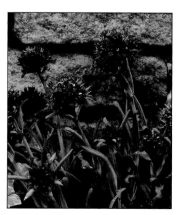
Lychnis alpina

LYCHNIS
Campion, catchfly

The genus is familiar in cottage-garden plantings, but the species described here is better suited to an alpine trough or rock garden.

L. alpina
Alpine catchfly, alpine campion

This charming tufted perennial, which is native to a large part of northern and central Europe, has narrow, grassy foliage. Clusters of bright rose-purple flowers are held at the tops of short, leafy stems, each petal neatly notched. H and S 15cm (6in). Hardy/ Z 4–7.

PENSTEMON

This large genus is often represented in gardens by the border perennials, but the species described here are ideal for rock and scree gardens.
Cultivation Grow in gritty, well-drained soil in sun.

P. alpinus

This clump-forming species from North America has broad leaves, which form dense rosettes, and blue or purplish, white-throated flowers from summer to autumn. H 25cm (10in), S 20cm (8in). Hardy/Z 5–9.

P. hirsutus var. pygmaeus

The typical species is an evergreen subshrub, large enough for a border, but this naturally occurring variety is compact and mat-forming. It has purple-tinged leaves and purplish flowers in summer. H and S 10cm (4in). Hardy/Z 5–8.

PHLOX

This is a large genus, which includes many perennials, some of which are semi-evergreen or evergreen, grown for summer colour in the border. There are also a number of low-growing, mat-forming species, which can be grown in rock gardens, raised beds and walls.
Cultivation The plants described here are best in fertile, moist but well-drained soil in light shade. *P. divaricata* and its forms and *P. subulata* can also be grown in full sun.

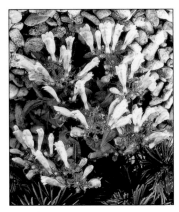

Penstemon hirsutus var. pygmaeus

P. divaricata subsp. *laphamii* 'Chattahoochee'
(syn. *P.* 'Chattahoochee')
This rather lax perennial, which is native to wooded areas in North America, has spreading stems bearing pairs of elliptical, deep green leaves, which are often flushed with purple. The saucer-shaped flowers, which are deep lavender with a crimson eye, are produced in summer over a long season. H 20cm (8in), S 30cm (12in). Hardy/Z 5–9.

P. douglasii
Also from North America, this low mat- or cushion-forming, evergreen perennial has small, tooth-like leaf-pairs. The fragrant, saucer-shaped flowers, borne in late spring and early summer, solitary or several, are clustered together close to the foliage, and they vary in colour from pink to lavender, purple, red or white. H 10cm (4in), S 20cm (8in). Hardy/Z 5–7. 'Boothman's Variety' has violet-pink flowers with dark blue centres. H 8cm (3in), S 20cm (8in). 'Iceberg' is white with a bluish coat.

P. subulata
Moss phlox
This species, which is native to the eastern United States, is a mat-forming, evergreen perennial with much-branched stems and numerous linear, pointed leaf-pairs. The saucer-shaped flowers, in shades of pink, purple, red or white, appear in late spring and early summer and are borne in clusters at the shoot-tips, close to the foliage. H 15cm (6in), S 50cm (20in). Hardy/Z 4–9.

PLATYCODON
Balloon flower
The single species in the genus comes from China, Korea and Japan. The common name derives from the shape of the buds from which the flowers open.
Cultivation Grow in fertile, moist but well-drained soil. These plants must have full sun.

P. grandiflorus
This clump-forming herbaceous perennial has erect, pale stems and oval to elliptical, toothed leaves. The deep blue flowers open from balloon-like buds. H 60cm (2ft), S 30cm (1ft). Hardy/Z 4–9. There are several selected forms, of which the dwarf 'Apoyama' is particularly suitable for a rock garden. It has deep violet flowers. H and S 20cm (8in).

PRIMULA
Primrose
Besides the many valuable border perennials, the genus includes many species that are suitable for rock gardens or alpine houses.
Cultivation Grow in very well-drained, humus-rich soil in a sunny position.

Primula marginata

P. auricula
Bear's ear
The common auricula, native to the Alps, is a low, tufted perennial with rosettes of deep green, rather fleshy leaves. The scented, yellow flowers, up to 2.5cm (1in) across, are clustered at the stalk-tips in spring. H 7.5–15cm (3–6in), S 10–20cm (4–8in). Hardy/Z 5–7. There are many named forms, including 'Chocolate Soldier', which has double, brownish-purple flowers, the petals edged with golden-yellow; and 'Marie Crousse', which has double, violet flowers edged with white. H to 15cm (6in), S 25cm (10in).

P. marginata
This tufted, evergreen perennial from the Alps has rosettes of leathery, green or grey-green leaves, which are coarsely toothed and often have whitish powder along the margin. The pink to bluish-lavender, primrose flowers are clustered at the end of short stalks. H 13cm (5in), S 20cm (8in). Hardy/Z 4–7.

P. vulgaris
Common primrose
This more or less evergreen perennial, native to Europe and western Asia, has rough, elliptical, bright green leaves borne in lax basal rosettes. The fragrant, yellow flowers are borne in profusion in late winter and spring. H 10–20cm (4–8in), S 35cm (14in). Hardy/Z 3–8. Named selections include 'Alba Plena', with double white flowers, and 'Lilacina Plena', with double lilac flowers. Some plants sold under this name may be hybrids with other species.

PULSATILLA
Pasque flower
These lovely perennials have large, bell-shaped flowers, which are followed by silky seedheads. Plant in a raised bed or rock garden where the exquisite flowers can be appreciated.
Cultivation Grow in gritty, well-drained, chalky soil in full sun.

P. alpina
Alpine pasque flower
The species, which is native to mountainous areas of central Europe, has dark green, finely divided foliage. The white flowers, borne in spring, are tinged with bluish-mauve on the outside and have a central mass of bright yellow stamens. H 30cm (12in), S 20cm (8in). Hardy/Z 3–5.

P. vernalis
(syn. *Anemone vernalis*)
The leaves of this clump-forming species, which is native to Europe and Siberia, are dark green and finely divided. The beautiful white flowers, flushed with pale purplish-blue on the outside, have bright yellow centres. Protect from winter wet. H 10cm (4in), S 20cm (8in). Hardy/Z 5–8.

P. vulgaris
(syn. *Anemone pulsatilla*)
The species, found across Europe, has tufts of finely divided, deep green, rather feathery leaves. The solitary, half-nodding to erect, bell-shaped flowers, which are borne in spring, may be white, red, violet-blue or purple and have silky hairs on the outside. H 20cm (8in), S 30cm (12in). Hardy/Z 5–7. 'Alba' is the white-flowered form.

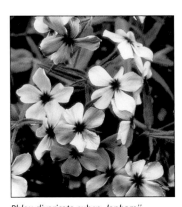

Phlox divaricata subsp. *laphamii* 'Chattahoochee'

Platycodon grandiflorus

Pulsatilla vulgaris

Saponaria ocymoides

RAMONDA

The small genus includes three species of evergreen perennials. They are suitable for rock gardens, raised beds or walls, where they can be grown sideways on. They resent winter wet and for this reason are often grown in alpine houses.
Cultivation Grow in rich but very well-drained soil in partial shade.

R. myconi
(syn. *R. pyrenaica*)
The species is native to northern Spain. It has dark green, hairy leaves in neat rosettes above which dark purplish-blue, yellow-centred flowers are borne in late spring to early summer. H 10cm (4in), S 20cm (8in). Hardy/Z 5–7.

SALIX
Willow
Better known for its larger shrubs and trees, the genus also includes dwarf species, which are suitable

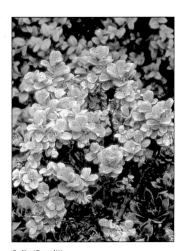

Salix 'Boydii'

for rock gardens or alpine troughs.
Cultivation Grow in gritty, well-drained soil in full sun.

S. 'Boydii'
(syn. *S. × boydii*)
This slow-growing, twiggy, deciduous shrub develops a thick trunk, which eventually looks rather gnarled. The rounded and crinkly leaves are grey-green, paler beneath. Small, brownish, upright catkins are produced in spring. H 30cm (12in), S 25cm (10in). Hardy/Z 4–7.

SAPONARIA
Soapwort
A genus of annuals and perennials from mountainous areas of Europe and south-western Asia. The well-known *S. officinalis* is suitable for a mixed border, but the plants described below can be grown in a rock garden, alpine trough or raised bed.
Cultivation Grow in gritty, well-drained soil in full sun.

S. 'Bressingham'
This mat-forming perennial hybrid has mid-green leaves and clusters of deep pink flowers in summer. H 8cm (3in), S 30cm (12in). Hardy/Z 4–8.

S. ocymoides
Rock soapwort, tumbling Ted
A mat-forming, evergreen perennial, this is native to central and south-eastern Europe. It has numerous, small, oval, deep green leaves. In late spring and summer, spreading clusters of pink or purplish flowers appear. Cut back

after flowering to keep plants neat. H 10cm (4in), S 30cm (12in). Hardy/Z 4–8.

SAXIFRAGA
Saxifrage
This is a large genus of more than 400 species of mat- or cushion-forming, evergreen or deciduous perennials that are widely distributed in the northern hemisphere, where they are found in mountainous regions. They show considerable variation in habit and leaf form and are widely grown in rock and scree gardens, raised beds and alpine troughs.
Cultivation Grow in rich, gritty, well-drained, neutral to alkaline soil in full sun.

S. cochlearis
A mound-forming, evergreen perennial from the south-western Alps, this has numerous, crowded rosettes of greyish, lime-encrusted leaf-rosettes. In summer, airy sprays of dainty, white flowers are produced on slender, reddish stems. H 25cm (10in), S 15cm (6in). Hardy/Z 6.

S. 'Kathleen Pinsent'
The spoon-shaped, silvery leaves form rosettes above which the pink flowers are borne in arching clusters. H and S 20cm (8in). Hardy/Z 5–7.

S. oppositifolia
Purple saxifrage
This saxifrage, native to many cold regions in the northern hemisphere, is a dense, mat-forming, evergreen alpine. It has

Saxifraga cochlearis

Saxifraga paniculata

deep green, scale-like leaves densely clothing the spreading stems. In late winter and early spring, solitary pale pink to rich purple flowers appear close to the foliage. H 2.5cm (1in), S 20cm (8in). Hardy/Z 2–6.

S. paniculata
(syn. *S. aizoon*)
This tufted, evergreen perennial, which is native to Europe, Canada and Greenland, has crowded rosettes of grey-green, lime-encrusted leaves. In summer, airy sprays of small, white or cream flowers are borne on stiff, arching stalks. H 15cm (6in), S 30cm (12in). Hardy/Z 4–6.

S. 'Tumbling Waters'
This slow-growing, mat-forming, evergreen hybrid grows in tight rosettes of narrow, lime-encrusted, silvery leaves. When the plant matures after several years, dense, arching, conical heads of small, open cup-shaped, white flowers are produced, after which the main rosette dies and the small offsets grow on. H 60cm (2ft), S 30cm (12in). Hardy/Z 5–7.

SEDUM
Stonecrop
The large and diverse genus contains around 400 species including perennials and succulents. They are from the northern hemisphere, where they are found in mountain and arid regions, and they are ideal plants for withstanding drought and strong sunshine. Some of the alpine types have a creeping,

scrambling habit, which will cover rock edges.

Cultivation Grow sedums in neutral to slightly alkaline, very well-drained soil in full sun.

S. acre
Wallpepper, biting stonecrop
This species, which is found in Europe, North Africa and western Asia, is a familiar little plant of old walls and rooftops. It is a bright green succulent with tiny, closely overlapping leaves. In summer, the shoot tips burst with flat-topped heads of tiny, star-shaped, yellow-green flowers. H 5cm (2in), S 60cm (2ft) or more. Hardy/Z 4–9.

S. pulchellum
Native to the south-eastern United States, this is a laxly tufted, succulent perennial with erect to ascending stems adorned with narrow leaves. The starry pink flowers are freely produced in summer. It is often grown as an annual. H 5cm (2in), S 25cm (10in). Hardy/Z 8.

S. spathulifolium
This compact species from western North America grows into rosettes. It is a mat-forming perennial with spoon-shaped, fleshy, brittle green or silvery leaves, often tinted with bronze and purple. In summer sprays of short-stemmed, tiny, star-shaped bright yellow flowers are produced. H 5cm (2in), S indefinite. Hardy/Z 5–9.

SEMPERVIVUM
Houseleek
The 40 species in the genus are mat-forming, evergreen succulents, largely from mountainous regions of Europe and Asia. There are many hybrids, some differing only slightly (if at all) from each other. They are ideal for rock and scree gardens, alpine troughs, walls and containers.
Cultivation Grow in gritty, very well-drained soil in full sun. Protect from winter wet.

S. arachnoideum
Cobweb houseleek
This mat- or mound-forming evergreen perennial is native to

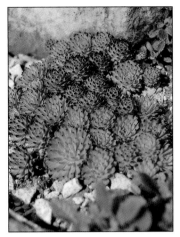
Sempervivum montanum

central and south-west Europe. It has numerous, greyish leaf-rosettes, tipped with red and enveloped in a cobweb of whitish hairs. The starry, pinkish-red flowers are clustered at the top of a short, leafy stem in summer. H 10cm (4in), S 10cm (4in). Hardy/Z 5–9.

S. montanum
(syn. S. helveticum)
An evergreen perennial from central and southern Europe, this forms low mounds of dull green, downy, succulent leaf-rosettes. The wine-red, starry flowers are borne at the tips of erect flowering shoots in summer. H 10–20cm (4–8in), S 20–40cm (8–16in). Hardy/Z 5.

S. tectorum
Common houseleek
This rather coarse, evergreen perennial from mountainous areas of central and southern Europe has large, succulent leaf-rosettes, the leaves usually green or grey-green with reddish or purplish

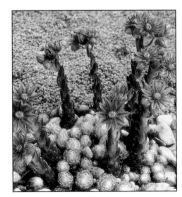
Sempervivum arachnoideum

tips. A mass of star-shaped, dull pink to purple flowers is borne on stout, leafy stems in summer. H 20cm (8in), S 50cm (20in). Hardy/Z 5–9.

VERONICA
Speedwell, brooklime
The genus contains about 250 species of diverse plants, originating mainly in Europe, where they are found in a range of habitats. Some are cushion-forming or mat-forming species, which are suitable for the rock garden, where they can be exploited to soften unsightly edges. Others are border perennials. They are easy to grow.
Cultivation Grow in fairly poor, well-drained soil in full sun.

V. prostrata
Prostrate speedwell
This mat-forming perennial, from the mountains of Europe, has deep green, narrow-oblong leaves. In summer, spikes of rich blue or purplish flowers are borne above the foliage on stiff, somewhat leafy, stems. 'Trehane' has lime green leaves, a sharp contrast to its darker blue flowers. H 15cm (6in), S 40cm (16in). Hardy/Z 4–7.

VIOLA
Pansy, violet
There are pansies and violas for every position in the garden, from the front of borders to alpine houses. They are ideal for summer bedding, and the smaller species are perfect for rock gardens, raised beds and containers.

Veronica prostrata

V. cornuta
Horned violet, viola
This spreading plant, ideal for groundcover and growing with blue-leafed hostas, has deep violet flowers among the copious leaves in early summer. Shearing these off triggers a second crop in late summer. H 15cm (6in), S 60cm (24in). Hardy/Z 5–8. Plants belonging to the **Alba Group** have white flowers. H 15cm (6in), S 60cm (24in). **'Alba Minor'** is similar but more compact. **Lilacina Group** plants produce flowers in shades of lilac.

V. lutea
Mountain pansy
This tufted perennial, native to the mountains of central and western Europe, has bright green, oval leaves and pansy flowers, which are yellow, violet or bi-coloured and appear in spring and summer. H and S 15cm (6in). Hardy/Z 4–8.

Viola cornuta Alba Group

Recommended planting lists

The following lists offer a guide to plants adapted to certain conditions. Most of the entries relate to entire genera. For more detailed information as to preferences of individual species, refer to the relevant entry. Remember that some plants are tolerant of a range of conditions, hence their presence in more than one list.

PLANTS FOR DRY SOIL IN SUN

PERENNIALS
Acanthus
Achillea
Anthemis
Artemisia
Aster
Dianthus
Echinops
Eryngium
Euphorbia
Helichrysum
Kniphofia
Lychnis
Nepeta
Osteospermum
Papaver
Penstemon
Phlomis
Salvia
Sedum
Stachys
Verbascum
Verbena
Zauschneria

ANNUALS AND BIENNIALS
Calendula
Cleome
Cosmos
Erysimum
Eschscholtzia
Limnanthes
Oenothera
Papaver
Salvia
Tagetes

BULBS, CORMS AND TUBERS
Allium
Crocus
Nerine
Tulipa

ALPINES
Armeria
Aubrieta
Aurinia
Cerastium
Dianthus
Gypsophila

PLANTS FOR DRY SOIL IN SHADE

ANNUALS AND BIENNIALS
Bellis
Digitalis
Lunaria

BULBS, CORMS AND TUBERS
Cyclamen
Eranthis
Hyacinthus
Muscari
Narcissus

PLANTS FOR MOIST SOIL IN SHADE

PERENNIALS
Aquilegia
Aruncus
Astilbe
Astrantia
Calla
Cimicifuga
Convallaria
Digitalis
Helleborus
Heuchera
Hosta
Lysimachia
Polygonatum

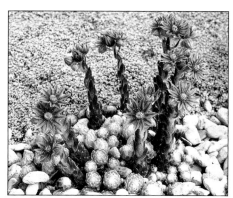

Hosta 'Golden Prayers'

Primula
Pulmonaria
Rheum
Rodgersia
Thalictrum
Tiarella
Tricyrtis
Trillium
Trollius
Viola

PLANTS FOR EXPOSED SITES

PERENNIALS
Achillea
Ajuga
Bergenia
Cimicifuga
Coreopsis
Iris
Persicaria
Primula
Pulmonaria

ANNUALS AND BIENNIALS
Hesperis

BULBS, CORMS AND TUBERS
Allium
Crocus

ALPINES
Campanula
Sempervivum

PLANTS FOR ACID OR LIME-FREE SOIL

PERENNIALS
Iris
Tricyrtis
Trillium
BULBS
Lilium

ALPINES
Corydalis
Gentiana
(autumn-flowering)
Lewisia
Phlox
Primula

PLANTS FOR CHALKY SOIL

PERENNIALS
Anemone
Anthemis
Aquilegia
Campanula
Convallaria
Delphinium
Dianthus
Iris
Paeonia
Pulsatilla
Rudbeckia
Salvia
Verbascum
Viola

ANNUALS AND BIENNIALS
Bellis
Lobularia
Papaver
Salvia
Viola

Stachys byzantina

Lilium 'Royal Class'

Sempervivum arachnoideum

Anemone coronaria 'Lord Lieutenant'

Narcissus 'Carlton'

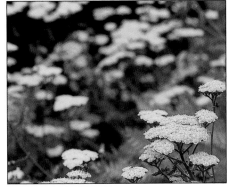

Achillea

BULBS,
CORMS AND
TUBERS
Anemone
Colchicum
Crocus
Gladiolus
Iris
Narcissus
Tulipa

ALPINES
Aubrieta
Campanula
Dianthus
Pulsatilla
Saxifraga

**PLANTS FOR
CLAY SOIL**

PERENNIALS
Aconitum
Astrantia
Digitalis

Helenium
Hemerocallis
Lysimachia
Lythrum
Persicaria bistorta
Rudbeckia

BULBS,
CORMS AND
TUBERS
Anemone
Camassia
Leucojum
Narcissus

**PLANTS FOR
COASTAL
SITES**

PERENNIALS
Achillea
Agapanthus
Anthemis
Artemisia
Dianthus

Eryngium
Euphorbia
Geranium
Penstemon
Phormium
Sedum
Stachys

ANNUALS AND
BIENNIALS
Antirrhinum
Matthiola

BULBS,
CORMS AND
TUBERS
Canna
Chionodoxa
Crocosmia
Crocus
Narcissus
Zantedeschia

ALPINES
Aubrieta

Gypsophila
Sedum
Sempervivum

**PLANTS FOR
AUTUMN
AND WINTER
COLOUR**

PERENNIALS
Helleborus
Ophiopogon
Tiarella

CLIMBERS
Celastrus
Humulus
Parthenocissus
Vitis

**PLANTS FOR
CONTAINERS**

PERENNIALS
Agapanthus

Argyranthemum
Bergenia
Gazania
Hosta
Lamium
Lilium
Liriope
Penstemon
Primula

ANNUALS AND
BIENNIALS
Myosotis
Nicotiana
Petunia
Verbena
Viola

BULBS,
CORMS AND
TUBERS
Chionodoxa
Crinum
Crocus
Cyclamen

Hyacinthus
Narcissus
Tulipa

**PLANTS WITH
SCENTED
FOLIAGE**

PERENNIALS
Chamaemelum
Melissa
Mentha
Monarda
Origanum
Pelargonium

**PLANTS WITH
SCENTED
FLOWERS**

PERENNIALS
Hosta
Paeonia
Phlox
Primula

Iris reticulata

Tulipa 'Fantasy'

Campanula portenschlagiana

Plant Hardiness Zones

Plant Hardiness Zones
This map was developed by the Agricultural Research Service of the U.S. Department of Agriculture. Every plant in the directory is given a zone range. The zones 1-11 are based on the average annual minimum temperature. In the zone range, the smaller number indicates the northern-most zone in which a plant can survive the winter and the higher number gives the most southerly area in which it will perform consistently. Bear in mind that factors such as altitude, wind exposure, proximity to water, soil type, snow, night temperature, shade, and the level of water received by a plant may alter a plant's hardiness by as much as two zones.

Zone 11 Above 4°C (40°F)

Zone 10 -1 to 4°C (30 to 40°F)

Zone 9 -7 to -1°C (20 to 30°F)

Zone 8 -12 to -7°C (10 to 20°F)

Zone 7 -18 to -12°C (0 to 10°F)

Zone 6 -23 to -18°C (-10 to 0°F

Zone 5 -29 to -23°C (-20 to -10°F)

Zone 4 -34 to -29°C (-30 to -20°F)

Zone 3 -40 to -34°C (-40 to -30°F)

Zone 2 -45 to -40°C (-50 to -40°F)

Zone 1 Below -45°C (-50°F)

Index

Acknowledgements

Author's acknowledgements

I would like to thank all the editors who worked on the book, especially Claire Folkard and Penelope Goodare. I would also like to thank all my friends and neighbours who allowed me to invade their gardens in pursuit of those elusive plant portraits.

Picture acknowledgements

Photography by Peter Anderson, Jonathan Buckley, Helen Fickling, Michelle Garrett, Simon McBride, Marie O'Hara.

The publisher would like to thank the following picture libraries for permission to use their photographs:

A–Z Botanical 53bl.

Jonathan Buckley 54, 122, 70.

Andrew Mikolajski 6, 10t, 11t, 17tc, 69tl, 75br.

Peter McHoy 18tc, 19tl, 20bl, 21bl, 22br, 26tl, 27tl, 27tr, 27br, 36br, 37bcl, 38tcl, 38tcr, 38b, 39tl, 39bl, 39br, 40br, 46tl, 46bl, 46bc, 47tr, 47bl, 47bt, 48b, 49tr, 50bc, 51tc, 51tr, 51bl, 52tl, 52tr, 52bl, 52br, 53tr, 58tr, 58bl, 59tl, 59tc, 59bl, 60br, 61tc, 62tc, 63bc, 64b, 65t, 65bl, 65bc, 66br, 69bl, 69br, 76tr, 79bl, 88tr, 88b, 112bl, 113br, 114tr, 114bl, 114br, 115tl, 115tr, 116tr, 116tr, 116bl, 116br, 117tr, 117bc, 117bc, 117br, 118tl, 119tl, 119br.